UNTOUCHABLE
JIMMY
SAVILE

SHAUN
ATTWOOD

JIMMY SAVILE BOOK 1

SPELLING DIFFERENCES: UK V USA

This book was written in UK English, so USA readers may notice some spelling differences with American English: e.g. color = colour, meter = metre and pedophile = paedophile

DEDICATION

This book is dedicated to Claire McAlpine, a Top of the Pops dancer who committed suicide, to Sheila Terry-Bailey of Duncroft Girls School and to all of the brave survivors who came forward in the hope that measures would be taken to prevent this from happening again

CONTENTS

CHAPTER 1

MOLESTING TEENAGERS ON AN INDUSTRIAL SCALE

Kelly Gold was a 15-year-old dancer and actress, attending stage school in London. When she wasn't studying, she would audition for parts in adverts and films or for modelling and dancing roles. Kelly was a regular dancer for the BBC's most popular music show, *Top of the Pops*. It was the early seventies and, every week, the young people of the nation would gather round the TV to watch the likes of David Bowie, The Rolling Stones, Cliff Richard or T Rex perform their latest releases, while teenage girls bopped chaotically on the show's crowded dancefloor.

It was at one of these shows that Kelly met Claire McAlpine, another 15-year-old dancer. "She was a good dancer," Gold told me, "and she was very beautiful. That's one of the things that stood out about Claire, she was a very pretty girl, and she was funny. She also had quite a serious side. She kept a diary and she wrote down any of her experiences. Even at auditions, I would often see her writing, I don't know what, she always put it in the diary."

The two girls quickly became friends, seeing each other regularly at *Top of the Pops* and other auditions. They would chat between acts and share titbits about their private lives. Schoolgirls like Kelly and Claire would be driven to the TOTP studio at the BBC's Television Centre in Hammersmith, west London. There, they would change out of their school uniforms and into the hot pants, mini-skirts, short dresses and high heels that they would wear for the show.

After the performances, some of the girls would go back to the dressing rooms of the DJs who hosted the show, to continue the party. Floor managers would whisper invites in the girls' ears on the dancefloor and they would make their way to the appropriate dressing room after the show. "I only went there once to a dressing room and I can't remember which DJ's dressing room it was," Gold said, "but there were a few people in the dressing room at the time drinking, and slightly what I might consider inappropriate behaviour with the girls. I only had someone try it on with me once and I sort of smacked their hand down and I made excuses to go to the toilet. And that was the only time I ever went into a *Top of the Pops* dressing room. I knew that what might be happening in there isn't what I wanted to happen to me."

One day, Claire received an invite from one of the floor managers and disappeared even before the performances had finished. Claire told Kelly that she had been invited out for a drink by one of the stars performing on TOTP and asked if she could stay over at Kelly's house that night. Kelly agreed and waited at home for Claire to arrive, but her friend never turned up. When Kelly next saw Claire, her friend told her she had spent the night with the famous singer.

Similar invites now started coming Claire's way, thick and fast. As she recorded in her diary, she was now having trysts with a Radio One DJ and one of the TOTP presenters. Claire's mother, Vera McAlpine, subsequently told the press that the diary entries involving the TOTP presenter were "so shocking that I would rather not repeat them."

"I think she had found when she was turning up at some DJ's places that she had got herself in a bit deep, "Kelly Gold said, "and didn't really know how to get out of it. And I told her then, 'Just don't go there.' But I think she'd found that she was already on a spiral of being obliged to meet these people. And then a few weeks on, she was very worried… that she might be pregnant. Meanwhile, her mum had found her diary… and she was really upset that her mum now was taking matters further… she was going to go to the BBC."

A month after Claire's mother found her diary, Claire was found dead on her bedroom floor. Lying next to her were two empty bottles of sleeping pills and her red diary. The BBC did nothing about Vera McAlpine's complaints. Neither did the police, who kept Claire's diary as evidence, until it mysteriously disappeared. In the inquest into her death and the subsequent press reports, Claire was branded a fantasist. *Top of the Pops*, meanwhile, carried on as usual, except that a minimum age was introduced for the dancers.

Claire's half-brother, Mark Ufland, told the press that the DJ presenter named in Claire's diary was Jimmy Savile, TOTP's main host and one of the most well-known and popular celebrities in the country. On the day before the inquest into Claire's death, Savile was interviewed by the *Daily Express*. He told the newspaper, "Many a time, I have dated a good-looking girl I have met on the show. But what I say to them is, 'Ask your folks if I can come round for tea.' I much prefer being with a family, with a pretty girl in the centre, than a session in the back of my car. For one thing, you can't see how pretty the girl is in the back of my car."

This was 1971. Jimmy Savile already had a long career of sexual abuse, rape and paedophilia behind him, and an even longer one ahead.

Jimmy Savile was the darling of the British nation. Host of *Top of the Pops*, he was a long-running disc jockey on Radio One, and the presenter of the immensely popular TV show, *Jim'll Fix It*. He was a household name, from the sixties until his death in 2011. Over his six-decade career, he raised over £40 million for charities and charmed and bamboozled a nation with his eccentric dress sense, his quirky sense of humour, and his trademark Cuban cigar.

But beneath the glamorous exterior, Savile led another, hidden life, one that lasted as long, perhaps longer, than his celebrity one. Its scale rivalled the magnitude of his public success, its numbers were equally eye-popping, but its toll was counted not in pounds, but misery and the destruction of innocence.

Savile was a serial sexual abuser and paedophile on a scale

seldom seen before. Spanning six decades, his career of abuse affected at least 500 victims. According to a 2014 NSPCC report, the victims were mostly in the 13-to-15-year-old age range, but the oldest was 75 and the youngest was just two years old. At least 72 of Savile's victims were at the BBC, of whom 34 were under 16, the UK's legal age of consent. Over 80 allegations came from the various hospitals Savile volunteered in, including Leeds General Infirmary, Stoke Mandeville Hospital, and Broadmoor, a high-security psychiatric hospital, holding some of the most dangerous criminals in the UK. Summing up Savile's career of abuse, the NSPCC report concluded, "There's no doubt that Savile is one of the most, if not the most, prolific sex offender that we at the NSPCC have ever come across."

Perhaps even more staggering than the scale of the abuse is the fact that Savile got away with it for so long. Right up until his death in 2011, the millionaire celebrity never faced a single criminal charge or a single exposé in the press. And all this despite constant rumours, as well as frequent and none-too-subtle hints from the man himself. Savile had access to some 40 hospitals across the nation and had his own offices, rooms and beds in at least three of them. At Broadmoor, he was given the keys to the entire high-security facility. And at Duncroft Approved School for girls with behavioural problems, he would often be seen taking the teenage girls out for rides in his Rolls Royce.

Savile's influence ranged from police to politicians to prime ministers and even the top echelons of the royal family. And all the while, he was abusing, molesting and raping underage girls and boys on a scale hitherto unknown.

The ultimate question, when faced with such a career of abuse, cover-up and manipulation has to be – how did he get away with it for so long?

What made Jimmy Savile untouchable?

James Wilson Vincent Savile was born on Halloween, 1926. He was the youngest of seven children, growing up in a working class family in Leeds. His father, Vince, worked as an illegal bookmaker, taking bets on horseraces off-course, an activity that was illegal until 1960. His mother, Agnes, was a supply teacher from the north east. She met Vince when he was working at a rural Yorkshire train station she passed each day on her way to work. The two got married in 1911 and moved in with Vince's parents in Leeds. They had their first baby a year later.

Jimmy Savile arrived five years after his next oldest sibling. In every way, he appeared the runt of the litter. As a young child, he was undernourished and sickly and almost didn't survive. "He was like a miracle child," said Boris Coster, the author of the book, *Broadmoor Sinister*, which details many of Savile's crimes. "[At] about three months old... he was actually being pushed in the buggy and he fell out of the buggy, causing substantial injuries, which resulted in Savile being placed into a hospital for three months. They actually thought they were going to lose him."

According to Savile's mother, Agnes, when baby Jimmy fell out of the pram, one of the muscles in his neck had been severed. The injury meant Savile could no longer sit up or close his eyes. He lay on his back, staring perpetually at the ceiling, suffering intermittent spams, in which his head would twist so far round, he would be staring over his back.

The hospital wanted to perform an operation but Agnes refused. She chose instead to pray for him at Leeds Catholic Cathedral. She had been praying unsuccessfully for six months when, in desperation, she tried an appeal to a little-known Scottish nun called Margaret Sinclair, who had been credited with several miraculous cures, according to a leaflet Agnes picked up at the cathedral. When Agnes got home later that day, little Jimmy's eyes were closed for the first time in six months. When he woke up, he was cured.

The miraculous healing became a central feature of Savile's personal mythology. He had somehow, he felt, been chosen. His life was to have a special purpose. "He was a sort of dream child," Coster told me. "Of all the brothers and all the sisters, he was the one that they all sort of rallied around. He was that type of special kid to them."

Contrasted with this feeling of specialness was a lonely childhood, in which Savile had little contact with other children. As the youngest child by five years, Jimmy didn't get to hang around with his older brothers and sisters much, instead spending most of his time with his parents. In an interview with journalist and Savile biographer, Dan Davies, Savile said that, as a young child spending so much time in the company of adults, he learned to watch and listen, taking everything in and filing it in his growing brain.

Starved of company, the young Savile spent much of his time across the road from the family house at St Joseph's Home for the Aged. He would chat with the elderly patients and smuggle in gifts for them. According to Davies, this is where Savile first developed his fascination with death, a morbid curiosity that would last his whole life and may have led to some of his darkest crimes, including necrophilia. "They were always dying," Savile told Davies in an interview. "I'd ask, 'Where's Mrs so-and-so?' and one of the nuns would tell me that she'd died." Savile would say goodbye to the old people as they lay dead and would even ride along in their hearses.

As he got older, Savile's isolation only grew. At 14 years old, the Savile children were expected to fend for themselves. Savile would come home to an empty house and have to cook dinner for himself – usually a tin of baked beans and an egg. Savile's relationship with his father doesn't seem to have been particularly close and was something of a mystery. He hardly ever spoke about the man, who died when Savile was 26 years old. One thing we do know is that Vince Savile was a formative influence on one aspect of his son's life. Savile's father introduced him to cigars at the tender age of seven, by giving him a drag of his own cigar in the misguided hope that it would put the young Jimmy off smoking. Instead, it had the opposite effect. Cigars would be a lifelong passion and would become one of Savile's trademarks. When he was found dead at his flat in 2011, there was a half-smoked Cuban cigar in the ashtray.

In contrast to the distance between father and son, Jimmy's relationship with his mother couldn't have been closer. He was her miracle child and her favourite of the seven siblings. He called her 'the Duchess' and, later in life, kept a room in his Leeds flat dedicated to her memory, complete with a wardrobe full of her clothes.

There were certainly some odd hints that emerged later in Savile's life, several coming, characteristically, from his own lips. In interviews, Savile always maintained that his mother was the "only true love" of his life. Later in life, he and Agnes spent a lot of time together, often going on holidays and cruises with each other.

It also raises the question of sexual abuse in Savile's childhood. Many sexual abusers were themselves abused as children, so it would certainly make some sense of Savile's lifelong career of offending. "I don't know what else, of course, took place in his relationship," Williams-Thomas told me. "He's saying there was a possibility of incest. I leave that to people to make their own determination."

Savile was twelve years old when the Second World War broke out. As a big industrial city, Leeds was a potential target for the Luftwaffe, so Savile was initially evacuated to rural Lincolnshire. But his time in the countryside didn't last long. When his parents found out that the house he was staying in was next to several large gas storage tanks, Agnes decided to move him back home. Leeds wasn't badly bombed during the war but, during one rare heavy bombing raid, Savile and Agnes were caught out in the open. As bombs fell all around them, the pair had to take shelter in a doorway. When the raid was finished, Savile stepped outside to help with the damage and picked up a black leather glove, only to find it still had a hand inside.

At 14, Savile left school and got a job as an office boy for a company that manufactured military uniforms. In his spare time, he would accompany his parents to the local Mecca Locarno dancehall, where the adult couples would dance in pairs to the big band music. But as well as being a social hub, the dancehall was the centre of an underground culture of crime, prostitution and gangs. Savile once again applied his habit of silently watching, listening and learning, and received an informal education in all aspects of criminality. As an example of this parallel underworld, Savile recounted in his autobiography how, one day, he found the dead body of one of the dancehall's female clients chopped up and left in a ditch.

Savile was growing up fast, and he soon secured a job as a percussionist at the Mecca Locarno, accompanying a female pianist, who played in an all-girl band. It was the beginning of a dancehall career that would eventually lead him to the big time. Another part of growing up was accelerated by the shortage of older males, who were off fighting the war. In his autobiography, Savile recalled scoring his first date with a woman when he was just 12 years old. His partner was a 20-year-old woman from the dancehall box office. Jimmy took her to the cinema, where there was some inexpert fumbling in the dark. He lost his virginity sometime between the ages of 13 and 15 to a woman who, he said, picked him up at the dancehall. Savile accompanied her home on the train, where she attempted to have sex with him. The act was finally consummated in a bush at the back of her house. Savile described the process giving rise to feelings of "terror mixed with embarrassment."

Savile was training part-time with the Air Training Corps and hoped for a call-up to the RAF when he was old enough to begin his national service. However, when he turned 18 in 1944, he failed a sight test, which ruled him out of the air force. Instead, he was destined for a rather less glamourous role. His name was selected for conscription as a so-called 'Bevin Boy,' after the Minister of Labour, Ernest Bevin. Bevin Boys served down the pits, mining coal for the nation's energy supply. It was down the mines that Savile said he learned his first lesson in "the power of oddness."

Savile was working at South Kirkby Colliery, where he was

given a job none of the other miners wanted. He was stationed on his own, down a tunnel that linked two of the larger chambers by rail. Savile's job was to lever back onto the tracks any coal trucks that became derailed. The eight-hour shifts alone in the darkness used to drive the other superstitious miners mad, imagining ghosts and potential disasters. But Savile thrived off it. He sewed a hidden pocket into his jacket and smuggled down books on science, languages and travel, which he would devour by the light of his single lantern.

One day, he arrived late for work, still dressed in his suit from the night before. With no time to change, he rushed into the pit cage, still wearing his suit and holding a newspaper. Ignoring the stares of his fellow miners, Savile walked blithely to his station down the lonely tunnel.

"I was a mile and a half away from the pit bottom and two miles from the coal face," Savile later recounted in a TV interview. "So what I did, I took all my clothes off, because it's very warm down the pit. I took all my clothes off and folded them in the newspaper and worked in the noddy, right. And I saved a little bit of water in the bottle. And just before it was knocking-off time, I cleaned my hands off and cleaned my face off, right. And I got back into the pit bottom immaculate. Now then, nobody but nobody ever did eight hours down a pit and came back as immaculate as they set off with white shirts. They were quite convinced that I was a witch. And I never said a word. And I suddenly realised that if you were different, and you didn't say anything about it, you'd see it had a tremendous effect on people. And that stayed with me."

By the end of the war, Savile had been transferred to Waterloo Main Colliery in Leeds. It was here that he claims he had the accident that ended his coal-mining career. Savile told biographer, Dan Davies, that he was assigned to shovelling dust off the conveyor belt and was lying on his side in a cramped, 18-inch-high space, when the tunnel was suddenly detonated. Half buried and concussed, Savile managed to call for help and the other miners dragged him out. Savile's back had been injured and, he claims, he was discharged from hospital with two walking sticks and the prognosis that he would never walk unaided again. Savile claimed he had spent seven years down the pits, followed by three years recovering from his injury. But this timeline, as well as the injury itself, are highly contentious.

Dan Davies pointed out that seven years in the mines would have timed Savile's release to 1951 or 1952, a period when he was already on record as taking part in long-distance cycling competitions, hardly the pastime of someone recovering from a major back injury. In another timeline, Savile reported that he had suffered the injury when he was 20 years old which, as Davies noted, would date the accident to 1946/47. But again, Savile is on record looking fit and healthy in 1948, appearing as a cyclist in the British film, *A Boy, a Girl and a Bike*. So when did the accident happen? Or did it happen at all?

Davies has uncovered newspaper reports that cast significant doubts on Savile's story. In the 1980s, Savile gave an interview with *The Sun* which stated, "In 1948, Jimmy was finally allowed to leave the pits when a chest cold showed up on X-ray." And in a 1981 article in *The People*, Savile said, "When I was James Wilson, working down the pits for £2 a week for six shifts, it didn't matter to anyone." As Davies pointed out, James Wilson was the name of Savile's dead cousin. It seems plausible then that the accident was just another of those myths that Savile used to dine out on. It may even be possible that, for most of the time he was supposedly working down the mines, Savile was actually using a dead relative's identity to evade the work altogether.

"That was a very short period of his life," Savile researcher, Boris Coster, told me. "That wasn't something to brag about extensively. I mean literally a couple of months down the mines. He used that quite a lot with people. I mean, he played on the downtrodden bit."

The fit and healthy Jimmy Savile had, in fact, taken up cycling as a serious sport by the late forties, and by the early fifties, he was competing in some big races. Savile had received his first bike aged 11 and had done some long cycles to the east coast and to Scotland during the war. After the war, he joined a local cycling club under the name Oscar 'The Duke' Savile, a supposed company director, and soon he was competing in major races. In 1950, he came second in the annual Edinburgh-Newcastle race. Now he set his sights on the big one.

Modelled on the famous Tour de France, the first Tour of Britain was due to take place in 1951. Savile aimed to qualify as part of the four-man team representing Yorkshire. To do so, he had to prove himself in a seven-day series of races between Butlins holiday camps in the north.

Savile earned his place in the Tour of Britain by finishing third in the qualifiers. But perhaps more importantly, this is where he first established his knack of off-the-wall showmanship, which attracted publicity wherever he went. Rather than wearing the usual cycling kit, Savile would show up to races wearing a suit and tie and smoking one of his trademark Cuban cigars. His bizarre antics even landed him a front page on *The Daily Express*, the newspaper which sponsored the Tour.

When it came to the big race, Savile fared less well. More interested in gaining press attention and chatting up women he met along the route, he came last in some stages and missed the start of others. By the Morcombe-to-Glasgow stage, 'The Duke' had had enough, pulling out of the race after a gruelling climb to the top of Shap Fell Peak in the Lake District. But Savile had made such a name for himself as a character that *The Daily Express* asked him to stay on and act as a race commentator, entertaining live crowds of up to 50,000 people. Savile went on to commentate for next three Tour of Britain races. It was his first introduction to broadcasting. It was also the start of a life-long trend of putting showmanship before sportsmanship, especially when it came to his later hobby of long-distance running. "I think he finished two marathons," Williams-Thomas told me. "All the other marathons, he got in the car and he got driven to the end. I mean, the man's just a complete liar."

Alongside his racing antics, Savile was experimenting with the other great passion of his early adulthood – DJing. While he was still using walking sticks, according to Savile's account, he was introduced to a new invention that would eventually revolutionise dancehalls – amplified music. Spotting the potential of the technology, Savile organised a 'Grand Record Dance' at a local Catholic social club in Leeds. Instead of dancing to a live band, for the first time, attendees would be bopping to records played on a gramophone and transmitted through speakers.

The night turned out to be a bit of a disaster. Only twelve people turned up and the revolutionary technology malfunctioned, causing a blackout in the hall and toasting the gramophone. But Savile was upbeat. He had got his first taste of the power of the DJ – the ability to control people's actions and emotions by the music he played.

Soon after, with an improved device, Savile and some friends put on a record dance for a girl's 21st birthday in the nearby town of Otley. The event was a success and Savile picked up one of the girls to boot. It was the start of a trend that would continue throughout his life.

In 1953, Savile's father died of cancer. Savile was working in the scrap metal trade, earning a handsome £60 a week, while cycle racing and DJing on the side. But his dad's death spurred Savile to think more deeply about the direction of his life, and he quickly decided it went beyond selling scrap. What he really wanted was the big time.

The answer to his prayers came when he saw an advert for a job at the Mecca Locarno, the local dancehall where, as a boy, he had worked as a percussionist. Savile went for the interview and got the job, becoming the dancehall's assistant manager.

According to Coster, Savile's older brother, Vince, played a major part in his introduction to the dancehall scene. Vince had served in the navy during the war and was a 'face' (i.e. well known within criminal circles) in the Leeds underworld that centred around the dancehalls. "His brother Vincent got Jimmy into nightclubs, being a disc jockey," Coster told me. "His brother is a key to a lot of things. Not a lot of people know, but Vincent was a bit of a villain. He was well known in the underworld scene. He had money, he had power, which I think is what Jimmy Savile played on… Cigarette rackets, booze rackets, the nightclub game would have been one of them as well because you can hide a lot behind a nightclub."

With his new career underway, Savile soon moved out of the family house, first sleeping in the dancehall's cloakroom under a pile of coats, then moving onto a lifeboat moored on a canal near the city centre.

Savile became an instant success at Mecca, wearing colourful vibrant clothes instead of the usual staid suits and ties. He experimented with new music and record dances and began to draw in the crowds. His success soon earned him a promotion – taking over a struggling Mecca dancehall in Ilford, East London. At his new post, Savile immediately went about organising a regular record dance, like those he was famous for in Leeds. 'Off the Record' would be an eclectic night at which punters would be encouraged to bring their own records, for the simple reason that the club didn't have any of its own. The first night saw hundreds of young customers turn up, a huge improvement on the pitiful trickle before Savile took over.

High on his success but homesick for Leeds, Savile asked for a transfer back to the north. He was handed a gig managing The Plaza, a Mecca club in Manchester. At The Plaza, Savile applied the same Midas touch, launching a weekly talent contest and introducing the new craze for skiffle music. He also opened the club on weekday lunchtimes for record dances, which attracted hordes of local teenagers, many of whom got in trouble for returning late to school.

It was at The Plaza that Savile's two-sided nature really became apparent. As the flamboyant face of the club, he wore see-through shirts and carried a roll of (fake) twenty-pound notes in his breast pocket; he drove a Rolls Royce (faked using an old Bentley with a Rolls Royce radiator grill welded to the front); and smoked his trademark giant cigars. But on the less-public side of things, he was using his power in darker ways. By his own admission, Savile would tie up and gag troublemakers in the basement of the club and have them beaten up by the bouncers at the end of the night. Other unwanted guests were slung out, their heads used as battering rams to open doors on the way.

Savile was hanging around with local gangsters, such as the notorious Bill Benny. His underworld connections secured the safety of his club from extortion, racketeering and gang violence. And it seems that Savile too was dabbling in the murky world of underground crime. He even admitted to biographer, Dan Davies, that in Manchester, he hired three "Hungarian heavies," who had worked in the death camps in Europe, dispatching bodies for their Nazi overlords. Savile called them his 'Sonderkommandos' and used them to do his dirty work. "Well, these guys," Savile told Davies. "All I'd need to do was ask and they'd go and knock someone off, that was all there was to it." It was an astonishing admission, if true – that Savile was having his underworld enemies killed in 1950s Manchester.

If so, conspiracy to commit murder wasn't Savile's only crime. The vast hordes of teenagers flocking to The Plaza gave him the opportunity to develop his taste for underage girls. Savile explained the possibilities for picking up girls in typically cold fashion. "I would stand on the stage with a record player with a thousand people in the room for four or five hours," he told Davies. "Of the thousand people, 700 were girls. If half of them can't stand you, that leaves 350 who can stand you. If half of them are not too keen on you at all, then the other half is. That's 125 people. If half of them actually don't fancy you, that leaves around 65 girls that might want to go off with you. You don't have to be a brain surgeon to work out that you're never going to be short of ladies' company."

Of course, not all of these girls were over the age of consent. In the early 1950s, word was already getting round that Savile was more than just your average 'ladies' man'. One colleague told Davies he had joked with Jimmy that he "was either going to be a huge success or in prison for screwing 14-year-old girls". Another said, "He was a naughty man, a naughty man. He'd go with teenagers... I don't know how he got away with it." Savile was frequently seen disappearing into his car or his office with the young girls. Other witnesses told of wild parties at his flat in Leeds, where Savile and his friends would invite all the girls on his street, some as young as 13.

That Savile's name was already familiar to the police is clear from further witness testimony. One of Savile's bouncers, Dennis Lemmon, told Davies that, one day, Savile had come to work in a bad mood. When Lemmon quizzed colleagues about it, they told him Savile was due in court the following day for "messing about with a couple of girls." When Lemmon later enquired about the court case, he was told Savile had paid them off, and not for the first time.

Savile's meteoric rise through the ranks of Mecca continued. He became the regional manager for the north west in 1954. His flamboyant character and style were becoming so well known that, in 1959, he got the call up for his first TV appearance as a guest on *Jukebox Jury*, a panel show in which guests would predict whether new music singles would become a 'hit' or a 'miss'. Savile appeared on the show in his usual exuberant attire – a light-brown suit, pink shirt, green shoes and gold bowtie. At his home club of Mecca in Leeds, Savile was well-known as an outrageous showman, sometimes wearing suits that were half black, half white and hair that was similarly dyed down the middle. On other occasions, he would wear tartan clothes and have his hair dyed to match. He once turned up to an interview for Tyne-Tees Television sporting pink hair. All of this was in the fifties when such things were unheard of. It was around the same time that Savile made the switch in appearance which would remain a permanent trademark throughout the rest of his life – he had his hair bleached blonde.

The publicity of the Jukebox Jury appearance helped Savile's rising star, and he was soon offered the big break that would set him up for the rest of his career. Radio Luxembourg was a pirate commercial radio station, broadcasting into the UK from across the Channel. Compared to the stuffy BBC, it appealed to young people, offering light-hearted entertainment and, mostly importantly, the new Rock 'n' Roll music that was taking the world by storm. Savile was contacted by a representative from Decca Records, who wanted a DJ on Radio Luxembourg to showcase their new releases.

Savile turned up at the interview for Radio Luxembourg with tartan-coloured hair. Two days later, while on holiday in New York, he was summoned back to start working for the station immediately. Savile began his first ever radio show with what would become a trademark greeting, "Hi there, guys and gals..." With his non-received pronunciation, non-BBC accent and his quirky delivery, Savile was a breath of fresh air and an instant hit. He quadrupled his listeners in just one month and soon had five different shows running on the pirate station, including the Teen and Twenty Disc Club, which went on to become one of the station's most successful shows. To add to his success, Tyne-Tees Television commissioned him to co-present a weekly popular music show for teenagers.

Savile even got the chance to fly to the US to present Elvis Presley with a gold disk on behalf of Decca. He had his photo taken with the King and distributed copies to the press, posting others outside the Mecca Locarno dancehall. Savile's name was duly featured in newspapers up and down the land, with headlines like "Jimmy and the King."

Savile also sold some of the pictures through his Radio Luxembourg shows, donating the proceeds to the National Playing Fields Association. His charitable work earned him the admiration of the charity's patron, the Duke of Edinburgh, and, according to Savile, launched the start of a lifelong friendship between the two.

The same period saw the beginning of another lifelong association, this time with Leeds General Infirmary, the city's main hospital. Chief porter, Charles Hullighan, invited Savile to help launch the hospital's new radio station and Jimmy agreed, throwing in several days' voluntary work as a porter. It was the beginning of a career of healthcare fundraising, which would provide convenient access to young vulnerable people.

As part of his continued rise, Savile was made an associate director at Mecca. He celebrated the promotion by purchasing a brand-new Rolls Royce, this one genuine. He also released a music single and followed it up with another the following year. He then went on tour around the country, accompanying the band, Johnny & The Hurricanes.

Bizarrely, despite his new-found wealth, Savile decided to move into a rented one-bedroom flat in Manchester in a derelict Victorian mansion. He painted the whole flat black and it came to be known as the 'Black Pad' – a suitable name for some of the activities that no doubt took place there. While hiding himself away in run-down properties, Savile chose to flaunt his wealth in other ways. Parked alongside his Rolls Royce, he had an E-Type Jaguar, and his neck, wrists and fingers were weighed down with gold. The ostentatious jewellery would become another Savile trademark, one that some say inspired the 'bling' style of future American rappers.

In Manchester, Savile set about opening a club night at the New Elizabethan Ballroom in Belle Vue, an amusement park and zoo. Savile replaced a tired old dance night, held every Sunday, with a new rock and pop event that played all the latest hits, hosted by the UK's 'DJ of the Year,' Jimmy Savile himself. The Top Ten Club opened in May 1963 and was soon drawing crowds of around 2,000 every Sunday, with live acts that would include The Rolling Stones, Jimi Hendrix, Stevie Wonder and Ike and Tina Turner.

To top his success, Savile was given his own column at *The People* newspaper, where he was encouraged to share anecdotes about his colourful lifestyle, alongside prognostications about the music industry. Savile's *People* column would become a source of some almost unbelievably brazen admissions of the dark activities he was getting up to.

Bizarrely, 1963 also saw Savile get into wrestling. It started as a stunt to raise money at a benefit contest for a recently deceased wrestler. Savile was asked to referee the event but instead said he wanted to compete. He trained for six weeks before entering the ring with 'Gentleman' Jim Lewis, the undefeated welterweight champion of the world. Who knows how much of the contest was staged but Savile lasted until the seventh round and managed to score some points against Lewis before finally succumbing to defeat. Savile broke a toe but described it as "about the best experience of my life." He was hooked and began a wrestling career that would last several years.

His DJ and broadcasting career was also about to take a stellar turn. The BBC wanted to produce a new pop music show aimed at teenagers, to rival ITV's immensely popular *Ready Steady Go*. The BBC decided to mimic *Ready Steady Go's* format of bands miming in front of live teenage audiences. But, unlike *Ready Steady Go*, the Beeb decided to base its acts around current chart hits. The show now needed a charismatic frontman, and Jimmy Savile's name was quickly bandied about. However, there were already doubts about Savile among the BBC executives, with one or two saying they didn't want him on television. Savile's crowd-drawing appeal ultimately won the day and, on New Year's Day 1964, he presented the first episode of *Top of the Pops* from a converted church in Manchester. The show kicked off with The Rolling Stones' new single, 'I Want to Be your Man' and ended with The Beatle's number one hit, 'I want to Hold your Hand.'

Top of the Pops went on to be the most successful UK music show ever, spanning five decades. But for Savile, with its live audience of teenage girls, it was just another hunting ground, one that would lead, seven years later, to the suicide of Claire McAlpine. Those few BBC executives were right to worry about Savile, it turned out. And no wonder. Despite his relatively unsullied public image that year in 1964, there were already lots of rumours and several allegations.

A 2013 Her Majesty's Inspectorate of Constabulary (HMIC) report into Savile found that, in 1963, a man had gone into a Cheshire police station to report a rape, naming Savile as the perpetrator. Incredibly, the man was told to go home and forget about it. In the same year, another man went to a Metropolitan Police station in Westminster to report that his girlfriend had been sexually abused by Savile at a BBC studio. According to Williams-Thomas, the man was told, "You know how serious it is to make allegations like that? You could get yourself arrested. Go away."

In 1964, the Metropolitan police received another tip-off about Savile. In 2012, an intelligence report by the Paedophile Unit of the Met police was discovered, dating back to 1964. It included details of a vice ring, centred on a house in Battersea Bridge Road in London. The house was used by teenage girls absconding from Duncroft Approved School for girls. The vice ring involved several Duncroft girls and a younger boy and was run by three "coloured" men, according to the report, who were arrested for living off the immoral earnings of their charges. One of the men was imprisoned for two years, the second was found not guilty, and the third failed to appear at court. In the file, it was stated that Jimmy Savile was a regular visitor to the house.

"Savile was connected at that address," said Williams-Thomas. "So, as a result of that, that intelligence went into the police system in 1964. But nothing happened with it. So, if you take it in its simplistic form, the very first time that people knew that Jimmy Savile was connected to the sexual abuse of children was 1964."

The allegations didn't just involve underage girls. In an interview with Dan Davies, Savile admitted that Leeds police officers had entered his dancehall in the 1950s to tell him he had been reported hanging around public toilets in Leeds. Savile dismissed the police officers in his usual offhand manner and the matter was dropped.

In October 1963, two boys appeared at Salford Juvenile Court for stealing a £152 watch from Savile's Manchester flat. One boy, aged 14, received two years' probation and the other, aged 11, a fine of £10. It was conveniently not mentioned what they were doing in Savile's flat. In another 1963 allegation, a 10-year-old boy said he had approached Savile for an autograph outside a hotel and had subsequently been "assaulted by penetration".

All in all, according to the 2014 NSPCC report into Savile's crimes, 13 separate allegations of sexual abuse had been made against Savile by the end of 1963. None of these allegations were followed up or shared with Savile's home force, West Yorkshire Police. All of them were quietly filed, the victims told to "go away," "move on," or "forget about it." Rumours about Savile already abounded in the club scene and at the BBC, yet the organisations he worked for continued to provide him access to more and more teenagers.

It was 1964. Jimmy Savile's career as a serial sex abuser had only just begun. Yet already, it seemed, he was untouchable.

CHAPTER 2

THE LUNATIC IN CHARGE OF BROADMOOR ASYLUM

It is 1977, three men are playing football in the exercise yard of Britain's most notorious psychiatric hospital. One of the men is a murderer, the other a violent psychopath, and the third a child molester.

The game finishes in good spirits and the men ask one of the nurses to open the boot room so they can return the football. The three men enter the boot room together, the door slams shut, and the air of innocent fun suddenly evaporates.

A trap has sprung shut. Two of the men quickly barricade the doors with footlockers. They then turn on the third man – the paedophile – and tie him up using boot laces while he screams desperately for help.

The first two men – Robert Maudsley, confined for 20 years for the murder of a homosexual man, and David Cheeseman, incarcerated for the attempted murder of a nurse at another psychiatric hospital – now proceed to beat and torture the child molester, David Alan Francis, for the next nine hours. The two patients repeatedly punch and kick the third man before Maudsley fashions a makeshift pointed weapon from a plastic spoon and begins repeatedly stabbing Francis with it. Francis's screams become louder and more desperate while the staff outside can only listen and watch through a small toughened-plastic peephole.

After nine hours of torture, Maudsley puts an end to Francis's misery by, according to one staff member, ramming the pointed weapon into his ear until it penetrates the brain. Accounts differ as to what happens at the end, with rumours surfacing that Maudsley eats parts of his victim's brain, earning him the moniker 'Hannibal the Cannibal' in the next day's press.

Once their victim is dead, Maudsley and Cheeseman surrender themselves to staff. Both men are convicted of murder and Maudsley is transferred to HMP Wakefield, a maximum-security prison in Yorkshire, where the following year he murders two fellow prisoners in one day, stabbing one and garrotting the other.

Maudsley is sentenced to life in prison with a recommendation that he never be released. He is still behind bars today having spent years locked inside an underground glass cell, and is the UK's longest-serving prisoner in solitary confinement.

The psychiatric hospital where Maudsley and Cheeseman committed their horrific crime was Broadmoor, the oldest and most infamous of the UK's high security psychiatric hospitals, where some of the country's most dangerous offenders are housed. Other patients have included Peter Sutcliffe, Ronnie Kray, Charles Bronson, and James Kelly – one of the prime suspects behind the Jack the Ripper killings. Maudsley and Cheeseman's murder of their fellow patient is by no means the only – or the worst – violent act to have occurred within Broadmoor's high Victorian walls.

And yet this is the institution where Jimmy Savile, a television presenter, DJ and serial sex offender, was given free rein, including his own accommodation and set of keys. "He had total run of Broadmoor hospital. He had a house just outside the walls, he had a caravan inside the walls, he could come and go as he pleased," said Boris Coster, whose book, *Broadmoor Sinister*, looks into the lives of some of the institutions most dangerous patients, and includes a section on Savile.

As part of Savile's charity work he managed to worm himself inside one of the UK's highest security institutions, getting round-the-clock access to some of the country's most vulnerable patients, and even landed himself the job of 'Honorary Assistant

Entertainments Manager'. In the 80s he would outdo even this by becoming the self-appointed 'head' of a taskforce commissioned to turn around the failing institution. And of course, being Savile, he used his unprecedented access to prey on the patients who had been trusted to his care. During his time at Broadmoor there were 11 formal accusations of sexual abuse, six of whom were patients, two staff, and three minors. "He was almost at will able to walk round and touch and sexually assault the females within there," Mark Williams-Thomas told me, "without any repercussions because none of those people would ever be believed." Boris Coster put it more bluntly: "It was another one of his sweetshops."

So how did a TV star and disc jockey with no medical, psychiatric or criminal qualifications get free run of one of the world's most infamous high-security psychiatric hospitals?

Like many of Savile's other 'sweet shops' it began with a fan letter. In 1968, Savile received a highly unusual object in the mail. It was a Brazil nut set on a wooden plinth inscribed with the words "NUTTERS INC – Jimmy Savile". Accompanying the ornament was a letter from a patient at Broadmoor asking the DJ if he would open a fête at the hospital. Savile wrote back saying he would gladly do so if he got the boss's permission. He subsequently did so and took his first of many trips to Broadmoor. "I had an immediate affinity with the place," he told his biographer, Dan Davies.

Savile began visiting Broadmoor regularly where, he said, he would be allowed access to the patients in order "to chat" which he saw as "a form of therapy". He soon had earned the job title 'Honorary Assistant Entertainments officer'. He organised concerts every Thursday evening and put on a regular disco night. Every week after recording *Top of the Pops*, Savile would drive to Broadmoor where he would let himself in and watch the show with the psychiatric patients. He would sometimes even bring TOTP guests with him, including the musicians of Pan's People on one occasion.

In his usual manner, Savile also managed to inveigle his way into the system in order to start enjoying privileges which he no doubt felt his celebrity demanded. He was given two attic rooms inside the high-security compound for his personal use as well as his own set of keys and seemingly unlimited access to patients. "He comes and goes as he pleases," Coster told me. "He has a massive palatial caravan in the ground. He gets his gold-plated Rolls Royce serviced by the mechanics there. Not just that, his Hustler mobile home – it's called The Hustler – serviced at Broadmoor."

The mechanical favours may have come from one particularly strong relationship Savile built up with Broadmoor's transport manager, Donald Bennett. Savile practically took Bennett onto his books with Bennett acting as one of Savile's chauffeurs. Bennett even claimed the Department of Health gave him double the amount of leave in order to ferry Savile around the country. In 1971, Savile walked the length of the country from John O'Groats to Land's End with his motorhome trailing behind. Bennett was one of the people who shared the driving of the vehicle. Bennett was also one of the eight private beneficiaries of Savile's will, receiving the annual interest from a £600,000 trust fund.

It is unclear whether Savile enjoyed such close relationships with the doctors and psychiatrists at the hospital. In an interview with Channel 4, one member of staff said that most of the staff distrusted Savile as he seemed to attract the paedophiles at the hospital. The head doctor, Patrick McGrath, disliked Savile, according to McGrath's son who met Savile at Broadmoor, but tolerated his presence because of the benefits it brought to his patients. But despite McGrath's seeming innocence about Savile's motives, McGrath appears to have had enough awareness to remark "over my dead body" when Savile offered to give his young teenage daughter a ride in his Rolls Royce. One thing Savile did manage to get out of Broadmoor's psychiatrists was a Mensa IQ test performed under professional supervision. Savile scored 150, putting him in the top one percent in the country in terms of IQ.

Not long after Savile's appointment at Broadmoor, he received a similar role at Rampton, another high-security psychiatric hospital in Nottinghamshire. This suited Savile's peripatetic lifestyle, as he travelled around the country in his motorhome, popping into one of his nearest 'sweet shops' at his convenience.

Savile followed a similar modus operandi at Rampton as at Broadmoor, parking his caravan in the grounds and taking staff and patients on day trips to Scarborough, where he had a flat. During his time at Rampton there were several reports of Savile being seen walking to and from his caravan with different females, but nothing was acted on or, it seems, officially recorded. In an article for *The People* Newspaper in 1972, Savile described his relationship with the Rampton patients in unnerving terms, writing, "The sub-normal patients come and hang off me like presents off a Christmas tree. I gather up great armfuls of them. I have got a great way with sub-normals."

Despite the extremely high security at Broadmoor, it seemed that Savile was also taking patients outside the walls at the UK's highest security mental hospital. In a 2012 *Daily Mail* article the daughter of one of the Broadmoor nurses told the paper that Savile used to take trusted patients out for trips in his Rolls Royce. Further evidence came from Mark Williams-Thomas's follow up *Exposure* programme for ITV which gave an update on the Savile investigation and included a section on Broadmoor. Williams-Thomas unearthed a letter from a Broadmoor patient to Savile thanking him for taking him on a supervised day trip. Even more shocking, the programme showed footage of a *Clunk Click* episode in which Savile let slip that some of the girls in the audience were from Broadmoor.

In Savile's early days at Broadmoor, the security might have been too tough even for him to abuse patients at will. Thus, perhaps, the need for the excursions and day trips. There is also evidence that he was preying on visitors to the hospital. The daughter of the nurse also told *The Daily Mail* that Savile would try it on with young women who were visiting relatives at the hospital and would stand outside his caravan in the grounds trying to entice them inside.

One such outsider was the daughter of a local journalist who often covered Savile's visits to Broadmoor. The girl was in her teens in 1975 when Savile asked her parents if she would like to come and watch him film an episode of *Top of the Pops*. They agreed and the girl travelled to London to meet Savile at his flat. After filming, Savile took her back to the flat where she said he forced his tongue down her throat. When he asked her if she was enjoying it, the girl said she wasn't which, she said, caused him to stop, but only, she thought, because he was worried about her parents knowing. Another member of staff reported seeing Savile take a 16-year-old girl into his flat inside Broadmoor who he had picked up at the local festival in the nearby village of Crowthorne.

Whether or not Savile found it difficult at first to offend inside Broadmoor's grounds, within a few years he had gained enough access and influence to have a more-or-less free rein inside the hospital. Two former psychiatric nurses from Broadmoor told the Exposure Update programme that Savile had keys to the female ward in Broadmoor and that he would often turn up there "unaccompanied and unannounced". Williams-Thomas interviewed one of the former female patients at Broadmoor who revealed just how shocking Savile's access to the female section was.

"He'd actually come in the bathroom while I was having a bath," the former patient told the *Exposure* programme, "and it was like two separate baths. There was no screens or anything and he just walked in. There was nothing you could do." She added, "He was just joking with the staff and looking at you, and he would look at you while you're in the bath."

But Savile's access didn't stop at watching female patients in the bath. The patient, referred to as Kate in the *Exposure* show, went on to explain how Savile sexually assaulted her. She said she was sat in the day room one day when Savile put his arm around her. She said she didn't feel comfortable with the close contact but that none of the other patients or staff seemed bothered and she thought it was Savile just being friendly. But Savile went further.

"He tried to touch my breast," Kate told *Exposure*, "and I just sort of moved my hand away, and I thought maybe he's made a mistake, maybe his hand's just, you know, trying to reason. I didn't want anybody touching me there whatsoever, you know. Then he tried to put his hand between my legs, tried to move his hand up, and I just stood up and I just said, 'No.'"

Kate said she reported the incident to hospital staff and as a result was placed in solitary confinement for several months. She told the show that the incident affected her so badly that she tried to kill herself but was prevented from doing so by staff.

The combination of freedom to touch patients, even in front of staff, combined with punishment of victims who dared speak out is familiar from other institutions Savile targeted, such as Duncroft school, Leeds General Infirmary and Stoke Mandeville hospital. It shows the incredible level of access and power Savile had at the high-security mental hospital, which was truly, as Boris Coster said, one of his "Sweet shops".

Williams-Thomas confirmed this opinion in an interview with me where he said he believed Savile had an almost free rein to wander around the hospital touching women at will. One case of sexual assault at Broadmoor that Williams-Thomas shared with me illustrated Savile's complete lack of empathy for his victims, which contrasted starkly with the caring veneer he put on in front of others:

"One girl we interviewed… she gave one account – when she was quite young she went there [Broadmoor], I think about 19, something like that, and she gave us an account when she was on her period and she didn't really know what she was doing. It was quite early, she was in a very distressed state, and Savile just stood there, watched her and then later he indecently assaulted her. And the way she gave us the account was just like, there was no sense of care in any way at all. He literally didn't care."

The Department of Health's 2014 inquiry into Savile's behaviour at Broadmoor threw up 11 cases of sexual assault. However, it concluded that there were likely to have been many more that went unreported. One of the accounts was from a former female patient who said she was assaulted by Savile around 1971 or 1972 during a screening of *Top of the Pops*. The patient, referred to as 'B' in the report, said that patients and staff were watching *Top of the Pops* with Savile in the day room. She said staff would sit at the back of the room and patients would sit at the front along with Savile where they were shielded from view by a large sofa. B said she was sat beside Savile on the floor beside the sofa when he assaulted her by "placing his hand between her legs and groping her genitalia while she was watching the television." According to the report the assault lasted for two or three minutes. B said she didn't report the incident for fear of being "punished as a troublemaker".

The report documented another female patient who had told a nurse at another hospital that Savile had sexually assaulted her under the stage at Broadmoor, where live acts would perform. Another former male patient told the inquiry he had passed on complaints to staff from three female patients who had all been assaulted by Savile in a single day. None of the senior staff to whom the patient said he had reported the assaults could remember the incident, according to the report.

Two female patients mentioned in the report alleged having been assaulted by Savile on repeated occasions. One of these patients, D, reported being assaulted by Savile on four or five separate occasions in 1987. D described the first assault as happening in the lounge area where she was on her own after having showered. The other patients were still showering at the time and the staff were either with them or having tea. Savile entered the lounge area unaccompanied, according to the patient, and put his hands up her nightgown. "He had his fingers inside of me," she told the inquiry, while at the same time, "he had his hands down his trousers and he was like playing with himself." D said after the assault Savile got up and walked out like nothing had happened. She said that the same thing happened on two or three occasions. She reported the first assault to the staff but, she said, had been told to "'stop making things up or [she] would be in serious trouble".

Another patient described being assaulted by Savile on multiple occasions in the early 90s. The assaults would occur in the day room when Savile would enter unaccompanied by staff and sit and talk to patients. This patient, 'E', told the report that Savile would put his hand on her leg while talking to her then slide it upwards and grope her genitalia while still talking. He would then move onto other female patients and do the same thing to them. E told the inquiry that Savile's clothes were "shabby and dirty" and that she felt repelled by him but always froze when the attacks happened, and felt guilty about not saying anything. However, on the one occasion she did report the abuse to a member of staff she was told she must have imagined it. E told the inquiry that she believed two patients had committed suicide as a direct result of Savile's assaults.

Savile's abuse was not only confined to patients, the report found. Two female members of staff reported being assaulted by Savile. One of them described him pinning her up against the wall in the central hall and thrusting his groin into hers. She said she struggled and he immediately released her. The staff member said that the hall was filled with patients and staff at the time and she was angry and embarrassed about the assault but didn't think it was worth reporting "given the climate at the time".

The inquiry also confirmed stories of Savile abusing young visitors to the hospital, referring to police reports from two female visitors who had been 14 and 15 at the time, who both claimed to have been sexually assaulted by Savile.

And Savile's activities weren't just confined to female victims. The report documented the testimony of one former male patient who said he regularly visited Savile's caravan to collect payment for washing Savile's cars, accompanied by Broadmoor's transport manager – and Savile's friend – Don Bennett. The patient, 'A', described how on one occasion in 1972 Bennett was absent so another staff member encouraged him to go to the caravan on his own. The report described what happened next:

"A described to us being coerced into giving Savile oral sex, recounting clearly the inner turmoil that this caused him, as well as the feeling that he had no alternative but to proceed, albeit unwillingly. Savile's penis was not fully erect, and A kept stopping through fear of being caught. After some minutes, Savile said 'ok' and stopped him, without ejaculating."

A told the report he had felt unable to say no or report the incident for fear of being branded a troublemaker. Bennett told the report he had no memory of the patient or his regular visits with him to Savile's caravan.

Another male victim, this time a young pre-teen boy who was visiting the hospital, told the report how Savile had exposed himself to him when they were alone on the hospital's minibus. The little boy rapidly made his escape from the minibus and told nobody. However, he told the report, he felt the incident was one of the contributing factors to his later need for counselling.

The allegations of sexual abuse against Savile ranged across most of his time at Broadmoor, which lasted from 1968 to 2004 when security changes meant he would no longer be allowed his own set of keys. There were likely to have been many more cases than the ones reported because, as the inquiry made clear, the culture at the time meant patients were discouraged from reporting such incidents for fear of being punished as troublemakers.

What is almost as shocking as the assaults themselves is the knowledge – or at least suspicion – among staff that there was something wrong with Savile. Many of the interviewees told the inquiry how Savile, on first meeting a new female, would kiss them on the hands, followed by kisses all the way up their arms, sometimes ending with a kiss on the lips. He would also often make inappropriate comments such as how the men on the ward had been "lusting after [her] body". They told the inquiry that there was a "steady stream" of young female nurses going into Savile's caravan and even some rumours that he used it as a "brothel". Another interviewee told how she had overheard a conversation in the staff room about how Savile would knock on nurses' doors at night and expect to be allowed in to have sex with them. It was also made clear that Savile's interest in younger women was widespread knowledge across the hospital. "I'd say it was fairly widely commented that he had, if you like, a penchant for younger women," one interviewee told the inquiry. Other former staff members told how older nurses would warn the younger women not to spend time alone with Savile. One former nurse told the inquiry she was told, "Don't leave young nurses alone with him, especially if they look about twelve years old."

All of which makes it seem incredible that Savile was allowed to carry on with his unrestricted access to the high-security hospital. What becomes even more incredible is that, after two decades of abuse at the hospital, Savile's power and influence over Broadmoor would escalate, when he became the self-appointed head of a six-person taskforce commissioned to overhaul the hospital's failing systems.

The explanation of how a TV presenter and disc jockey came to be in charge of reforming the UK's oldest and most infamous high-security mental hospital involves a look back at the convoluted history of Broadmoor.

Built in 1868 near the village of Crowthorne in Berkshire, Broadmoor was originally known as a 'Criminal Lunatic Asylum'. It was designed and built by Sir Joshua Jebb, an officer in the Royal Engineers and the country's Surveyor General of Prisons. Jebb's time in the army had made him an expert on siege warfare, on which he had written several books. He had also designed Pentonville Prison in London, Woking Convict Invalid Prison, and Mountjoy Prison in Belfast. All of which made him the ideal person to create the UK's first wholly independent prison for convicts who had been found 'not guilty by reason of insanity'.

Built on a ridge overlooking the Berkshire countryside, the asylum spanned 53 acres. It was surrounded by high walls that enclosed five imposing red-brick blocks with narrow arched windows, as well as gardens and other administrative buildings. Its situation in the Berkshire countryside gave Broadmoor a healthy and tranquil air. It was suitably isolated but close enough to

London, to which it was connected by rail, to make transferring prisoners reasonably simple.

In 1949, Broadmoor was transferred to the jurisdiction of the Department of Health, marking the beginning of its slow transformation from asylum to hospital. In 1959, the transition became official, with Broadmoor being redesignated as a 'special hospital' under the new Mental Health Act. Broadmoor was tasked with treating patients with mental illnesses which made their behaviour dangerous, violent or criminal. In 1957, the medical psychiatrist Dr Pat McGrath was put in charge of Broadmoor and given the unenviable task of modernising an institution that was overcrowded, understaffed and still run more like a prison than a mental hospital.

It was under Dr McGrath's regime that Savile first became involved with the hospital in 1968. It was McGrath who Savile wrote to asking for permission to visit the hospital following the patients' request. It was McGrath who rubber-stamped Savile's role as Honorary Assistant Entertainments Officer, and who agreed to Savile having unrestricted access to the hospital, as well as accommodation within the grounds. Dr McGrath's son, the novelist Patrick McGrath, insists that his father disliked Savile but he realised at the same time that Savile provided an opportunity for his patients to experience a wider and healthier access to the world at large, especially with his weekly discos and regular concerts, as well as his occasional day trips. Whatever McGrath thought of Savile privately, publicly he spoke of him in the most glowing terms, saying in a 1978 article about Savile's level of access to Broadmoor that, "in a special security hospital... [it is] the highest mark of trust the management can offer".

The kind of patients Savile was getting access to were truly some of the most dangerous psychopaths in the country, including serial killer Peter Sutcliffe aka The Yorkshire Ripper, and the legendary London gangster, Ronnie Kray. Broadmoor's history had been littered with such unstable psychopaths from the moment it accepted its first case in 1863 – a woman who had killed her own baby.

Among the many others, there was Alan Reeve, who battered a 15-year-old boy to death in 1968. Sectioned in Broadmoor, Reeve then strangled another prisoner and went on to escape the hospital. He went on the run in the Netherlands and killed a policeman in a gun fight before fleeing to Northern Ireland where he was extradited back to England and finally re-incarcerated in Broadmoor.

Then there was John Straffen a child serial killer who strangled his first victim – a five-year-old girl – in Bath in 1951. Later that year Straffen strangled a nine-year-old girl who he met at the cinema. At his trial Straffen was found unfit to plead due to his mental health and committed to Broadmoor. However a year later, he was in sound enough mental health to escape the hospital by climbing the ten-foot wall while wearing civilian clothes under his uniform. Within hours of escape, Straffen had killed a five-year-old girl he found riding a bicycle in nearby Farley Hill. Straffen was recaptured and this time found guilty. He was sentenced to death but later in the year was reprieved by the Home Secretary and was sent to Rampton, Broadmoor's sister hospital in Nottinghamshire. Straffen died in prison in 2007 and, at the time, was the UK's longest serving prisoner.

Another was Graham Young aka the 'Teacup Poisoner'. Young was a serial killer who started early. He experimented with poisoning his friends and relatives as a young boy and by the age of 14 had been convicted of three non-fatal poisonings, also admitting to the murder by poison of his stepmother. He was detained in Broadmoor until his release in 1971 when he immediately started poisoning people again, this time with greater success. He poisoned several of his colleagues at a factory in Hertfordshire, killing two of them and causing severe illnesses in others. He was caught and sentenced to life in prison for two murders and two attempted murders. He died in Parkhurst in 1990.

Of Broadmoor's most notorious patients, Savile met quite a few, even becoming friends with some. Savile was particularly close with Peter Sutcliffe, aka the Yorkshire Ripper, and indeed shared a bizarre connection with the hunt for the serial killer.

The Ripper part of Sutcliffe's nickname was appropriate because, like his predecessor Jack the Ripper, Sutcliffe had targeted women, including prostitutes. But Sutcliffe's reign of terror was much worse than the East End serial killer's. Sutcliffe murdered 13 women and attempted to murder seven others between 1975 and 1980, compared with Jack the Ripper's five murders. Similar to the previous Ripper, Sutcliffe's modus operandi was to stalk the streets late at night, often in red light districts. He would target lone women, often prostitutes, and strike them over the head with a hammer before slashing or stabbing their bodies with a knife. Several of his victims survived his attacks but required brain surgery, most died.

Sutcliffe was arrested in 1981 in Sheffield when police found him with a prostitute. He was taken to Dewsbury police station in West Yorkshire and questioned in connection with the Yorkshire Ripper murders as he matched the physical description of the Ripper. After two days of questioning, Sutcliffe confessed to the murders, saying that the voice of God had told him to punish prostitutes. He was charged with 13 murders and seven attempted murders and sentenced to 20 concurrent life sentences. This was later converted to a whole life order in 2010, ensuring that he would never be released.

Sutcliffe was transferred to Broadmoor in 1984, after being diagnosed with paranoid schizophrenia. It was here that he became friends with Savile although, intriguingly, there had been a link between the two men before the serial killer's arrest. Two of Sutcliffe's killings had been committed in Hyde Park in Leeds. At the time Savile had a flat overlooking Hyde Park, situated not more than 150 yards from where the murders took place. Savile was actually brought in for questioning by West Yorkshire Police in relation to the murders, which raises the obvious question – why would the police see him as a potential suspect? In any case, Savile was released after a test failed to match his dental records with the teeth marks of the Ripper, found on the body of one of his victims.

Boris Coster raises the intriguing question of whether Savile and Sutcliffe knew each other prior to Sutcliffe's arrest. Considering the two shared the same interests and stomping grounds it's not out of the question. Also there was Savile's bizarre offer of making himself an intermediary between the Ripper and the police should the killer give himself up. In any case, Broadmoor was not Savile's first meeting with Sutcliffe. They had originally been introduced at Parkhurst Prison on the Isle of Wight where Sutcliffe was first incarcerated. In 1982, Savile had led 30 prisoners in a sponsored jog around the prison grounds to raise money for his Stoke Mandeville appeal. Sutcliffe was one of the men Savile met on that day. Savile later mentioned to the press that he had spoken with Sutcliffe for several minutes and that the serial killer had been "terribly friendly" and "in high good humour".

But it was in Broadmoor where Savile and Sutcliffe's relationship would truly blossom. Staff and patients both remarked how Savile and the Ripper would often be found deep in conversation, and that the two clearly shared some kind of bond. "It's a very close relationship," Coster confirmed, "these two get on like a house on fire."

But why? Dan Davies suggests in his Savile biography, *Hidden in Plain Sight*, that Savile used his contacts with people like Sutcliffe and the Krays to find out about the darker side of human nature, in order to delve into his own dark side and, importantly, to observe how they thought, spoke and behaved – in short, how they gave themselves away – so that he wouldn't make the same mistake. Coster on the other hand suspects that Savile and Sutcliffe were close because they shared a prior knowledge – and perhaps complicity – in each other's crimes.

One thing is for certain: Savile spoke highly of Sutcliffe and even used him as a bizarre kind of PR attraction. Such was the unfortunate case of heavyweight boxer Frank Bruno who Savile befriended in the early 90s. After Bruno's loss challenging Mike Tyson for the World Heavyweight Championship, Savile became a kind of mentor to the big man, taking him on charity runs and fundraisers around the country. On one such occasion in 1991, Bruno accompanied Savile to Broadmoor where he helped unveil the new gym. On a tour of the secure ward Savile introduced Bruno to one of the patients and the two shook hands while a photographer snapped a picture of the moment.

Only after the meeting did Savile tell Bruno that he'd just shaken hands with the Yorkshire Ripper. Bruno was understandably angry, even more so when the photograph emerged of him shaking hands amiably with the murderer of 13 women. It seems reasonable that Savile had set up the meeting to get the shot as a kind of PR stunt, perhaps in an attempt to improve Sutcliffe's image. But why? Perhaps for the same reason Savile defended Sutcliffe whenever asked about him in the press – the two were friends. But then Savile defended another serial killer, the Moors Murderer Ian Brady, too. Further in this Savile book series, we will explore why Savile became a suspect in the Ripper case and the possibility that he had met not only Sutcliffe, but also the Moors Murderers.

In 1988, Broadmoor's board of directors was suspended and an interim taskforce was assembled to turn around the failing hospital. At the time, Broadmoor was in a dispute with the Prison Officer's Association, a trade union which most of the hospital's nurses belonged to. Trade union actions such as a ban on daytime overtime work meant that patients were being left alone in secluded cells for long periods of time. The appointment of the taskforce came just in time, according to a leaked article, to head off the damaging effects of a highly critical report by the Hospital Advisory Service on Broadmoor's management, its nurses, and the lack of care for patients. "Time is running out for Broadmoor," the report was later revealed to say, painting the hospital as an institution as outdated as its peeling Victorian façade, where patients were treated without human dignity and kept in line through an atmosphere of suspicion and fear.

Savile told his biographer, Dan Davies, that his name was first nominated for the taskforce by the "top civil service boss" who ran

Broadmoor. This was probably Brian McGinnis, the senior civil servant who ran the mental health division of the Department of Health just prior to Savile's appointment. McGinnis was subsequently arrested for two separate rape allegations, one on a child with learning difficulties. McGinnis, although uncharged on both accounts, was subsequently banned from working with children. McGinnis was also at the centre of a scandal in the 1980s when his department helped block the introduction of tougher legislation governing sexual assaults on people with learning difficulties and mental health problems.

Savile's nomination to the taskforce was ratified by Edwina Currie, a conservative MP in Margaret Thatcher's government who was then under-secretary of state for health, and the politician in charge of the UK's special hospitals. Savile claimed he was placed on the taskforce for his knowledge of the hospital and because of his ability to "get things done". He also claimed that he had been made chair of the six-man team, an assertion that the Department of Health moved quickly to contradict, stating that its under-secretary, Clifford Graham, was the chairman. Undeterred, Savile commented, "Because I live here, I call myself the chairman of the taskforce. Technically, I could be anything. I live here, I am the boss. It's as simple as that."

Savile quickly outlined a plan to improve the hospital, including smaller wards, private rooms and individual therapy sessions for patients. He didn't mention that he also got a new office just outside the hospital's wall.

Savile certainly worked quickly and within weeks had met with Edwina Currie at The Athenaeum, a private members' club, to present a list of problems he had found. Savile told Currie, according to her diaries, that he had unearthed evidence of staff being fraudulently overpaid, including false overtime claims of up to £800 a week. He had also found staff accommodation being used by family members who didn't work at the hospital, and even claimed the existence of a hidden IRA terrorist cell within the hospital. In an interview with Mark Williams-Thomas for the *Exposure Update* programme, Currie said she had come to believe that Savile was using the information he had gathered to blackmail staff into complying with his demands.

Currie told Williams-Thomas, "He had put himself in the position where he could say to that member of staff, 'I know that you're fiddling your overtime and I know you've been doing it for years. I know that you've got your sister living in one of our houses here and that she's not been paying rent. I know what you've been up to. You will get the sack. Don't be a whistleblower, don't even think about it. You know what happens to whistleblowers.'"

Although Currie was critical of Savile's behaviour on the *Exposure Update* documentary she failed to mention her earlier approval of his blackmail tactics. The under-secretary of state had written in her diary at the time "Attaboy!" in approval Savile's unconventional methods.

Currie claimed she had never liked Savile but then so did everybody after Savile's exposure. In my interview with David Icke for my Savile documentary, *Untouchable*, Icke told me that Savile wasn't Currie's only association with known paedophiles, nor did she seem to mind working in close association with them.

"Edwina Currie's note in her diary just shows her callous disregard for the kids who've been abused," Icke told me, "because towards the end of the Thatcher premiership she gave a role, a job, an official title to Peter Morrison – Peter Morrison who they all knew was a paedophile. 'Likes little boys' – that's the kind of code they use. And Edwina Currie wrote in this diary of hers… that she was concerned that Thatcher had given Morrison this role because he's a known paedophile… Miss Currie, you knew that Peter Morrison was a paedophile and you said nothing, you did nothing… And then she says in the diary that the chairman of the Conservative party had asked Morrison about the paedophilia and he'd promised to be discreet! … It shows the cavalier, almost commonplace nature of it."

As if the dodgy connections around Savile's appointment to the taskforce weren't enough, they went one step further when, at

Savile's recommendation, his friend Alan Franey was appointed as Broadmoor's new General Manager. Franey had been an administrator at Leeds General Infirmary during Savile's time volunteering there. The two had become close friends, often running marathons together, with Franey even appearing as a guest on Savile's *This is Your Life* tribute programme. Franey was also one of the last people to contact Savile before Savile's death, calling him at his Leeds flat in October 2011, just a few days before the end.

Franey had no experience of mental health institutions or the prison system so his appointment seems a bit of a mystery. Savile had originally put Franey's name forward and he was present at the meeting of civil servants that confirmed Franey's appointment, so the DJs influence was clear. Why was Savile so keen to have his old friend from Leeds General Infirmary running Broadmoor? It seems reasonable that Savile was worried that the new regime would affect his free access to patients. He needed a trusted hand at the helm to make sure his reign of abuse could continue unaffected. And indeed Savile continued to have free access to the hospital throughout Franey's eight-year tenure.

Mark Williams-Thomas confirmed this in an interview with Ray Rowden, a senior NHS executive supervising Broadmoor in the 90s. Rowden told Williams-Thomas he was astonished to discover that Savile still had his own set of keys to Broadmoor. Rowden was so concerned that he brought the matter up with Franey who, he says, merely shrugged it off.

In the 2014 Department of Health report on Broadmoor, staff told interviewers that Franey "put it about a bit" and used his accommodation for "inappropriate activities". According to various staff, Franey had had up to "50 affairs" during his time at the hospital. The report went on to point out that three sexual assaults by Savile were reported to Franey in the 90s, all of which he brushed under the carpet. Franey claimed not to remember any of them. The report concluded, "In our view, it is impossible to examine Savile's position in the hospital and his ability to exploit it without understanding Franey's role in the management of the hospital."

Mark Williams-Thomas spoke to Franey for the *Exposure Update* programme, an interview in which Franey insisted he got the job on his own merits and that he had no knowledge of Savile's behaviour. "I remember interviewing Franey," Williams-Thomas told me, "and I said to him, 'So what role did you give him?' And he said, 'Well, he already had a role at the place.' And I said, 'Yeah, but what role was that?' He said, 'Assistant Entertainment Manager.' I said, 'Well, what did that involve?' He went, 'Well, I'm not really sure.' I said, 'You're the general manager, you're the boss. How did you not know what this bloke was doing?' I said, 'He had a set of keys.' He said, 'Well, he didn't have a set of keys to bedrooms.' I said, 'He had a set of keys to everywhere, It might not have been the bedrooms but he had a set of keys to go wherever he wanted.'"

Whatever the case Savile's hardball tactics with the Broad-moor staff were soon paying off. Most of the taskforce's proposed reforms were pushed through without response or strike action. Savile was, unsurprisingly, unpopular with Broadmoor staff. Mark Williams-Thomas told me about the depth of feeling that Broadmoor staff had towards Savile. "There was staff that called us who were there at the time who hated him, hated him with a vengeance because he effectively thought that he was the boss. He could come and go, he could do what he wanted, he ignored things. The keys for example – you had to hang the keys up at the end of every shift. He didn't, he took the keys with him."

Management and staff who were unwilling to adapt to the new structures Savile and 'his' team were putting in place were told to consider finding jobs elsewhere. They had no choice but to comply or leave. Savile was protected from any come back by his official role in the taskforce, as well, it seemed, as his personal support from powerful figures within the government like Edwina Currie and Margaret Thatcher herself.

One of the more controversial changes implemented was the

transferral of 60 patients to other institutions around the country. It was the largest transfer of patients in the hospital's history and caused a ruckus in the press, especially when it was revealed that two of the patients were convicted murderers. *The News of the World* ran with the headline: "Jim Fixes it for 60 Psychos to Go Free". Savile also announced plans to turn Broadmoor into a kind of halfway house that would focus on preparing patients for reintegration into society. One of the ways of doing this would be to abolish the old male and female wards and have patients of both sexes mingle together, as Savile said "falling in love" was one of the strongest motivations in rehabilitation.

Franey went on to serve as General Manager then CEO of Broadmoor for eight years. These were years in which Savile had unrestricted access to the hospital and its patients, despite the reforms he had himself forced through. They were years in which his offending continued, some of which was documented in the 2014 Department of Health report, but doubtless was on a far greater scale than any formal inquiries will ever uncover.

In 1997, allegations surfaced that a child paedophile ring was operating inside Broadmoor and that patients had access to child pornography. The Department of Health launched an inquiry but found no evidence to back up the allegations. Nevertheless, later the same year, Franey resigned from his position at the hospital. With Franey's resignation came major security shake ups at Broadmoor. In 1998 the Department of Health launched an inquiry into all three of the UK's high security psychiatric hospitals and found serious shortcomings. It implemented a new system whereby the Department of Health directly provided the security protocols which all three hospitals must follow. This, along with Franey's resignation, finally spelled the end of Savile's three-decade reign of terror at Broadmoor.

Under the new security rules, Savile would still be allowed access to the hospital but his days of owning his own set of keys were over. Access to the hospital would now be much more restricted and he would no longer be able to come and go as he pleased. As the 2014 Department of Health report described, once Savile was briefed on the new security arrangements, he stopped visiting the hospital altogether. His formal right to access the hospital wasn't withdrawn until 2009, but it was no longer one of his sweet shops, so he dropped it – along with his supposed care for all its patients.

Savile's exposure came too late for his Broadmoor victims to receive any justice in his lifetime but, when the truth began to surface in 2012, Broadmoor was one of the institutions which came under the spotlight. Edwina Currie was quick to admit that the Department of Health had been guilty of allowing Savile free rein at Broadmoor, saying on Williams-Thomas's *Exposure Update* programme, "We gave him every instrument that he needed in Broadmoor to prey on some extremely damaged individuals. If Savile were alive now I'd want to see him locked away for the rest of his life."

The Department of Health conducted its own inquiry into Broadmoor in 2014 which found 11 allegations of sexual abuse against Savile by patients and staff, while admitting there were probably many more that had gone unreported. But despite the findings, no heads rolled and no one was found to have colluded with or enabled Savile's behaviour. Rather the hospital seemed to be distancing itself from the culture and security of its former incarnation, repeatedly pointing out the differences between the modern regime and the one in which Savile thrived. Much of what enabled Savile to freely abuse patients at the hospital was put down to the different culture of the times which was more permissive about touching women. The repeated failure of staff to report their suspicions, despite the consistent rumours, was put down to their respect for Dr Pat McGrath who had sanctioned Savile's presence and who "must know what he's doing".

"I've seen the 148-page report on Broadmoor," Boris Coster told me, "and the first 10 pages... is like 10 pages of nothing. And then it gets down to the last 10 pages of, well, at the time we lived in a different era, we could get away with touching someone up the backside. They actually turned around and basically said, well it's acceptable. No one's ever been brought to account for it. It was, just write a report and just brush it under the carpet."

Coster and his fellow true-crime writer, Christopher Berry-Dee, wrote several freedom of information requests to Broadmoor but said they were consistently "fobbed off" by the institution with quibbles over whether the requests should be answered by the NHS or Department of Health.

Broadmoor today is still one of the country's three high-security psychiatric hospitals. It comes under the West London NHS Trust and treats patients with mental illnesses and personality disorders who are deemed a risk to themselves or others. It is now much more a hospital than it has ever been, with the focus on rehabilitation and therapy of all kinds including psychiatric medicine, psychological therapy, occupational therapy and even arts therapy. It has been given a rating of 'Good' by the Care Quality Commission. Yet in many ways it is still the Broadmoor of the past. It still has the high walls, the formidable security, and the forbidding air of a Victorian mental asylum. Many of its patients are still convicted criminals and many of its nurses are still members of the Prison Officers Association.

Perhaps more than anything, Broadmoor is still haunted by the ghosts of its past, ghosts such as Peter Sutcliffe, Robert Maudsley and Ronnie Kray. But perhaps Broadmoor's most tenacious, and most unpleasant, ghost is that of Jimmy Savile, the man who haunted its corridors for more than three decades, bringing terror and suffering to its most vulnerable residents – a ghost who wasn't even a patient and should never have been there.

CHAPTER 3

DUNCROFT GIRLS SCHOOL
SAVILE'S SWEET SHOP

The first person to publicly expose Jimmy Savile wasn't a reporter from the BBC or ITV or a journalist from a national newspaper. It was a 57-year-old woman writing her memoir online under the name Keri.

It was 2009, a full three years before ITV's *Exposure* documentary would reveal the shocking truth about Britain's favourite TV personality and Keri, or Karin Ward as she is now known, was writing her memoir on Fansite.com, an online writing community for budding authors. It was partly a writing exercise and partly an act of therapy for Keri, who had suffered sexual abuse throughout her childhood and teenage years. One of her abusers was Jimmy Savile who Keri thinly disguised in her memoirs as 'JS', an extravagant and outgoing celebrity with a penchant for outsize cigars who regularly visited the school she attended, Duncroft Approved School for Girls in Surrey. It hardly took a Sherlock Holmes to work out who she was talking about.

In her memoir, Keri described Savile's first visit to the school in the early 70s. 'JS' turned up in a flashy sports car and the Duncroft girls flocked around to help clean it, a task they were rewarded for with cigarettes and a rare trip outside the school grounds. JS always brought large numbers of duty-free cigarettes, Keri recalled, which he would give to the girls, along with records and other presents. She recounted that JS was friendly with Duncroft's headmistress, Margaret Jones, and that the usually stodgy school meals were better prepared and presented on the days when JS would visit.

Keri soon joined the other girls in looking forward to JS's visits along with the promise of free cigarettes and rides in his car. However, she soon became acutely aware that there was a price attached to these benefits. "Sadly," she wrote, "it also meant one had to put up with being mauled and groped when he pulled into a lay-by some five miles along the road. I wasn't the only girl that JS favoured with this either. In fact, on the several occasions when he chose to take me out, he often tried to press me to 'go further' than simply fondling him and allowing him to grope inside my knickers and at my almost non-existent breasts. He promised me all manner of good things if I would give him oral sex."

Keri was 14 years old at the time. She soon gave into JS's requests for oral sex in return for a trip to watch the filming of his *Clunk Click* programme at BBC headquarters in London. The act occurred in JS's car and caused Keri to gag violently, leading JS to fling the door open and urge her to vomit "outside the car".

Keri got her visit to the BBC but it just led to further abuse and humiliation. Over the course of half a dozen visits to watch Savile's shows, Keri suffered and witnessed more abuse at the hands of JS and his friends, all of which she recorded in her memoir. However, little did she know at the time, but another person with vivid childhood memories of Savile and Duncroft was reading her memoir with great interest, and that this person, Meirion Jones, was a journalist working for the BBC's current affairs show, *Newsnight*. It was when Jones contacted Keri that the first spark was lit that would lead, ultimately, to Savile's exposure.

When that happened in 2012, Keri's experiences at Duncroft would become headline news. But what was less well known was that Duncroft wasn't the first time Keri had met Savile. She had first bumped into him during a trip to Haut de la Garenne, a notorious children's home on the island of Jersey where Savile also preyed on underage victims. That first meeting with Savile had led to Keri suffering a string of sexual assaults and rapes at the hands of strangers.

Keri's life story was certainly harrowing. She was born of a failed marriage, the pregnancy becoming apparent after her mother and biological father had split up. Keri's mother was encouraged to keep the baby by her own adoptive parents but she became an unwanted reminder of the failed relationship, leading Keri's mother to resent and hate her own child who, she believed, had ruined her life. As a young child, Keri became the victim of a double life, loved and spoiled in public and with her grandparents, but abused and neglected behind closed doors. Keri records in her memoir how she was slapped, dragged around by her hair, and called all manner of names by her mother from an early age including "disgusting, vile, scrawny, useless, stupid, revolting, selfish, greedy, worthless and ugly".

Keri and her mother lived in a tiny caravan in Norfolk. Keri's bedroom was no bigger than a cupboard with a tiny bunk atop a storage area and just 18 inches of floor space. Every night the three-year-old would be locked inside this 'bedroom' to prevent her escaping to curl up on the sofa in the lounge.

As a toddler, Keri developed a life-long phobia of vomiting which originated one night when she was violently sick all over herself. Her mother was furious at being woken by the crying and showed no sympathy for the young Keri, merely stripping the girl of her clothes and blankets and leaving her with a potty, a blanket, hair full of dried vomit, and a threat not to disturb her again if she didn't want a beating. Keri vomited again during the night and filled the potty almost to overflowing. She slept fitfully in the stinking room curled up in one corner of the bed, feeling alone and afraid until she was woken by her carer who unleashed another string of abuse for being so selfish as to make such a mess.

Things only got worse when Keri's mum met a new man. Her new stepdad regularly beat Keri by laying her across his lap, removing her knickers and spanking her bare bottom while her mother looked on with a "triumphant sneer".

Keri had been kept apart from other children so when she started attending a primary school in rural Norfolk her manner and 'posh' accent made her the target of bullying. The abuse caused her to start wetting herself which then caused further abuse from her mother when she got home and another dreaded spanking from her stepdad.

However things would soon get far worse. One day at school Keri was attacked by one of the bigger boys in her class. The bully kicked her between the legs and she was sent home in pain, barely able to walk. She had wet herself again and when her stepdad returned from work, he came up to her room and began verbally abusing and beating her, demanding to know what had happened. When she told him that a boy had kicked her between the legs, he dragged her out to look at the area concerned, which, she wrote, he stared at for a weirdly long time. Then he struck, sexually abusing her and penetrating her with his finger. This caused the five-year-old girl incredible pain, drawing blood and making her retch which, in turn, set off her panic about vomiting.

The only safe haven in Keri's childhood was her nana, her mother's adoptive mum. Visits to her nana's house would mean a break in the verbal, physical and sexual abuse and being taken care of, loved and nurtured like a normal child. In her book, *Victim Zero*, Keri wrote, "I truly believe that if Nana had not been such a presence in the background, one of the beatings would have resulted in my death and Mother (possibly her husband too) would have ended up in jail."

Keri's nana didn't know about the abuse she suffered behind closed doors and was confused by all the trouble she seemed to get into. Keri was always such a mild-mannered and pleasant girl whenever she saw her. Later on when Keri did try to explain what was happening to her, she realised she was putting her grandmother in an impossible position because, of course, the abuser was her nana's own daughter so it was difficult for her to accept that she could be doing such terrible things.

In the meantime, the family moved to London and the sexual abuse intensified. Every evening while her mother was at work, Keri's stepdad would give her a bath where she would be forced to wash her "stinking fanny" in a specific way, standing up with a flannel and perfumed soap. She would then be forced to masturbate her stepdad and later to give him oral sex. If she gagged during the act she would be beaten.

At her new school in Chingford, she was soon the target of bullying again. The other children found out about her fear of having her head submerged in water, developed from her mum pouring cold jugs of water over her head as a punishment as a young child. They soon began lying in wait and pouring buckets of water over her head. On one occasion, she was pinned down by a gang of kids and targeted with a hose, water guns and buckets of water while she writhed, screamed and wet herself.

Keri's mother got pregnant by her stepdad and she soon had a baby brother, who, unlike herself, was the apple of her mother's eye. The family moved to a three-storey house in Norwich back in Norfolk, and here the sexual abuse ramped up even further.

Keri's stepdad planned to use the top floor of the house for a model railway set. To her surprise, he enlisted her help, getting her to exercise her creative side by making model trees, bridges and buildings for the model landscape. He even began taking Keri on shopping trips into Norwich to buy things for the train set. Stunned by the change in attitude, Keri started spending most of her time in the 'playroom' at the top of the house which became a kind of refuge from her mother, who increasingly began to sulk. Strangely Keri's stepdad seemed to encourage the animosity between mother and daughter, often sticking up for Keri against his wife.

Unfortunately, the change didn't last long. Keri didn't realise it but she was being carefully groomed. The change came suddenly and unexpectedly on the day the set was complete and the train ready for its maiden voyage around the track. Keri was happily watching the model wend its way around the scenery she had made when her stepdad attacked her from behind and raped her, silencing her screams with one of her mother's silk scarves.

From then on trips to the 'playroom' meant only one thing and the room that Keri had used as a refuge now became a place of pain, fear and dread. Noticing the sudden change in her daughter's attitude, Keri's mother, incredibly, merely sneered. "Mother took obvious pleasure in sneering at me," she wrote in *Victim Zero*, "while telling me it was too late to change my mind now and other such things: serves you right; you're stuck with it now; that'll teach you… Obviously by then she knew what Daddy was doing to me up in the attic room."

Keri was soon expelled from her new school in Norwich for stealing money from other girl's coats. She was sent to a boarding school run by nuns where she was briefly happy because she was away from home and the constant abuse. However, she was soon expelled for hitting another girl. She was sent back home, which was now a cottage in a village in rural Norfolk. There she fell in with the school troublemaker and began bunking off school to shoplift and hitchhike on day trips away.

Keri was now a young teenager. Her new friend, Charlie, would help her bunk off school and take her into town where they would shoplift trendy clothes. For Keri, who had always been dressed by her mum in dowdy clothes fit for a middle-aged spinster, her new sexy look was a refreshing change. She felt more confident and the two friends would hang out in the local park with Charlie's friends who were often drunk or high. Charlie would sometimes disappear with men, according to Keri, and return a little later, flushed but with money in her pocket to buy more alcohol.

But Keri's new freedom didn't change the situation at home. The sexual abuse continued and began to take a new turn. One day, her stepdad took her into Norwich and bought her a number of sexy outfits. He then took her around to a friend's house where he left her after a brief whispered conversation. Her stepdad's friend gave her cola to drink and asked to see her new clothes. The man took photos of Keri while she tried on the short skirts and skimpy tops with no underwear. Soon she started to feel dizzy and nauseous. She suddenly suspected that the cola had been spiked. Fortunately for her the man's wife returned in time to stop anything more sinister happening.

Keri knew her mum would go mad about the skimpy clothes her stepdad had bought her so he had promised to hide them in his room. Unfortunately, Keri's mum found them and did go mad – at Keri, of course, not her stepdad. She called social services and had Keri taken away to a children's home run by Norfolk county council called Garfield House.

At first Keri enjoyed the atmosphere at Garfield House. She was taken shopping and bought a lot of trendy new clothes and she seemed to get along well with the half dozen other teenage residents, alongside the younger children. But soon another side to the home began to become apparent. One of the male staff, a young man called Alan, used to brush and dry the girls' hair after bath time and he would touch and caress Keri's neck with his fingertips while he combed her hair. Alan was nice to Keri and gentle with her so she didn't complain when the touching became more intimate. However, it turned out that Alan, along with his younger brother Joseph, was doing similar things with all the girls.

At weekly meetings with the resident housefather, Mark, the children were given drinks of their choice, including alcohol, and encouraged to talk about sex and masturbation. At one meeting, Mark became angry when he asked Keri how she "pleasured herself" and she responded that she didn't know what he meant. The housefather exploded and loomed over her shouting that she shouldn't try to be funny.

It was while at Garfield House that Keri visited Haut de la Garenne, a similar children's home located on the Channel Island of Jersey. It began innocently enough as a camping holiday. The children spent days on the beach and nights singing along to Alan's guitar under the stars. On the second or third day, they visited a castle in the morning then were driven to a children's home to meet the residents. While the children were still on the driveway of the magnificent building, an incredible thing happened – Jimmy Savile stepped out of the doorway and came to meet them. The famous DJ and TV presenter wore his trademark shabby tracksuit and fat cigar and his arms were bulging with bags full of gifts. The children all ran to surround him and he sat down on the grass among them, distributing his bounty. Keri joined the crowd and was handed a paper bag that contained sweets and a five-pound note along with a wink from the celebrity.

Keri played games with the rest of the children all day long and when it came to dinner time ate with the other children in the dining hall, where Savile was the centre of attention. It is here that events took a sudden and horrific turn for the worse. She wrote in her book, *Victim Zero*:

"And that is where my memories suddenly and inexplicably became fractured and strange, as if I'm trying to peer through thick, frosted glass. There are brief snatches of absolute clarity as if the recall had moved inexplicably closer to the other side of the glass: my being locked inside a St Helier hotel room with a Frenchman who required me to perform fellatio upon him before he penetrated my body in every way possible, multiple times; the beach at St Brelade's Bay being covered all over with giant hornets and the pain I felt because I stood on one before the beach was evacuated; the hugely muscled boxer on the beach at St Ouen's Bay one night, who carried me into the sea until he was up to his chest in water and told me he would drop me and stand on my head if I didn't stop screaming. I stopped screaming; he raped me and left me alone in the dark on the beach. Other fleeting and far less clear memories of sex acts with faceless, nameless people… and other vague memories of feeling almost permanently nauseous, although also of never being short of cigarettes or money. The adults from Garfield House were either absent, turning a blind eye to teenage smoking, or complicit in the provision of cigarettes, alcohol and who knows what else."

After the trip to Haut de la Garenne, Keri began regularly running away from Garfield House. On these excursions she would sometimes have sex with strangers for money. Her time in Jersey had taught her that this was a surefire way of always having money and cigarettes. On her escapades, she met a Hell's Angel who treated her kindly. He had promised to help her run away to Ireland where they would wait until she turned 16 then get married at Gretna Green in Scotland. But on the night of her planned escape, Keri was caught sneaking down the drive of Garfield House. The Hell's Angel had already been apprehended by the police. Keri's social worker was called in and the next day she was shipped off to a new home, one that would renew her acquaintance with Jimmy Saville on far more intimate terms.

Keri arrived at Duncroft Approved School for Intelligent but Emotionally Disturbed Girls in 1974. She was 14 years old and already had enough horrific experiences under her belt to last a lifetime. Yet at Duncroft the horror story would continue.

When Keri arrived at Duncroft, it had just transitioned from being run directly by the Home Office to locally-controlled social services. The school had begun life as something of a cutting edge experiment within the care services of the 1950s, using psycho-therapy to help the girls overcome their emotional and behavioural problems. The intake of Duncroft was also kept to a minimum so it had a small population of around two dozen, generally middle class, intelligent girls who could have a greater fund of attention and resources focussed on them. The school's principle, Margaret Jones, held a passionate belief that the girls under her care could turn their lives around in the nurturing environment of Duncroft.

The uplifting ideals clashed somewhat with Keri's first impressions of the half-Jacobean, half-Georgian stately home. What she noticed more than anything else was the bars on all the windows, the locked doors, and the staff walking around with huge bunches of keys like jailers. After an initial look around, Keri was taken to an impressive-looking office where she was introduced to Miss Jones, the school's principle. In her memoir, Keri describes Jones almost like a real-life Cruella Deville: "She was very slender and tall; her black hair was cut in a bob styled to curl around her ears – and she had a most pronounced under-bite, along with the brightest red lipstick I'd ever seen. She was smoking a very long cigarette."

Keri says she took an instant dislike to Jones who, she said, gave her "the creeps" and reminded her of a "perfect vampire queen". Jones introduced herself and explained the school rules about behaviour which centred around the provision of cigarettes. As a newcomer, Keri would be placed in Grade 3, which would allow her 20 cigarettes a week. Bad behaviour would result in being dropped a grade, meaning fewer cigarettes, while good students would be upgraded and receive more. Rations were doled out every Saturday and Keri quickly learned to keep a close eye on her pack at all times as the precious commodity was always the target of the other girls' attentions.

Despite the 'cutting edge' reputation of the school, the curriculum was anything but progressive, especially given the fact that it was specifically for intelligent girls. It seemed tailored to funnelling the students into traditional female roles such as secretaries and housewives with lessons confined to typing, shorthand, home economics and English. The timetable stunted Keri's prospects of becoming a vet, and her repeated requests to study maths, science and history were met with the same response – the school didn't have the resources.

Alongside the basic education were endless chores which included cleaning the toilets, bathrooms, staircases and endless floors. Despite the prison-like conditions girls often absconded from Duncroft. When they were recaptured they would be placed in the isolation room, a small padded cell from which screams would often be heard. More than once the screams were silenced abruptly by what Keri deduced must be some kind of injection.

Keri herself was given tablets which made her drowsy and detached, and affected her ability to remember much of what happened at the school. These were administered after a brief initial chat with the resident psychologist and Keri was not informed what they were. She found out later that the medication was lithium and that the psychologist had diagnosed her with bi-polar disorder despite little evidence to back up the diagnosis.

It wasn't long after Keri's arrival that Savile made his first appearance at Duncroft. Keri remembers his first entrance in a low-slung sports car wielding armfuls of duty-free cigarettes. She soon found out that 'JS' was a regular fixture at the school, often staying for weekends and sometimes sleeping overnight. He was great friends with Miss Jones who, Keri wrote, "overtly simpered and smirked whenever she was in his company". The two would spend hours talking and laughing in Jones's room and gossip was rife among the students about their relationship.

Keri soon began joining the other girls in the car trips with Savile and soon was being sexually abused by him on a regular basis. But after the horrors she had been through, Keri hardly even considered this abuse, and she was sure none of the other girls considered it particularly untoward, all of whom laughed and sniggered about it between themselves. When Keri told her friends about giving Savile oral sex in his car, there was no sign of shock or disgust. The only memorable reaction was from one girl who admonished her for not securing the trip to the BBC before performing the act.

Savile was, at least, true to his word and Keri soon found herself on the set of *Clunk Click* at BBC headquarters in London and would go on to visit the BBC on five further occasions. The Duncroft girls would get to watch the show, making up the audience, then they would be invited back to Savile's dressing room where he and the show's guests would drink alcohol and make lewd jokes. The girls would also be plied with drink and passed around between the men to be fondled and made the subjects of sexual innuendos. Savile would be the centre of attention. As Keri wrote in *Victim Zero*, "He sat on his throne-like chair, generally with a child or young person jouncing on his knee, holding court with his foul cigar smoke weaving through the air as he pontificated and laughed."

Keri described how she was sometimes the girl unfortunate enough to be bounced on Savile's knee and how she could feel him becoming aroused through his clothing. "More than once," she wrote in her memoir, "if I was wearing the right clothing, JS would slip his hand up inside my blouse or jumper. Like everyone else, I smiled and did not complain. After all, he was the great JS and every one of us 'owed' him because we were about to be on telly."

Keri met lots of famous celebrities on her visits to the BBC, many of whom signed her special autograph book. She recorded in her memoirs that not all of the men she met at the BBC were interested in young girls but she made it quite clear that many of them were. One of the worst was the rock star, Gary Glitter, a man who made her "feel sick". Keri said when he was a guest on *Clunk Click* he showered the girls with presents of "expensive perfume, cigarettes and promises of tickets to one of his shows". In return, he expected free rein to touch and sexually abuse the girls. "He didn't touch me," Keri wrote, "although I watched in a detached fashion as he had full sex with one of the other girls half hidden behind the curtained off alcove in the dressing room into which we were all crammed."

This curtained alcove was a familiar scene of sexual abuse and rape in Savile's dressing room as was verified by several other victims, including two former Duncroft girls who appeared on the ITV *Exposure* documentary.

Another famous guest on *Clunk Click* was the comedian, Freddie Starr, who Keri said, "absolutely stunk of old sweat and the same cologne my stepfather used to use". Starr, like many of the male guests on the show, had wandering hands and apparently he had no qualms about the other girls seeing what he was doing. One girl later recounted how she had asked the comedian to give her a memento to remember him by. Starr offered the girl a lock of his hair and when she said yes he put his hands down his trousers and plucked out a couple of pubic hairs which he handed to the shocked girl. According to the girl, Savile had then chimed in, saying that pubic hair was a good present for the girls as "they like to give head".

Keri had her own horrifying brush with Starr when the funny man 'goosed' her. Goosing was a practical 'joke' that was common – and considered acceptable – back in the 70s, according to Keri, in which a man would pinch a woman's buttocks shouting, "Goose!" When the woman jumped, thus pushing her chest out, the man would grope both breasts and say, "Honk, honk!"

When Starr did this to Keri, he didn't get the usual reaction of forced laughter and blushes. Instead Keri reacted hysterically, breaking down into sobs and screaming at him to get off. As Keri explained in her memoir, the reaction was less due to the goosing itself than the smell of Starr, which brought back horrific memories of her stepfather and his abuse. Her response didn't go down well in Savile's dressing room however and the other girls started laughing at her hysterics. Starr encouraged the ridicule by stating loudly, "I wouldn't touch you anyway, you're a tit-less wonder!" Keri said the remark compounded negative feelings she already had about her lack of breasts and contributed to a lifelong sense of stigma and humiliation about her flat chest.

Later in 2015, after Savile's exposure, Keri's writings about her encounter with Freddie Starr would lead the aging comedian to sue her for libel, claiming that the incident had never occurred and that he had never met her.

In between Savile's visits and trips to the BBC, life continued pretty much as normal at Duncroft. Keri would get occasional breaks from the school and in one she tried to tell her nana about the abuse she had suffered at the hands of her mother and step-dad. She was saddened but not particularly shocked to find that her nana didn't believe her. Although her grandmother loved her, she simply couldn't process the fact that her own daughter could do such things.

Keri met with a similar response when she tried to tell the resident psychologist back at Duncroft, who suggested that Keri's stories were the fantasies of an overactive mind. Not long after-wards Keri was told she was doing well enough that she could soon leave Duncroft and return home. It was the last thing she wanted to do, so she decided to run away, taking advantage of a fight between two girls to climb through a window and make off down the drive.

Outside the grounds, Keri managed to hitch a lift from a lorry driver who was heading north. On the journey they got chatting and Keri told the truck driver her life story. Shocked and sympathetic, the man offered to put her up in his house in Bradford where he lived with his wife. Keri agreed and ended up spending several weeks living with the couple. The man's wife even found her a job in a local factory and Keri began to find her feet in the distant northern town. However, after eight weeks, the man came home from work saying he and several other truck drivers had been questioned over the disappearance of a girl. Keri realised her presence could get the couple into serious trouble so she decided to head back to Duncroft, getting a lift back down south with the lorry driver.

Keri's escape had the one benefit that she was no longer deemed rehabilitated enough to return home, so she was able to stay at Duncroft. When she turned 16, she was transferred to the 'Lodge', a separate building where she would learn job skills and be prepared to enter the workplace. She soon found a role working as a secretary and general assistant in an office. She would work in the days and return to Duncroft for the evenings and weekends. It wasn't long before Keri was able to leave the school for good and re-enter society fully. However, after the traumas she had suffered, life was never easy for Keri. She went on to have three marriages and seven children by five different fathers. Four of her children were taken into care and in 1982 she spent a year in jail, while pregnant, for fraudulently signing cheques.

In 1998, the past finally caught up with Keri and she had a nervous breakdown that left her incapable of functioning. She also began to suffer from uncontrollable diarrhoea followed by crippling constipation. Her psychologist suggested she write down all the things that had happened to her as a form of therapy. Keri had always enjoyed writing, so she decided to give it a go and soon found that it worked – the process of writing about her traumas was helping her mind to process them. From then on Keri began a regular writing practice which led to the writing of her memoir. In 2006, she found a writing website called Fanstory. com where aspiring writers could post their work and have other members read and critique it. Keri soon began posting sequences from her memoir including passages about 'JS' and his abuse of the Duncroft girls. Keri said she never expected anyone to read the memoir and, as the website was American, didn't expect anyone to recognise JS as Jimmy Savile. She would soon be proved wrong.

In 2011, Keri was diagnosed with bowel cancer and received an intense treatment of radiotherapy. While still recuperating from the treatment she was contacted out of the blue by someone from the BBC. Hoping this was someone wanting to do something about her memoir, she called the number she had been given with trembling fingers. Unfortunately, her hopes were dashed. The caller was the journalist Meirion Jones working for *Newsnight*. Jones told Keri he had read her memoir and would like to speak to her in connection with a *Newsnight* investigation to expose Savile as paedophile.

In fact Jones and Keri shared a lot of similar memories of Duncroft. He too had been a regular visitor to the school in the 70s but in a different capacity. Meirion Jones's aunt was Margaret Jones, the school's headmistress and shared a house in the grounds with Meirion's grandmother.

Jones remembered trips to the lavish summer garden parties thrown at Duncroft with trestle tables laden with food and visiting dignitaries that included film stars and minor royalty. Jones visited the school regularly with his parents between 1970 and 1974 to visit his grandmother and aunt. On these visits he remembered seeing Savile on at least half a dozen occasions and spotted his Rolls Royce parked on the drive many more times. Jones was a teenager at this point and remembered Savile as being something of a mystery, a man with some kind of secret. This impression was deepened when Jones witnessed the celebrity drive off the school grounds with three girls in his convertible sports car.

Jones told Savile biographer, Dan Davies, that his parents confronted Margaret Jones about this and it led to a huge row which caused a long-term rift in the family. Jones said his aunt adored Savile and that he had invited her to stay in one of his homes on the south coast for a holiday. Savile would often turn up unannounced at Margaret Jones's house on the Duncroft grounds and, on one occasion, Jones's mother remembered being at the house when Savile dropped by and demanded to be cooked a meal. Another row had ensued and Jones's mum said she had found Savile intimidating. Jones's grandmother, who also lived in the house, didn't trust Savile. "She hated him," Jones told Davies. "She thought he was creepy."

Jones visited Duncroft less and less as he grew up and attended university then got a job as a newspaper journalist. In 1988, he moved into radio with the BBC and seven years later he transferred to television where he worked as a journalist and producer for the BBC's flagship current affairs programme, *Newsnight*. But although he stopped seeing Savile, Jones never forgot about the DJ and he kept his ears open for stories about him. There were plenty of these at the BBC, but Jones could never track the story back to an actual witness or victim. He also kept his eye on Friends Reunited, a pre-Facebook website that re-connected old friends from the same school. Jones would often read the comments on the Duncroft page of the website. There he found lots of dark hints about Savile, but again nothing concrete.

Then in 2011, Jones found Keri's memoir on Fansite.com. He immediately recognised her description of Duncroft with its mixture of stately home and prison, the weird celebrity visits and the trips to the BBC. And of course he immediately recognised 'JS'. Suddenly Jones had what he had been looking for all these years – a direct account from a victim about being sexually abused by Jimmy Savile. At the time Jones was working on a programme for *Newsnight* about catching paedophiles alongside Mark Williams-Thomas, and he mentioned the story to his colleague. Jones also mentioned rumours he'd heard of a Surrey police investigation into Savile and was surprised to find that Williams-Thomas, an ex-Surrey police officer in the child protection unit, hadn't heard about it. Williams-Thomas promised to find out more and Jones sidelined the Savile investigation while he concentrated on other projects.

On the 29th of October that year, Jimmy Savile died and Jones realised it was time to pick up the Savile investigation. He immediately spoke with *Newsnight's* editor, Peter Rippon, and sent him extracts of Keri's memoir. Rippon gave the go-ahead for Jones to start an investigation. Jones immediately turned to Liz MacKean, a *Newsnight* reporter he had worked with many times, to help with the story. Jones was in America at the time so MacKean began the investigation herself, contacting 60 ex-Duncroft girls who were active on the school's Friends Reunited page.

In the meantime, Jones was working on Keri to give an interview for the programme. Jones had first spoken to Keri when she had just finished radiotherapy and was fighting bowel cancer. Keri was ill and fully expected to die from the disease. After the initial disappointment that Jones wasn't contacting her about doing something with her memoir, Keri said she wanted nothing to do with *Newsnight's* Savile investigation. However Jones managed to keep her talking, telling her about his own relationship with Duncroft and praising her writing, which he said had brought back vividly his own childhood memories of the case. Jones asked Keri why she had waited until now to expose Savile and Keri responded that she had never made any secret of what the DJ had done to her, it was just that no one had really cared before. The two ended up having a long chat but Keri was adamant that she wouldn't do an interview. She also expressed scepticism that the programme would ever make it to air before it was shut down by the higher-ups at the BBC. Jones protested that the show had been given the go-ahead but Keri remained sceptical. She was to be proved right.

The call ended in a kind of stalemate, with Keri refusing to talk on film but with Jones managing to keep the line open for further communication. Meanwhile MacKean had found out some tantalising information from the Friends Reunited group – several of the women claimed they had received letters from Surrey police stating that the investigation into Savile had been terminated because of his old age and infirmity. On top of this, five of the 60 ex-Duncroft girls contacted claimed to have been sexually abused by Savile and one also said her sister had been assaulted by Savile at Stoke Mandeville hospital. Five more, though not directly affected, were able to give corroborating evidence.

MacKean was gradually building up a pattern of Savile's offending behaviour from talking to the victims and witnesses, and she was increasingly becoming convinced that Savile was everything these women claimed. Their stories all fitted together and painted a consistent picture of his behaviour, from random groping and kissing to oral sex in the back of his car in return for trips to the BBC. In fact three of the women confirmed Keri's story that the abuse had continued on BBC premises.

In the meantime Mark Williams-Thomas had contacted Jones asking to be part of the investigation and Jones agreed readily. Williams-Thomas had been able to confirm unofficially through his contacts that Surrey police had indeed investigated Savile over child sex abuse claims. Williams-Thomas would now be useful to the investigation, both in tracking down official proof of the Surrey police investigation, and as an expert on paedophilia and child sex abuse. The team filmed an interview with Williams-Thomas for the programme in which the ex-police officer confirmed that the pattern of abuse, as described by the victims, fitted the profile of a serial predator who had probably offended across a widespread number of institutions.

Rumours about the *Newsnight* investigation had already spread around the BBC and there were several furtive discussions about it, not all of them positive. Plans were underway for a special Savile tribute programme to air at Christmas, and the *Newsnight* programme threatened to derail it. One of the most vocal critics was one of *Newsnight's* own deputy editors, Liz Gibbons, who was opposed to the programme on "grounds of taste" because Savile had so recently died. In a meeting, MacKean was able to convince Gibbons to support the ongoing investigation but the editor remained wary, especially around the credibility of the witnesses, as did the programme's editor, Peter Rippon. It soon became clear to Jones and MacKean that they would need to get the programme on air before Christmas in order to head off the Savile special.

To this end it was great news when, after five separate telephone conversations with Jones, Keri finally agreed to give an on-camera interview. As soon as she had agreed, things moved fast, with Jones racing to do the interview before Keri changed her mind. An interview with MacKean was set up at Keri's home and while the *Newsnight* team scampered to make preparations, Keri's children and ex-husband-turned-carer, rushed to clean the house that had fallen into neglect since Keri's illness.

MacKean and the team travelled to Oswestry in Shropshire on the 14th of November to interview Keri at her home. She was about to have a major operation for bowel cancer and didn't expect to survive, which perhaps made her testimony all the more frank and determined. MacKean was in no doubt that Keri was telling the truth – her story fitted with the evidence they had gained from the other Duncroft women. "She wasn't pretending to know more than she did," MacKean told Dan Davies. "She wasn't pretending that her memory was perfect. She was a woman telling the truth."

MacKean gleaned from Keri a sense of how clever Savile was at grooming his victims. She got a sense of how he made these intelligent but disturbed girls feel like they were in control of the situation, in some way almost taking advantage of Savile in order to make them feel complicit in the abuse and therefore unlikely to ever speak about it. Keri made it clear that she and most of the other girls had not felt any shame or embarrassment at what they did with Savile or even, at the time, considered it abuse.

It was only as they got older and had children themselves that they began to truly understand the real significance of what had happened to them.

Keri's interview would be critical to the programme's success because none of the other Duncroft victims would agree to speak on camera. They were simply too scared, even after Savile's death, and were unwilling to come forward, even with the promise of anonymity.

On the plus side, the team had managed to secure footage of Gary Glitter appearing on an episode of *Clunk Click* which confirmed Keri's and several of the other women's claims. The grainy black-and-white footage showed Savile introducing his fellow celebrity paedophile to the teenage audience while they sat among the uncomfortable-looking girls. "I get two?" Glitter practically drooled as he draped his arms around a pair of teenage girls. It is easy to see why Keri said most of the girls were nervous of Glitter and found him unbearably sleazy.

Later in November, the *Newsnight* team managed to interview another Duncroft girl on camera. Rochelle Shepherd had been a student at the school in the late 70s and, while not a victim herself, had witnessed the groping and kissing firsthand and provided excellent corroborating testimony to Keri's interview, alongside quotes from seven other girls whom they had spoken to. By the end of the month MacKean had knocked up a first draft of the script, which was sent to Newsnight's editors and legal team. Rippon seemed enthusiastic and the BBC's Impact Team began working on versions of the story to roll out across the network. The organisation was clearly aware that the story was going to make waves.

Little did they know at the time but this was to prove the high watermark for the *Newsnight* investigation. Shortly after the interview with Rochelle Shepherd, Jones received an email from Rippon asking for confirmation from Surrey police that they had cancelled their Savile investigation because of his old age. This followed a conversation Rippon had had with Stephen Mitchell the BBC's Deputy Director of News. No one knows what was discussed during this meeting but the outcome seemed to have changed Rippon's attitude to the story rather suddenly. He was now asking for corroborating details that hadn't formerly been on his radar.

Suddenly there was a pressing need to produce the letter which several of the ex-Duncroft girls had said they received from Surrey police confirming that the Crown Prosecution Service had closed the investigation due to Savile's old age. The problem was none of these letters had ever surfaced. One of the women insisted that she still had the letter but despite repeated attempts by MacKean to see it, the woman failed to produce the document.

Jones believed that the CPS letter was just a sideshow designed to stall and ultimately stymie the *Newsnight* programme by BBC higher-ups who were worried about the fallout from the show. He insisted that the real story wasn't about the cancellation of the police investigation but the fact that the team had spoken to more than half a dozen girls who testified to having been abused by or of witnessing Savile's abuse. He pointed out that their star witness, Keri, had not even been part of the Surrey police investigation which focussed on the evidence of just two ex-Duncroft girls. The *Newsnight* team had far more evidence than the Surrey police investigation had gathered, but this didn't seem to matter to the BBC executives. The story had changed to focus on the failed police investigation and if no proof could be obtained that it was cancelled due to Savile's old age, the whole future of the programme was at stake.

This made for bad news when, on the 9th of December, the CPS released a statement in response to the *Newsnight* team's enquiries, stating that the Savile investigation had been closed due to lack of evidence, not Savile's old age. Jones forwarded the email to Rippon, knowing full well that this probably meant the show would be axed. The noises coming from higher up had already alerted Jones and MacKean that the BBC's attitude to the story had seismically shifted, especially when, during a conversation, the *Newsnight* editor had told the team that the Duncroft victims were "not the youngest" and that "it wasn't the worst kind of abuse."

It came as no surprise to Jones or MacKean therefore when, after the CPS statement, Rippon confirmed that they would be pulling the *Newsnight* programme. The two journalists felt crushed and betrayed and had no idea what to say to the victims, whose hopes they had raised about finding justice. Faced with the dilemma of what to say to Keri and the other ex-Duncroft girls, Jones and MacKean chose to do nothing. "We didn't because we didn't know how to say it," MacKean told Dan Davies. "… We just felt that our hands were tied. It was very uncomfortable indeed."

The *Newsnight* show may have been cancelled but rumours of the investigation were already out there and the story was now likely to come out one way or the other, the question was from which source. Jones gave his Duncroft contacts and blessing to continue the investigation to Williams-Thomas and ITV's *Exposure* programme, but there were also rumours that Sky were pursuing a similar story about Savile. Some stories about a BBC coverup of a Jimmy Savile investigation surfaced in the British press in the new year of 2012. These, it was claimed, were leaked from within the BBC and the finger of blame was immediately pointed at Jones who vigorously denied the accusations. In response to the stories, the BBC's PR team issued a press release admitting to the *Newsnight* investigation but claiming that the show was cancelled due to a lack of leads. The statement focussed on the Surrey police angle, completely omitting the fact that the *Newsnight* team had found victims outside the police investigation, and not including any comments from Jones or MacKean themselves.

It would take another year of investigating by Mark Williams-Thomas before the full truth would come out about Savile in ITV's *Exposure* documentary, but by then it would be too late for Jones and MacKean. They had been left out in the cold by the BBC following the programme's axing, and ultimately they would be thrown under the bus. Their experience of what had really happened was incompatible with the official line of a dead-end inquiry into a failed police investigation.

Neither Jones nor MacKean were sacked but both felt they were effectively forced out of the BBC. MacKean, who took voluntary redundancy, told *The Observer* in 2015, "The BBC tried to smear my reputation. They said they had banned the film because Meirion and I had produced shoddy journalism. I stayed to fight them, but I knew they would make me leave in the end. Managers would look through me as if I wasn't there. I went because I knew I was never going to appear on screen again."

Jones went on to work for BBC's investigative news programme, *Panorama*. In 2015, just after he had finished working on an exposé called *The Fake Sheikh Exposed*, he was told his services were no longer required on the show. His position as Head of Investigations at *Newsnight* had been filled in his absence so Jones was effectively out of a job. He considered suing the BBC but after consulting a lawyer who told him the case would drag on for at least a year, he decided to take voluntary redundancy instead. Jones said in a statement following his redundancy, "People said they won't sack you after Savile but they will make your life hell. Everyone involved on the right side of the Savile argument has been forced out of the BBC."

Jones went on to have a successful career in journalism, becoming the editor of the Bureau of Investigative Journalism. MacKean went on to work for the Channel 4 show, *Dispatches*. She died in 2017 of a stroke at the age of 52. As for Keri, she wasn't surprised when the BBC axed the *Newsnight* programme, it was what she had predicted all along. Anyway, she had more pressing things to worry about. In late 2011, she had major surgery for her bowel cancer. Although the operation was successful, there were complications and she was sent home to recuperate with a stoma bag and, essentially, an open wound in her stomach.

It was in this condition in early January 2012 that she was contacted by Mark Williams-Thomas who was now investigating the Savile story for ITV's *Exposure*. Keri was feeling ill as well as fed up with the Jimmy Savile investigations that she was sure would end up going nowhere. She declined firmly to do an interview. However Williams-Thomas kept calling, first on her house phone, then on her mobile and also by email. Keri kept saying no, either herself or via her carer, Peter. But in the following days she started to get more calls and emails from other journalists until she felt like she was being thoroughly hounded. She ignored the calls as best she could.

Keri gradually recovered from the operation and beat the bowel cancer. By the time Williams-Thomas's *Exposure* documentary was about to air in October 2012 she had recovered enough energy to have changed her mind about speaking out. She contacted Williams-Thomas and said she wanted to do an on-camera interview. It was too late for inclusion in the *Exposure* show but Williams-Thomas did the interview anyway, and, in the wake of the *Exposure* programme, Keri became one of the media's go-to sources for the barrage of Savile stories that would dominate the press for several weeks.

It was from these interviews and Keri's memoir that the story hit the press about Freddie Starr groping her at the BBC. Subsequently Starr sued Keri for slander and libel, claiming that the incident had never happened. The case went to the High Court in July 2015 and Meirion Jones, Liz MacKean and Mark Williams-Thomas all testified on Keri's behalf. After five days in court the judge dismissed Starr's claim, finding that Keri had told the truth about Starr groping her on Savile's *Clunk Click* programme. Starr, who was 72 at the time, was ordered to pay Keri's legal fees. However, the comedian had already moved to Spain and liquidated his assets in the UK thus avoiding paying the half-a-million-pound court costs to Keri's lawyers.

Keri, now in her sixties, is doing well and is a successful author. The memoirs that she originally published on Fansite.com in 2009, exposing Jimmy Savile, are now a series of eight published books called simply 'Keri'.

As for Duncroft and the BBC, it is the usual story. No one was found accountable, no heads rolled. In the wake of the *Exposure* programme there was a lot of finger-pointing and criticism of the organisation but little was actually done. When the BBC's director general, George Entwistle, was forced to resign in November 2012 it was more to do with a subsequent *Newsnight* investigation gone wrong than the Savile story itself. Later in the year, an independent inquiry into the BBC's handling of the Savile affair was conducted by the head of Sky News, Nick Pollard. In December 2012, the Pollard report was published finding that "chaos and confusion", a "lack of leadership" and adherence to "rigid management chains" had made the BBC "completely incapable" of handling the Jimmy Savile investigation. However, despite the report's damning conclusions, little actually changed at the corporation. *Newsnight's* editor, Peter Rippon, and his deputy, Liz Gibbons, were moved to other roles; the director of news, Helen Boaden, kept her position; and the deputy director, Stephen Mitchell, retired. That was it.

Surrey police launched Operation Outreach, an investigation into the Duncroft allegations, in 2012. The results were released in 2015, documenting that Savile had carried out 46 sexual assaults on 22 Duncroft residents and one visitor during the 1970s. Of the 46 attacks, 25 occurred within the Duncroft grounds, in the TV room, kitchen and dining room, and 13 occurred in Savile's various cars. The assaults ranged from non-consensual kissing to forced oral sex, according to the report.

Again the evidence was damning but as usual no one was held accountable. According to the report, in 2014 Surrey police had passed a dossier of evidence to the Crown Prosecution Service relating to two former Duncroft members of staff. However, six months later the CPS dropped the case after deciding there was no realistic prospect of prosecution.

As for Margaret Jones, headmistress of Duncroft throughout the 70s and close friend of Jimmy Savile, she was interviewed by *The Daily Mail* in November 2012 and admitted to having been "hoodwinked" by Savile. She said she had always thought Savile was an "odd bod" but had never known he was a predatory paedophile. Instead the 91-year-old chose to lay the blame mainly on her ex-pupils who, she said, had taken advantage of Savile for cigarettes and trips in his car. She told the paper that the girls were free to come forward about Savile at the time but had chosen not to, conveniently forgetting the testimony of one girl who had been locked in the isolation room after reporting being groped by Savile. Regarding the women making the accusations Jones said, "They had an opportunity to tell anybody. But it suited them – some of them, not all of them – to wait 30 years. They're looking for money ... they come out of the woodwork for money. I do object to my school being targeted .... wild allegations by well-known delinquents."

So much for the caring headmistress who was passionate about rehabilitating the girls in her care.

CHAPTER 4

PAEDOPHILE LORD MOUNTBATTEN INGRATIATES SAVILE INTO THE ROYAL FAMILY

On Wednesday 7th July, 1999, Jimmy Savile's cottage in Glencoe, Scotland was a hive of activity. His friend, Julie Ferguson, and two of her friends were buzzing around trying to get everything sorted for lunch. The dining area needed to be immaculately laid out and the locally sourced lamb and salmon cooked and served to equal perfection. Savile meanwhile was dressing up in his best attire – a kilt of Lochaber tartan, a green military shirt and his green Royal Marines beret.

The hustle and bustle continued until the last minute when the special guest arrived, then Julie and her friends donned their specially prepared waitress aprons bearing the individual monograms H, R and H and greeted their visitor with much-practised curtsies.

The special guest was His Royal Highness the Prince of Wales. Later that day, Charles was due to present a minibus to a local mountain rescue team. When Savile had heard of the visit he had invited the prince to lunch at his nearby cottage in Glencoe which he had bought from a famous mountaineer, Hamish MacInnes.

The lunch went well with the local salmon and lamb washed down with some Laphroaig whiskey which Savile knew was a favourite of the prince. Afterwards, Savile took Charles to his local post office where his royal highness watched, intrigued, as

Savile withdrew his old-age pension payment. Charles had never been inside a post office before, Savile told his biographer, Dan Davies, and asked Savile, "Does this happen very often?" "Yeah," Savile replied, "every week."

It would be no exaggeration to say that Jimmy Savile had a special relationship with the now-king of England. Alternatively described as a "friend", "advisor" and "mentor", Savile had the prince's ear and the prince's respect. Charles would often carefully follow Savile's advice on matters ranging as widely as how to deal with the press, who to appoint as staff, and even how to deal with his failing marriage to Princess Diana.

And it wasn't just Charles. Diana also was initially said to be "fond" of Savile, calling and writing to him often, asking for his advice and helping him out with his various charity projects. Then there was Prince Philip, Charles's father and the queen's husband. Savile would address the Duke of Edinburgh as "boss" and spoke about them having a "a great rapport" and "amazing fun together". Savile once even picked Philip up from a train station in his bright yellow BMW Isetta bubble car.

Savile was also friends with Philip's uncle and protector, Lord Louis Mountbatten, and gave advice and help to Sarah Ferguson, Prince Andrew's wife. He was a regular visitor to Kensington Palace, the official London residence of the Prince of Wales, often letting himself in uninvited. He had his own room in Clarence House, another of Charles's London residences, and was even said to pop in for a cup of tea with the Queen at Buckingham Palace.

But how did a serial paedophile get so close to the royal family and have such unprecedented access to their homes and personal lives? As Boris Coster, the Broadmoor researcher told me, "If you try to get into a category A prison today, you will have the most stringent security checks done and then you still might not get in. You're telling me that Prince Charles, with MI5 and MI6 and his own security staff… and not one single one of them had the brains and the wits to think, let's do an in-depth security check on Mr Savile before we let him in here, let alone him within a hundred yards of the royal family. But no they didn't."

The answer to the riddle begins with Lord Louis Mountbatten, uncle and guardian of Prince Philip. Mountbatten's naval career had risen dramatically, with him becoming the First Sea Lord before his retirement. One of Mountbatten's various roles within the navy was colonel commandant of the Royal Marines, an honorary position appointed by the crown.

Savile first met Mountbatten in the 60s when he was earning an honorary green beret by completing the Royal Marines commando training course. Savile had first associated with the Royal Marines in the late 60s when he completed an endurance march across Dartmoor for charity that was part of the marines' training. Wishing to prove himself further, Savile completed every aspect of the Royal Marines commando training course, one of the toughest military courses in the world, and earned himself an honorary green beret. It was during his training with the marines that Savile met Mountbatten. According to Savile's own account to Dan Davies, Mountbatten was fascinated by the skinny figure of Savile training with the elite unit and wanted to know "what this long-haired geezer was doing with this crack fighting corps".

Savile and Mountbatten hit it off instantly according to Savile, who described it as an "attraction of opposites". With his usual alacrity, Savile was soon helping Mountbatten with official engagements, assisting him with the opening of a new sergeants' mess at the marines' training base in Lympstone in Devon. Mountbatten cut the ribbon, according to Savile, but got Savile to give the speech. Mountbatten would often rely on Savile's ability to deal with the press, Savile told Davies, quoting Mountbatten as saying, "I'll cut the ribbon but get Savile down. He can do the speeches. He does it better than me."

How much of what Savile claimed is true is open to debate but it seems clear that Savile and Mountbatten did have a friendly relationship. At a Variety Club luncheon held in Savile's honour in 1978, Savile was seated next to the Earl. Savile called Mountbatten "the Governor" and Mountbatten said of Savile that he was a "fixer" who could solve any problem.

Like many of Savile's relationships, on the surface his friendship with Mountbatten seemed a harmless mix of genuine affection and mutual expediency. But like Savile's other relationships, was there something more sinister going on beneath the surface? It might seem an odd question to ask of such a royal figure as Mountbatten if it weren't for his private life, because, just as with Savile, there was something extremely sinister going on beneath the surface.

To all appearances Mountbatten's life was one of glittering success and accolades. His full title, Admiral of the Fleet Louis Francis Albert Victor Nicholas Mountbatten, 1st Earl Mountbatten of Burma, KG GCB OM GCSI GCIE GCVO DSO ADC PC FRS, sums up perfectly the man's long record of achievements. During his long and distinguished career Mountbatten was a naval leader, a war hero and a major political player on the world stage, even seen by many as the true power behind the throne.

Mountbatten was born with the (comparatively) humble title Prince Louis of Battenberg on 25th June, 1900 in Frogmore House, Windsor. His parents were descended from German nobility, Prince Louis of Battenberg and his wife Princess Victoria of Hesse and by Rhine. His maternal grandparents were even more distinguished – Queen Victoria and her consort, Prince Albert of Saxe-Coburg and Gotha. The godparents at his christening give some indication of the world young Louis was born into – Queen Victoria, head of the British Empire and Alexander II, the last Tsar of Russia.

Mountbatten was destined for the navy from an early age, attending the Royal Naval college, Osborne, on the Isle of Wight at age 13 before graduating from the naval college in Dartmouth in 1916 just in time to see action in the First World War. He also changed his name to Mountbatten at this time. The German family name of Battenburg sounded unpatriotic, given the nature of the enemy.

Mountbatten's first naval role was as a junior midshipman on the battlecruiser, HMS Lion. He was stationed on the fore bridge which was an excellent place to watch the captain and other commanding officers as well as any action going on at sea. In August that year he did see his first action. Lion was ordered to defend the port city of Sunderland from a German naval bombardment. The destroyer narrowly escaped being hit by a mine and a torpedo during the engagement. In 1917 Mountbatten transferred to HMS Queen Elizabeth and for the last months of the war he was promoted to sub-lieutenant, second in command of 50 officers and men aboard the small escort and anti-submarine vessel, P31.

After the war Dickie, as Mountbatten was known to family and friends, was sent to Christ's College, Cambridge for two terms as part of a scheme to improve the education of 400 young officers whose training had been interrupted by the war. It was here that Dickie made the first of his royal contacts and, like the rest of his life, made the most of them for his own advancement. Two of the king's sons, Bertie (the future king) and Henry were also studying at Cambridge at the time and Mountbatten befriended them. Hearing that their brother and heir to the throne, David (officially known as Edward) was setting off on a world tour the following year, Mountbatten asked Bertie if he could request the Prince of Wales to join him. The heir to the throne agreed and Dickie was ready for his next adventure.

On the trip the two became close friends and, according to Dickie, shared things with each other that neither of them had said to anyone before, especially about affairs of the heart. Although he attracted the jealousy of other officers aboard the ship, Mountbatten had made such a good impression on the Prince of Wales that he was invited to accompany him on another tour, this time of India and Japan, in 1921, where the friends' relationship deepened even further.

In the meantime Dickie had fallen in love with Edwina Ashley, the granddaughter of the Earl of Shaftesbury on one side and Sir Ernest Cassel, a merchant banker and one of the richest men of his day, on the other. The two had met several times across various social functions and both had been fascinated by the other, but it was on a cruise along the coasts of Belgium and France that the two fell in love, sitting up late at night on deck holding hands and visiting the local night clubs at each stop on the tour. Edwina travelled out to meet Mountbatten in Bombay during his tour with the Prince of Wales. They spent three days together in February and on Valentine's Day Dickie proposed. They were married in St Margaret's church next to Westminster Abbey on 18 July 1922. Most of the royal family were in attendance and the Prince of Wales was the best man.

During the interwar years, Mountbatten enjoyed a meteoric rise through the ranks, so that by 1934 he had been given his first ship, HMS Daring, to command. In 1936 he was made a personal aide de camp to his old friend David who had now become King Edward VIII. However the new king's reign didn't last long and in May the following year Mountbatten attended the coronation of his other royal friend, Bertie, as King George VI, following Edward's abdication. By the time the Second World War broke out, Mountbatten was a full captain and in command of the destroyer HMS Kelly.

On the outbreak of war, Mountbatten took charge of the 5th Destroyer Flotilla. Close scrapes appeared to follow him wherever he went. In May 1940 Kelly was hit by a German torpedo off the Dutch coast. Mountbatten was unharmed but the ship was seriously damaged so he switched his command of the flotilla to HMS Javelin. Later the same year Javelin was hit by two torpedoes in a fight with three German destroyers off the coast of Cornwall. Mountbatten returned to Kelly, which had since been repaired, only to have it sunk by German dive bombers in 1941 during the battle of Crete. Mountbatten was subsequently given command of the aircraft carrier HMS Illustrious which was docked in Norfolk, Virginia for repairs.

In October 1941, Mountbatten was promoted to Chief of Combined Operations, a staff role that would look for opportunities to mount amphibious assaults on Hitler's Fortress Europe with an eye to an eventual full-scale invasion. After two successful commando raids – Bruneval, which captured important intelligence information, and St Nazaire which destroyed the German's largest Atlantic dry dock, Mountbatten was promoted acting Vice Admiral. He and his staff planned the disastrous Dieppe raid in August 1942, which would see over 6,000 Canadian troops frontally assault the well-defended port city of Dieppe without adequate air or naval cover, losing over half the force as casualties.

Another transfer saw Mountbatten become Supreme Allied Commander of South East Asia Command (SEAC) and promoted to acting Admiral. In South East Asia Mountbatten managed to turn around the Allies' perilous situation. Consequently the Japanese advance in Burma was halted and British troops began to advance, eventually retaking the country in May 1945. Following the surrender of the Japanese on 15 August, Mountbatten led Allied forces back into Singapore, which had been humiliatingly captured by the Japanese in 1942. With British troops back in the city, Mountbatten personally oversaw the formal surrender of Japanese forces in the South East Asia region on 12 September, recording in his diary that it was, "the greatest day of my life."

After the war Mountbatten returned to England as a rear admiral. Later that year he was made a viscount with a seat in the House of Lords. But greater honours and responsibilities – perhaps overwhelmingly great – were about to be bestowed. In 1946 he was offered the position of Viceroy of India with a mandate to transfer power back to the Indians by no later than June 1948, with the minimum of turmoil and bloodshed. Mountbatten reluctantly agreed and In February 1947 he was appointed Viceroy of India.

The political situation in India was extremely unstable with constant violence against the British ruling regime as well as inter-faith clashes between Hindus and Muslims. Muslim League leader, Muhammad Ali Jinnah, was demanding a separate homeland for India's roughly 94 million Muslim inhabitants. Mountbatten privately voiced concerns that he and his wife Edwina would end up with bullets in their backs and his reluctance was justified. The Mountbattens' arrival in Delhi led to huge riots. Mountbatten was well-known for his diplomatic abilities and he required all of these to get all the conflicting factions pulling in something like a similar direction.

Mountbatten had soon befriended the Indian independence activists Nehru and Gandhi but the political situation was dire. Sectarian strife was becoming so bad that Mountbatten quickly came to the conclusion that there would soon be civil war. He decided that the deadline of June 1948 was too far away and that acceptance of partition and a prompt announcement of a quicker date for independence were essential to avoid outright armed conflict.

Mountbatten set the date for partition as 15 August 1947, just 72 days from the official announcement. Some thought that the haste of the plan showed decisiveness and a clear intent to hand over power, others that it was reckless and the product of an over-eagerness on the part of Mountbatten to wash his hands of the problem and get out of India regardless of the deaths and turmoil it would cause.

Nevertheless partition went ahead and at midnight on 15 August 1947 India and Pakistan gained their independence with three north-western provinces, Baluchistan, North-West Frontier and Sindh joining Pakistan and three other provinces, Punjab, Bengal and Assam being partitioned between Pakistan and India. Mountbatten became the first Governor-General of India in order to ease the transition of power, and was also promoted from a viscount to Earl Mountbatten of Burma. He stayed on as Governor-General of India for 10 months until June 1948, a period which saw terrible massacres committed by Indians, Muslims and Sikhs, particularly in the border territories. Many of these deaths were blamed on Mountbatten for keeping the decision on the geographical placement of borders a secret until partition.

When his time as Governor-General was over, Mountbatten left India and returned briefly to Britain before moving back to Malta where Mountbatten was made commander of the First Cruiser Squadron of the Mediterranean Fleet. He had been offered jobs as Governor of Malta, Governor General of Canada and ambassador to both Moscow and Washington, but he was more interested in his naval career even though it meant he was now further down the chain of command. As before, however, Mountbatten rose through the ranks quickly, becoming Fourth Sea Lord then Commander-in-Chief of the Mediterranean Fleet and NATO Commander Allied Forces Mediterranean. It wasn't long before he reached the top, becoming First Sea Lord, Chief of the Naval Staff in 1955, the same position his father had held.

Meanwhile Mountbatten's power and influence had extended in other directions. In 1952, following the death of her father, King George VI, Elizabeth was crowned queen. In 1947 she had married Prince Philip of Greece and Denmark. Philip was the son of Prince Andrew of Greece, brother of King Constantine I of Greece. After the disaster of the Greco-Turkish war, Constantine was forced to abdicate and Andrew and all his family were banished from Greece for life in 1922. Philip's childhood was itinerant and unstable. His father disappeared to Monte Carlo to live with his mistress and exercise his habit for gambling. His mother was diagnosed with schizophrenia and placed in an asylum. Philip, essentially an orphan, pinballed around Europe living with various relatives and receiving education in schools in France, Germany and finally Britain. In Britain, Mountbatten's older brother, George, acted as Philip's guardian while Philip was educated at Gordonstoun, the same Scottish Highlands school which Charles and Andrew would later attend. When George died of bone marrow cancer Philip, then 16, was placed in the care of Mountbatten.

Mountbatten had a close relationship with his charge and the Earl, who had two daughters of his own, thought of Philip as the son he never had. It was Mountbatten who had first arranged for Philip and Elizabeth to meet. In 1939 when 13-year-old Elizabeth was aboard the Royal Yacht cruising along the south coast, Mountbatten arranged for 18-year-old Philip, then a cadet at the Royal Naval College in Dartmouth, to escort the ship and have tea with the royal party. Philip and Elizabeth were seen to get along particularly well and Philip's was the last boat in the flotilla to turn away as they escorted the yacht on its departure.

From then on Mountbatten supported and encouraged the affair, writing to the king to persuade Philip to stay in the Royal Navy and not get mixed up in matters in Greece. Mountbatten was crucial in securing Philip's British nationality and getting him to sign a revocation to the throne of Greece, as well as Philip adopting the name Mountbatten from his mother's side of the family. All this was done with one eye on a possible marriage to Elizabeth and, no doubt, the raising of the Mountbatten name to the throne of England. His scheming was successful and in 1947 Philip and Elizabeth were married in Westminster Abbey. However his plan to have the Mountbattens become the ruling family of England was scuppered when the King insisted that Philip and Elizabeth's children would bear the name of Windsor after their mother's family.

With Elizabeth's accession in 1952 Philip became consort and Mountbatten's influence over the crown was extended. He was still Philip's guardian and mentor and played the same role to Philip's eldest son, heir to the throne, Charles. Charles referred to his great-uncle as 'Honorary Grandfather' and followed in many of Mountbatten's footsteps including a career in the navy and a lifelong love of polo. He also took Mountbatten's advice on affairs of the heart which, perhaps not surprisingly, included a potential marriage with Mountbatten's granddaughter, Amanda Knatchbull. Dutifully Charles did court the young woman and proposed in 1979, but Knatchbull rejected his offer.

By the time Mountbatten met Savile in the 60s, Mountbatten had achieved everything he could have hoped to achieve and more. But behind the gaudy façade of pomp and circumstance which marked the whole of Mountbatten's career, there were secrets – dark sexual secrets that he seems to have succeeded, for the most part, in covering up. It had been known for a long time, almost since the beginning, that his marriage to Edwina was a sham. It took less than three years before Edwina had her first known affair with former army officer, Hugh Molyneux. After a ten-month relationship she then started seeing a rich heir and polo player called Stephen Sandford. In 1926 her new lover was ex-cavalry officer, Mike Wardell. There followed an almost unbroken line of lovers throughout the rest of her life, including Hollywood star, Larry Gray, and possibly even Douglas Fairbanks Jr.

In 1931, things came to a head and Mountbatten threatened to leave, but Edwina persuaded him not to and they came to an agreement – Edwina could continue to have her lovers as long as she was more discreet. The marriage had become a one-sided open relationship. It became two sided in 1932 when Dickie met Yola Letellier, the third wife of Henri Letellier, a French newspaper magnate. She was young and beautiful and supposedly the inspiration for Colette's novella, Gigi. Yola became Mountbatten's main 'other woman' for the rest of his life but he had many other lovers besides.

Despite his many faults, Mountbatten seemed impervious to jealousy and many of his and Edwina's lovers became friends of the family, visiting openly and accompanying them on holidays. Still Edwina's actions caused controversy, especially when she was found to be having affairs with black actor, Paul Robeson, and black jazz singer, Leslie 'Hutch' Hutchinson – quite a scandal by the racist mores of the time. Edwina was attracted to people of colour and during and after Mountbatten's term as Viceroy of India she had a long-term affair with India's first prime minister, Jawaharlal Nehru, who may well have been the love of her life. When Edwina was found dead in her hotel room in Burma she was surrounded by Nehru's letters.

While an open marriage was a lot more shocking in Mountbatten's time than it is today, it seems there were other secrets and more sinister sides to Mountbatten's sexuality which remained hidden, sides that might explain Edwina's early infidelities and the lack of a sexual relationship between the two.

I interviewed Mountbatten biographer, Andrew Lownie, for my True Crime podcast. As Lownie told me, rumours about Mountbatten's bisexuality had followed him throughout his life. Mountbatten's close friend the gay playwright and film maker, Noel Coward, said it was "beyond doubt" that Mountbatten had male as well as female lovers. Mountbatten's tiny mews house in Kinnerton Street in Belgravia was, according to one source that Lownie quotes, "Awash with young, good-looking Naval ratings bustling about the place to no apparent purpose." And a woman who worked in a clothes shop opposite the Kinnerton Street property told Lownie that there was a constant procession of handsome young men visiting the flat. It seemed that Mountbatten used his position within the navy to obtain sexual favours from young servicemen in return for career boosts. Nicholas Davies, who was Robert Maxwell's foreign editor at *The Mirror*, stated in his book, Queen Elizabeth II, which Lownie quotes, that he headed a *Mirror* investigation into a homosexual sex ring centred on the Life Guards barracks in London in which a number of young guardsmen told him that Mountbatten was involved.

Several men claim to have been Mountbatten's lover or to have seen him with male lovers. The murderer and conman, Roy Fontaine claimed to have been Mountbatten's partner during the war. He even claimed, according to Lownie, that Mountbatten's gay friends all knew him as 'Mountbottom' while Fontaine himself called him 'The Queen'. And Lownie recounts another story from the actor, John Gielgud, who told how Mountbatten was caught in flagrante by his butler after he had invited a young man to strip and beat him. The man went about his business with so much enthusiasm, according to Gielgud, that Mountbatten's cries of pain attracted the butler who said, on finding his master in such a compromising position, "I thought you rang, sir".

Nothing is wrong with being a homosexual obviously, but

during most of Mountbatten's life it was a criminal offence punishable by imprisonment, which explains and justifies his secrecy (nothing of course justifies the coercing of young men into sexual activities in return for career progression).

However the secrecy may have concealed much worse. Mountbatten's driver from 1942-43, Norman Nield, revealed that he was paid extra to keep silent about Mountbatten's assignations with young boys who ranged from eight to 12 years old, using brandy and lemonade to help seduce the boys. Nield also claimed that Mountbatten sometimes dressed the young boys up in baby girl outfits before having sex with them. Another source, Anthony Daly, who wrote a memoir about being a high-class rent boy in the 70s, told of how he'd heard that Mountbatten had had sex with a young Burmese boy in the back of a Dakota cargo plane in Ceylon (now Sri Lanka). According to Daly, he was told that Mountbatten had a sexual preference for "well-bred and well-educated young men of good standing... ... from good families; or public school boys".

In 1980, stories surfaced that made even darker claims. Writing for *Now Magazine*, Northern Irish writer, Robin Bryans claimed that Mountbatten was part of a homosexual and paedophile vice ring operating over both sides of the Irish border in the 70s. Bryans claimed that Mountbatten, along with other top establishment figures, took boys from the Kincora Boys' Home in Belfast and Portora Royal School in Enniskillen and abused them in homosexual orgies held in various stately homes across Ireland, including Mountbatten's own residence, Classiebawn. According to the article, Mountbatten's preference was for public school boys around the age of 13 or 14.

Lownie managed to track down two of the survivors of Kincora who both remembered assignations with Mountbatten. The first, calling himself 'Sean', was 16 when he remembers being driven from Kincora to Classiebawn in 1977. There he remembers being led to a darkened room where an older man gave him oral sex. In an interview with Lownie, Sean said: "He was one of those men who wanted attention, wanted you to chase him… I think he felt some shame. He said sadly, 'I hate these feelings.' He seemed a sad and lonely person. I think the darkened room was all about denial." Sean only recognised the man from the encounter as Mountbatten when he saw a picture of him on the news following his death.

Another Kincora survivor, known as 'Amal', told Lownie he met Mountbatten four times in the summer of 1977 when he was 16. On each occasion Amal met the sea lord in a hotel room in Mullaghmore, the town near Classiebawn. Amal told Lownie that on one occasion, "I remember he admired my smooth skin. We gave each other oral sex in the 69 position. He was very tender and I felt comfortable about it. It seemed very natural. I know that several other boys from Kincora were brought to him on other occasions."

Lownie also found official confirmation of Mountbatten's dark predilections. An FBI file from 1944 containing an interview with an intimate of the royal family stated that, "Lord Louis Mountbatten was known to be a homosexual with a perversion for young boys." Although some of Mountbatten's FBI file was released following freedom of information requests, most of it is still secret. The same is true of British government files on Kincora which, although due for release in 2018, were extended for a further period. The official secrecy around Mountbatten's private life and the Kincora paedophile ring seem to indicate information that the authorities would rather not become common knowledge. According to Lownie, there is little doubt that what we currently know about Mountbatten's private life is just the tip of the iceberg.

Mountbatten died in 1979 in Ireland where he spent much of his last years in the home he had inherited from Edwina's family after her death, Classiebawn castle. Classiebawn was on the west coast of Ireland just 12 miles from the Northern Ireland border. Mountbatten had for several years been a target of the IRA and had survived at least one attempt on his life during his time in

Ireland. On the 27th of August 1979 during his usual summer holiday at Classiebawn the IRA succeeded.

That morning Mountbatten took some family and friends on his boat, Shadow V, to check the lobster pots they had placed the day before. Just as the boat reached the pots a deafening explosion ripped through the air as 50 pounds of gelignite stowed on board by the IRA detonated, tearing the boat apart and killing Mountbatten instantly, leaving him a legless corpse floating face down in the water.

Was it possible that the IRA knew that Mountbatten was abusing young Irish boys at Kincora and other homes? We may never know as the files around Mountbatten are so closely guarded. More pertinently, given their shared perversions, did Savile know what Mountbatten was getting up to in secret? Even more, did Savile help and enable Mountbatten by providing him with a source of young boys? We know from Kincora that children's homes were a source of victims for Mountbatten and we know that Savile used children's homes like Duncroft and Haut de la Garenne to provide victims for himself and others. Is it too much of a leap then to suggest that Savile might have been providing young boys for Mountbatten?

Mountbatten had called Savile a "fixer" who could fix any problems. This phrase takes on new light when we consider just what Savile might have been fixing for Mountbatten. Dan Davies said that in his conversations with Savile, the DJ had always claimed he had taken an oath of 'omerta' with the royal family. Omerta was the Italian mafia's oath of silence. He also claimed that his success with the royals came down to his ability to mind his own business. And on another occasion Savile told Davies that the royals liked him because of his ability to "get things done", adding that he worked "deep cover" saying, "People don't realise I'm deep cover until it's too late."

Whatever his true relationship with Mountbatten, it is clear that the aging Earl was the bridge by which Savile gained access to the rest of the royal family, starting with Mountbatten's nephew and ward, Prince Philip. Mountbatten was the man who sanctioned Savile as trustworthy to the other royals, according to Savile, telling Davies, "It meant what was good enough for Lord Louis was good enough for him. That's how I got to know all these people. Lord Louis was the governor.

Savile soon became as close with Prince Philip as he was with Mountbatten, laughing and joking with the Duke of Edinburgh, calling him "Boss" and playing pranks on the press with him, such as when he picked the prince up from a train station in his bright yellow bubble car. Like all of Savile's relationships, his friendship with Philip was one of mutual expediency. Savile, Philip thought, gave him and other royals access to the "common touch", making them seem more human and accessible, and Savile in return used Philip to further his various projects.

One such use of royal support almost beggars belief as to how much Savile could get away with in royal circles. During his fundraising activities for Stoke Mandeville hospital Savile was trying to get construction magnate, Victor Matthews, to rebuild the hospital's spinal injuries unit for free. Matthews wasn't keen so Savile used Philip's influence to convince him. According to Dan Davies, Savile dictated a letter to Philip's secretary addressed to Matthews on Philip's behalf. The letter stated, "I understand you are going to help Jimmy Savile build Stoke Mandeville Hospital. This is a wonderful thing and will be much appreciated by the country, Philip."

The letter was sent without Philip's knowledge and Matthews was effectively coerced into taking on the construction project. Savile's audacity in dictating official letters on the Duke of Edinburgh's behalf is stunning. Even more so is Philip's reaction on finding out about the ruse. When he discovered that Savile had sent the letter under his name, Philip merely asked, according to Davies, "Do you know the geezer?" To which Savile responded, "No, never met him before in my life."

Perhaps forging royal letters was what Philip considered all part of the "common touch". Whatever the case it seemed that

Savile could do no wrong in Philip's eyes. Indeed several commentators, including Savile himself, said he acted as a kind of court jester to the royals, goofing around and telling jokes with an air of irreverence that allowed him to say and do things no one else would have gotten away with.

It was because of this "human touch" that Philip thought Savile would be a useful friend for his son, the Prince of Wales and heir to the throne of England, Prince Charles. Charles, it seems, did indeed find Savile useful and came to consider him a friend, confidante, advisor and even mentor. In a meeting of NHS officials hosted by Charles at Highgrove House, the prince introduced Savile as "my health advisor". It was clear that Charles trusted Savile implicitly and valued his advice on a wide range of topics. This is made clear by a recorded telephone conversation between Charles's wife, Princess Diana, and her friend James Gilbey. In the conversation Savile came up in relation to Charles asking him to give advice to Sarah Ferguson, Prince Andrew's wife. Gilbey Asked Diana if Charles and Savile got on well to which Diana replied, "Sort of mentor."

In return, Savile flaunted and parlayed his relationship with Charles. Savile's personal assistant, Janet Cope, told Davies that Savile had once told her how much he respected the Prince of Wales for his honesty. "When he says something, you believe you are getting it straight from the heart," Cope said Savile had told her.

Savile and Charles's relationship rose to greatest prominence during Savile's Stoke Mandeville fundraising campaign. The hospital in Buckinghamshire housed the important National Spinal Injuries Centre (NSIC), but by 1979 the unit had become dilapidated and parts of the ceiling were beginning to cave in. Savile began fundraising to build a new NSIC and by his efforts and string-pulling managed to raise £10 million within three years, leading to the new unit's opening in 1983. Part of that string-pulling, as we have seen, involved forging a letter from the Duke of Edinburgh. Savile also used his influence with Charles to help the project, persuading the Prince of Wales to become patron of the appeal. In November 1981, Prince Philip laid the foundation stone of the new NSIC and was given a tour of the hospital by Savile. On the 3rd of August 1983, the new spinal injuries unit was officially opened. Standing beside Savile on the front steps as he cut the ribbon were Prince Charles and Princess Diana.

Proof of Charles's close relationship with Savile emerged in 2022 when the Netflix series, *Jimmy Savile: a British Horror Story*, was released. The documentary series revealed a number of private letters between Prince Charles and Savile from a correspondence that lasted 20 years, from 1986 to 2006.

Many of the letters involve Charles asking for Savile's advice often on how to deal with the public. Charles repeatedly praises Savile's "straightforward commonsense" and asks Savile for help advising other members of the royal family such as Prince Andrew and his wife, Sarah Ferguson. The extent to which Charles relied on Savile as an advisor is shown by Savile providing a hand-written five-page crisis management document in 1989 which Savile titled "Guidelines for members of the Royal Family and their staffs". In the letter, Savile spelled out rules for how the family should deal with national disasters and crises which would demand a response from members of the royal family.

Savile advised Charles, "There must be an 'incident room' with several independent phone lines, teletext etc. The Queen should be informed in advance of any proposed action by Family members." He added that the room should be run by "a special person with considerable experience in such matters," before seemingly offering himself up for the job by adding, "I get into St James Palace and Buckingham Palace on a regular basis."

Charles's appeal for help came after the Lockerbie disaster in which a commercial airliner, Pan Am Flight 103, exploded over the Scottish village of Lockerbie in December 1988 killing 259 passengers and crew and 11 Lockerbie residents after a bomb was detonated on the plane. Prince Andrew had visited the site the day after the disaster. But the gaffe-prone Andrew did nothing to assuage the grief of residents. Instead the prince caused anger by his lack of compassion when he said, "I suppose statistically something like this has got to happen at some stage ... Of course it only affects the community in a very small way." The Prince added that the disaster was "much worse for the Americans."

Apart from seeking Savile's help in preventing further gaffes, Charles looked to Savile for advice on outreach, writing in one letter in 1987, "Perhaps I am wrong, but you are the bloke who knows what's going on. What I really need, is a list of suggestions from you. I so want to get to parts of the country that others don't get to reach." It becomes clear that Savile was also helping Charles with his public speaking – probably following the example of Mountbatten – when he wrote to Savile in 1991 requesting Savile for help with a speech he was due to give at London's Guildhall. "You are so good at understanding what makes people operate," Charles wrote, "and you're wonderfully sceptical and practical... Can you cast an eye over this draft and let me know how you think we can best appeal to people?'

Later Charles wrote another letter thanking Savile for his help:

"Dear Jimmy, I can't tell you how grateful I am for the most useful assistance you have provided for my speech in the Guildhall the other day. It was really good of you to take the trouble to put together those splendid notes and provide me with considerable food for thought. Whether you think the final result is in any way worthwhile is another matter. With renewed and heartfelt thanks, Charles."

Probably the most appreciative and mysterious note from Charles came on the occasion of Savile's 80th birthday. Charles sent the ageing DJ a birthday card in which he wrote, "No one will ever know what you have done for this country, Jimmy. This is to go some way in thanking you for that." Accompanying the card was a box of Savile's favourite Cuban cigars and a pair of gold cufflinks baring the Prince of Wales's fleur de lys crest.

This wasn't the only card or gift Savile received from Charles and other royals. A charity auction of Savile's possessions after his death had an entire section devoted to the royal family which contained 35 items. Among the cards and gifts from Charles, Diana, Andrew and Fergie were a pair of American cowboy boots and numerous Christmas cards from Charles and his family.

Savile's ability to influence Charles was clearly evidenced by the way Savile guided many of the prince's public engagements. There was the lunch at Glencoe and the visit to the local post office in 1999. And in 1986, Charles was doing a tour of the north east of England when Savile managed to persuade him to change his schedule to include a visit to the Harton and Westoe Colliery Welfare Club to have a game of dominoes with the locals. In 1987, Savile persuaded Charles to attend a ceremony for carers in London, and in 1988 he organised a cocktail evening to be hosted by the Prince at Kensington Palace to thank various television producers for their help in a recent charity telethon. Charles made the arrangements for the evening from Charles's private office in the palace. In November of the same year, Savile was invited to Charles's 40th birthday party.

Savile seemed to have unrestricted access to royal palaces at this time. He boasted of popping into Buckingham Palace following the completion of one London marathon to have a shower followed by tea with the queen. He even smuggled a 14-year-old girl into a reception at Buckingham Palace in the boot of his car. This turned out to be a stunt for one of Savile's *Jim'll Fix It* episodes yet it illustrates the kind of access and influence he had. Savile constantly visited Kensington Palace, according to several witnesses, often popping in without an invitation or appointment. His behaviour, like his visits, was 'informal' to say the least and often trod a fine line between playful and downright unacceptable. On one occasion, a newly-appointed aide was shocked to see Savile licking up the arm of one of Charles's female clerks. When she asked what Savile was doing there she was equally shocked to hear that the DJ was "trying to patch things up between the Boss and Bossette."

Incredibly, Savile's influence even extended to royal job appointments. When Charles's private secretary, Sir John Riddell, resigned Charles asked Savile to interview one of the candidates, Sir Christopher Airy. On Savile's advice, Charles took Airy on as his new private secretary despite another of Charles's most trusted advisors expressing doubts about Airy.

But the apogee of Savile's influence on Charles came in 1988 when, incredibly, Savile was called in as a kind of marriage guidance counsellor to help fix the broken marriage between Charles and Diana. That Savile, a known 'ladies' man' who had never been married himself, was called in to 'fix' the royal marriage almost beggars belief.

As part of Savile's work to patch up the relationship, he arranged for the couple to meet in Dyfed in 1989 to comfort flood victims together in public. This was thought to be quite a coup as the couple weren't talking at the time. It didn't work in the long-run of course but it illustrates Savile's incredible power and influence over royal affairs that he could pull the royal strings so readily.

It seems that Savile's influence also extended to Princess Diana herself. As with Charles, it seems Savile and Di's relationship strengthened around Savile's Stoke Mandeville appeal. In 1987, he invited Diana to unveil a new MRI scanner at the hospital. On the day Savile greeted Diana wearing a T-shirt that said 'For Sale' which, according to witnesses, made the princess roar with laughter and playfully slap the DJ. Savile's secretary, Janet Cope, told *The Mirror* that Diana was "fond of Jim", adding that Diana would accompany Savile on tours around the hospital before retiring for a private chat. Cope also told Dan Davies that Diana wrote to Savile often, usually thanking him for his help and advice. It seems that Diana would also call Savile regularly. One of Savile's Friday Morning Club regulars, Joe Baker, told *The Times* in 2012 how Savile would "hold court" at the regular meetings in his Leeds flat, and about the admiring glances he would receive when the phone rang and he announced it was Princess Di calling for a chat. And according to the cardiologist who treated Savile for his heart condition, Diana had called Savile in hospital awaiting his operation and also to congratulate him on its success.

As with Charles, Savile seemed to have an influence over Diana's public engagements. In 1985, he persuaded her to make a television appearance on a two-hour charity telethon called 'Drugwatch' in support of the 'Just Say No' anti-drugs campaign. He also played the role of court jester with Di, often making her laugh, as with the 'For Sale' T-shirt. On another occasion at a 1984 Royal Variety Performance, he made the princess and the Queen Mother laugh when he greeted them dressed as a doorman. Savile confirmed with Dan Davies that he regularly played jokes on Diana.

Perhaps the most stunning illustration of Savile's closeness to Diana came in a recorded telephone conversation between the princess and her friend, James Gilbey. The conversation centred around advice that Charles had requested Savile to give to Prince Andrew's wife, Sarah Ferguson, on how to avoid the negative publicity she seemed to endlessly attract. In 1988, Charles had written a letter asking Savile, "I wonder if you would ever be prepared to meet my sister-in-law, the Duchess of York?" He added, "I can't help feeling that it would be extremely useful to her if you could. I feel she could do with some of your straight-forward common sense." In the phone call with Gilbey, Diana revealed that Savile had called her explaining the situation with Fergie in an apparent attempt to prevent any jealousy the princess might feel.

"Jimmy Savile phoned me up yesterday," Diana told Gilbey, "and he said, 'I'm just ringing up, my girl, to tell you that His Nibs has asked me to come and help out the redhead, and I'm just letting you know, so that you don't find out through her or him, and I hope it's alright by you.'" Savile went on to say about his mission with Fergie, according to Diana, "You can't change a lame duck but I've got to talk to her, 'cause that's the Boss's orders, and I've got to carry them out. But I want you to know that you're my number one girl."

Despite Savile's protestations, however, the relationship between him and Diana might not have remained as cosy as it appeared. In a 2021 ITV documentary about Savile, *Portrait of a Predator*, a former royal correspondent, Richard Kay, recalled how Diana told him she had found Savile's behaviour "creepy" and how he caused her to "recoil".

Kay told the programme, "He inserted himself into their marriage in the way that he was someone who made himself available. And Charles liked having him around. He would turn up, Diana told me, at Kensington Palace, where she lived, uninvited and would manage to persuade the police on the gate, who never let anyone in without an invitation, to walk in."

When Di asked what Savile was doing there, he would quip, "I'm just here just to check up on you," according to Kay. According to the royal correspondent, Savile would "walk in and drift around Diana's apartment". And, confirming Charles's aide's account, he stated that Savile would "kiss the hands of the secretaries" and "rub his lips up their arms." Even more shockingly, Kay claimed that Savile had done the same thing to Diana, saying, "He licked Princess Diana's hand and she recoiled from that. As she told me, it was something very creepy."

The fact that Savile would turn up at Kensington Palace uninvited was confirmed by Diana's former royal protection officer, Ken Wharfe, in an interview with *The Times*. Wharfe also revealed that Savile's unwanted appearances also extended to royal visits. "He used to just turn up at Kensington Palace and at functions," Wharfe told *The Times*. "When Diana was carrying out an engagement around the country, he would just turn up out of the blue like it was the Jimmy Savile visit rather than the Princess Diana visit." He added, "I don't think Diana was a great fan of his in the way that the Prince of Wales was."

Apart from his japes and his bombing of royal events, there might have been a more sinister reason why Diana found Savile "creepy". In one of my interviews with David Icke, he claimed that he spoke to a long-term friend of Princess Diana who told him that Diana knew about Savile's offending, even as far as his obsession with corpses. "This lady, who was Princess Diana's friend for nine years," Icke said, "she told me that Savile was a necrophiliac. She told me that and then it came out publicly."

If it is true, as David Icke claims, that Diana knew about Savile's behaviour then isn't it likely that other members of the royal family would also have known, including Charles, Philip and perhaps even the Queen? Could the royal family have been complicit in Savile's dreadful crimes?

David Icke thinks so. Not only this, he thinks that Savile was actually procuring children for members of the royal family. This, Icke claims, is the reason why Savile and Mountbatten first hit it off and why Mountbatten then sanctioned Savile's entry into the royal inner sanctum. "So why are the British royal family inviting… this record-breaking paedophile, and this procurer of children – why are they inviting him into the inner circle of their bosom?" Icke said. "Well obviously it's because of what [Savile] was doing. He wasn't invited into the inner circle of the royal family despite what he was doing; he was invited because of what he was doing. And what he was doing was procuring children."

Unlike Mountbatten, there is no evidence that Philip or Charles ever indulged in paedophilia. However Philip was known to have had had a string of indiscretions in his early life, some of which involved sex workers. In the 1940s, he would regularly attend a meeting called the Thursday Club which took place in a private room above a seafood restaurant in Soho, London's red light district. The meetings were described as "rip-roaring stag parties" by Philip's biographer, where prominent figures including members of the royal family would drink to excess and tell bawdy jokes and stories of their amorous adventures.

Among those who attended were Lord Louis Mountbatten's nephew, David Mountbatten; the British spy and Soviet defector, Kim Philby; London gangsters, the Kray twins; and high-society pimp, Stephen Ward, who would later become embroiled in the Profumo scandal, supplying prostitutes to British politicians.

After the Thursday Club meetings many of the participants would go back to David Mountbatten's house for more drinking and card games where they would be joined, according to the author of the blog, 'Royal Foibles', by "enough young, attractive women, one for each club member."

Louis Mountbatten would often be present at these parties. The writer, Miles Kington, later recalled in an article for *The Independent* a conversation with Mountbatten in which he asked why all the "showgirls" were present. Kington wrote:

"'Don't knock these girls,' said Lord Louis. 'These girls are all great ladies in their own right. The Duchess of Northumberland, the Percy, the Lady Devonshire . . .'

'These are their titles?' I said, amazed.

'No,' he said. 'They are the pubs they work at.'"

Given the location at David Mountbatten's home and the presence of Louis Mountbatten, not to mention the Krays, could some of these young prostitutes have been underage? It doesn't seem beyond the realm of possibility. And if so, might Philip have indulged? We will probably never know but the possibility is there.

As for Charles, there is less evidence of promiscuity and none of paedophilia, but his choice of friends and mentors is open to question to say the least. First there was Mountbatten, then Savile, then there was his friendship with the Bishop of Lewes and Gloucester, Peter Ball. Ball often boasted about his friendship with Charles and other establishment figures including, interestingly, Margaret Thatcher. Ball used these contacts, an inquiry later found, to make himself "impregnable". Sound familiar?

Ball was a paedophile who committed sexual offences against 17 teenage boys and young men. However, when he was first accused of child sexual abuse in 1993 by his victim, Neil Todd, Ball got away with just a caution after his high-profile friends, including Charles, rallied around to support him. Charles wrote a letter to Ball two years after his caution in which he wrote, ""I wish I could do more. I feel so desperately strongly about the monstrous wrongs that have been done to you and the way you have been treated." Charles then arranged for the Duchy of Cornwall to buy a house for Ball and his twin brother, Michael to rent.

It took until 2015 before Ball was finally convicted for his crimes. He was sentenced to just 32 months in prison and released in 2017 after serving half his sentence. A representative of Ball's victims told the Independent Inquiry into Child Sexual Abuse (IICSA), "The story of Peter Ball is the story of the establishment at work in modern times. It is the story of how the establishment minimised the nature of Peter Ball's misdeeds … and silenced and harassed those who tried to complain." A statement which could equally have applied to Savile.

Then there was Prince Andrew. As I have covered extensively in my book, *Elite Predators*, Charles's younger brother Prince Andrew is alleged to have had a taste for teenage girls. He allegedly had sex with Jeffrey Epstein's sex slave, Virginia Roberts (now Giuffre) when she was just 17, and at the time Epstein and Ghislaine Maxwell had joked that she was getting a bit old for Andrew. Andrew had an intimate relationship with both Epstein and Maxwell – both child sex traffickers and paedophiles – and he accompanied Epstein on many of his trips around the world, as well as staying at various Epstein properties. Like Savile, Ghislaine Maxwell had unprecedented access to Buckingham Palace and other royal residences where Andrew was staying. And like Savile, Epstein and Maxwell were procurers of children for the rich and powerful. Can it really be a coincidence that the royal family constantly attracts these kinds of people?

Due to the intense secrecy and protection around the royal family, we will probably never know the true extent of Savile's relationship with Charles and the rest of the royals but the bits and pieces we can pick up provide a trail of breadcrumbs that leads somewhere dark. Perhaps the words of the anonymous letter (examined in more detail in Chapter 10) sent to the Metropolitan Police about Savile in 1998 best express the extent of Savile's influence in the top echelons of society:

"When Jimmy Savile falls," the letter read, "and sooner or later he will, a lot of well-known personalities and past politicians are going to fall with him." Did those "well-known personalities" include members of the royal family? It seems highly likely that they did.

CHAPTER 5

HORRORS AT HAUT DE LA GARENNE

Madeleine was just five years old the first time she was called into Mr Tilbrook's office. She had only been at Haut de la Garenne, a children's care home on the island of Jersey, for a few days so when she heard the news that she had been called to the headmaster's office she instantly panicked that she was going to be punished.

She was trembling by the time she reached the office. She had seen Mr Tilbrook on a few occasions previously and he always had a stern look as he patrolled the corridors scanning for wrongdoing and misbehaviour. He also had a reputation as a harsh disciplinarian which was confirmed by the looks on the children's faces whenever his name was mentioned.

Given all this, Madeleine was pleasantly surprised when her escort dropped her in the headmaster's office to find that he had a welcoming smile on his face. Mr Tilbrook dismissed Madeleine's escort, an older boy who couldn't mask the look of relief on his face when he was allowed to leave, then beckoned her over to the other side of the desk where he was sitting.

Mr Tilbrook asked Madeleine how she was getting on as he stroked her hair and offered her a sweet. He told her they were going to be friends then lifted her onto his knee. Madeleine's legs shook as she stared into his mirror-black eyes and felt his hairy hand, that looked to her like a spider, running up and down her leg.

Madeleine froze with fear as the hand slipped between her thighs and under her knicker elastic to touch her in the private place she knew, even at five years old, was not supposed to be touched. Paralysed with fear she dared not move. Mr Tilbrook stood up, leaving her sitting on the chair. He told Madeleine to close her eyes until he said she could open them again. Her heart pounding with terror Madeleine did as she was told, even when something large and hot was forced into her mouth.

Madeleine stayed rigid with fear while the hot thing was shoved into her mouth repeatedly. When it finally ended, she felt a warm sticky substance on her face. Mr Tilbrook told her in a hoarse voice that she could open her eyes now and he wiped the stuff from her face with his handkerchief. Terrified and sickened, Madeleine couldn't control herself. She felt her stomach turn suddenly and vomit came flooding out of her mouth. Mr Tilbrook made a sound of disgust and held the wastepaper bin out for her, shouting harshly at her not to miss it.

Madeleine tried to do as she was told as she bent forward and retched and retched until nothing more would come out.

Haut de la Garenne had been the home of unfortunate children since 1867 when it was first opened as an industrial school for "young people of the lower classes of society and neglected children". Apart from a brief hiatus as a signal station during the German occupation of Jersey in the Second World War, the building functioned almost continuously as a children's care home until its closure in 1986. In the 1960s when Madeleine first attended the home, it housed up to 60 boys and girls aged five to 16 years.

Residents of Haut de la Garenne were orphans and children who had been removed from their homes due to behavioural problems or because their parents could no longer look after them. The latter category were usually from the poor underclass of Jersey's farm workers, made up mostly of poor immigrants from nearby Guernsey and France, and further afield from Ireland, Scotland and Portugal. All these immigrants had arrived on the sunshine-and-money-filled island with families hoping for a better life. Little did they know what would await them at Haut de la Garenne, a children's home filled with abuse, rape, torture, suicide and even murder. Haut de la Garenne would also come to be associated with the name of Jimmy Savile.

One of the immigrants searching for a new start was Madeleine Vibert's mother. Maureen had travelled all the way from rural Ireland in the 1950s seeking a more glamourous and adventurous lifestyle. Attracted by the promise of work and accommodation on the island, including a free ticket to get there, Madeleine's mother was disappointed to find that the shiny brochure-like description of the job didn't live up to the squalid living quarters and back-breaking farm work that greeted her when she arrived in Jersey.

Still, she made the most of it and had soon met a local man who was darkly handsome and charismatic. They were married, albeit in a registry office which wasn't recognised by her Catholic faith, and she soon had two children to look after. Unfortunately, like the work, Jim didn't turn out as good as he seemed. Within five years he had left Maureen on her own to look after two children. With no option but go back to working on the farms, Madeleine's mother had to place her two boys in care in order to scrape together enough money to live.

At a local dance held by the immigrants, Maureen soon met another man, this time a fellow Irish settler. She received a divorce from her first marriage and married her new man, this time in a proper Catholic ceremony. But, like Jim, her new husband didn't turn out to be as good as he seemed. He soon proved to be the kind of wastrel Maureen had sought to avoid by leaving Ireland, the kind of man who spent all his money on drink and expected his wife to serve his every need. Disillusioned by married life in their miniscule and squalid flatlet, Maureen herself turned to alcohol to dull the pain. Nevertheless the two conceived a child and Madeleine was born in 1960.

Just three months after her birth, an event happened that would characterise most of the rest of Madeleine's childhood. Her parents were drunk and fighting as usual and causing so much racket that neighbours called the police. Both parents were charged with drunk and disorderly behaviour and jailed for a month. Madeleine was placed in care for the duration of their stay and her mother was told she would not be allowed out until they found a bigger and more suitable place to live.

Madeleine was taken in by the Westaway creche, a care home for children under five, where she stayed until she was old enough to be moved on. In the whole five years, her impoverished parents hadn't managed to earn enough money to afford bigger accommodation. Nevertheless Madeleine was treated well at the creche. The female nurses were kind and caring and the head, Mrs Peacock, was like a surrogate mother to all the children. Madeleine was allowed to see her mother regularly and she waited eagerly for the time when, as her mum kept promising, she would be allowed to move back home.

But that day remained no more than a promise. When Madeleine reached five years of age, she was too old for the creche and had to be moved to a bigger care home. She was in tears of sadness and anxiety when Mrs Peacock dropped her off and left her at the large forbidding building that she would now have to call home. It was her first introduction to Haut de la Garenne.

As soon as Mrs Peacock left, the case of personal belongings, including Madeleine's favourite doll, was taken off her and she was whisked off by a female warden to visit the headmaster, Mr Tilbrook. She was given a quick rundown of the rules en route – no speaking unless spoken to and all staff had to be addressed as 'sir' or 'miss'.

Mr Tilbrook's office was completely bare of decoration except for a menacing-looking cane. Mr Tilbrook himself was just as intimidating. With a stern, unsmiling expression he explained that Madeleine was no longer a child and would have to learn discipline. He repeated the instructions about calling staff sir and madam and sent her on her way as swiftly as she had entered. After that Madeleine was taken to the storeroom where she was given the only clothes she would be allowed to wear in the home – a grey pinafore dress, two nightdresses and a grey set of underwear. She was then showed to her bed among a long line of others in the dormitory which she had to make neatly each morning or she wouldn't receive any breakfast. She was told by a friendly older girl that the warden who patrolled the corridors at night would whack the exposed feet of any children who were seen to have their feet outside the sheets. This punishment would be administered with her heavy duty torch, which would leave the children hobbling for days.

It wasn't long before Madeleine was called to see Mr Tilbrook in his office for the second time. This time it wasn't stern words and introductions, but false smiles and horrifying sexual abuse that awaited her. When she had finished vomiting, she ran back to her bed, curled up into a tight ball and cried as silently as she could. The next morning was her first day at school.

If she had hoped for a reprieve from the harsh atmosphere of Haut de la Garenne, she was to be disappointed. The other children in her class knew that she was one of the 'naughty' children from the care home and either avoided her or bullied her. And her sleepless and nightmare-haunted nights at Haut de la Garenne left her exhausted and unable to process what the teachers were saying, causing her to be labelled as backwards and lazy.

Meanwhile back at the care home, the abuse continued. She was soon called back to Tilbrook's office to undergo the same gruesome treatment at the hands of the paedophile headmaster. And it wasn't just her who was suffering. At night she would cower under her sheets as the sound of footsteps tapped through the dormitory, heralding the arrival of the tall dark figure carrying a pillow who would stop by the bed of his unfortunate victim. Then she would hear the stifled cries of protest followed by terror and pain, as well as the deeper guttural grunts of pleasure from Mr Tilbrook. She would try to concentrate on her few memories of happiness to drown out the horrifying sounds coming from the nearby bed.

When she was six years old, Madeleine saw her first dead body at Haut de la Garenne. It was 30th July 1966, a date she remembers well because it was a rare day of freedom for the children. The wardens were all watching the England football team in the World Cup final. Making the most of their freedom, Madeleine and a few friends had rushed out into the grounds to play with a skipping rope when suddenly one of her friends, a newcomer to Garenne, let out a shrill scream. When the others asked what the matter was, she pointed to a tree further down the field with something large and strange hanging from it. Nervously, the children approached the tree and saw a young boy dangling from his neck, his head bent unnaturally sideways and his eyes red with blood.

When the children ran inside the building screaming, they were quickly isolated from the rest of the children in a separate room and told to keep what they had seen to themselves. They were each given a shot of alcohol to calm their nerves and told to forget the incident. But of course Madeleine couldn't forget. She had seen the 10-year-old boy before his suicide. He had been with an older man, one of Mr Tilbrook's friends who had been visiting the school. Madeleine had seen the man leaning against a wall with one hand, his legs spread apart. Between his legs, she had seen the figure of a boy kneeling. With his free hand the man was pushing the boys head back and forth faster and faster until the man gave a grunt of pleasure then pulled up his trousers and left. The boy was left crying. His face was red. He ran from the room without glancing at Madeleine.

Despite her fear of Mr Tilbrook, Madeleine told her mother about the abuse at Haut de la Garenne, but only by accident. One day on a rare trip home, she was left alone in the living room with her mum's new partner, Frank, while her mother cooked roast dinner in the kitchen. As they watched TV together, Frank tried to ask her some questions about her time at the children's home. Receiving blank stares he ended up patting her hair awkwardly and telling her she was a good little girl.

Triggered by this, Madeleine thought Frank wanted what Mr

Tilbrook asked her to do and, fearing the consequences of not doing it, she began to undo his belt. Shocked, Frank pulled away and shouted for Maureen to come in. When her mum asked her to explain what she was doing, Madeleine told her it was what she had to do for Mr Tilbrook.

Frank wanted to go to the home and attack Tilbrook then and there but Maureen stopped him. They wouldn't believe Madeleine and they would take her away permanently. Instead they decided to redouble their efforts to find a bigger place as soon as possible. In the meantime, they made Madeleine promise that if the headmaster tried it again she would threaten to tell. Madeleine promised but she knew she wouldn't do it. Tilbrook had too much power to be denied.

When her mother dropped her back at the home, Madeleine watched her walking away with hunched shoulders as she tried not to cry. Then a warden ushered her back inside Garenne. That evening she was sent for by Mr Tilbrook.

True to their word, Maureen and Frank soon managed to get a bigger place, a small house next to a dairy farm. Madeleine had to share a room with her parents but it meant she could leave Haut de la Garenne so she didn't mind. She was also sent to a new school. It was a new start but things continued as they had before. Madeleine was bullied for being poor and Irish. At home things were better. Her mother gave birth and now Madeleine had a baby brother. But soon after things went wrong again. Maureen came down with glandular fever and soon afterwards the welfare services visited. They told Madeleine her mother was too poorly to look after her and the baby and that she would be taken back to Haut de la Garenne until her mother recovered.

Unfortunately, a few weeks later when Maureen was well enough to request Madeleine's return, the authorities told her the house was too small to bring up seven-year-old Madeleine and the new baby. Madeleine would be staying at Haut de la Garenne.

On her first night back at Garenne, Madeleine was abused, but this time not by Mr Tilbrook. She was woken in the middle of the night by two female wardens. Panicked that she was going to be made to stand in the corridor – the punishment for wetting the bed – Madeleine pulled away. But the wardens' voices were friendly. They told her to come with them to another room where they gave her a glass of the alcohol they had been drinking.

When Madeleine had swallowed the drink, the female wardens began touching her body. They slid her nightdress off and suddenly one of them was kissing Madeleine on the mouth. She was given another drink while the wardens took their clothes off, then she was forced to touch and kiss their breasts and other parts of their bodies until finally the two women had had enough. They dragged her back to her bed and dumped her there like a used sack of goods.

It wasn't just the adults who abused the children at Haut de la Garenne. Sexualised children mimicked the behaviour of the adults around them, with older children abusing the younger ones. One night Madeleine was woken by an older, ten-year-old girl slipping into bed beside her. The girl had seen Madeleine being taken away to Tilbrook's office and knew what was done to her there. She forced herself on top of Madeleine and mimicked the sex act while keeping her face pressed tightly against Madeleine's to stop her screaming out.

Yet nothing at night was as terrifying as the dark shadow of Mr Tilbrook as he wandered through the dormitory peering over beds to select his victim, a pillow clutched under one arm, which he would use to smother the girls' screams of terror and cries of pain.

It was over a year before Madeleine escaped Garenne for a second time. Her mother and Frank had managed to secure a council flat on a run-down estate. Madeleine was overjoyed to be home but she soon noticed the difference in her mother, who had begun to drink heavily, even at the expense of heating the flat and buying food. Even so anything was better than Haut de la Garenne. However, the children's home seemed to act like a black hole, endlessly tugging Madeleine back into its orbit.

It happened again when Madeleine was playing at the nearby Hotel le Coin, pretending to be one of the rich holidaymakers' children and enjoying herself with her friends. When she left the hotel, still laughing with her friends, Madeleine walked in front of a coach and woke up in intensive care with a broken collar bone and concussion.

Soon after the accident Madeleine received the news she always dreaded. She was being sent back to Haut de la Garenne. Because of the accident the authorities had decided her mother couldn't control her. Even worse, this time she was being made a ward of court. That meant her mother no longer had any legal rights over her. It also meant she must stay in care until she was 16.

This time there were new horrors waiting for her. Inside a cellar space beneath the floorboards, accessed by secret trapdoors and underground corridors, was a plunge pool where the rich men who visited Haut de la Garenne would have parties. One night Madeleine and some of her friends were escorted to the underground space where they were told some nice men were waiting with presents for them. But the girls were experienced enough to know that these presents wouldn't be ones they wanted. And they were right. When they reached the pool, they were ogled by grey-haired old men drinking alcohol and smoking cigars. They were told to strip out of their clothes, then they were told to get into the pool where they were each claimed by a man and made to do things of which they were all too familiar.

One small ray of light was that Madeleine's older friend, Frances, was back at Garenne. When she was a five-year-old newcomer, Frances had helped and comforted Madeleine, showing her how to make her bed properly and teaching her ways to stay out of trouble with the wardens. But later Frances had gone away with no explanation from the staff. Now she was back again but, Madeleine noticed, much of the brightness had gone from her smile and the cheeriness from her chat. She would later find out that Frances had been gang raped by a bunch of teenage boys in the home. Frances had been made pregnant and sent to the mainland to have the baby, which was promptly taken from her and put into care. Then she was sent back to Haut de la Garenne to go through it all again. Her experiences, like everyone at the care home, took their toll on Frances and when Madeleine caught up with her in later life she had suffered a debilitating nervous breakdown which left her too terrified to leave her house.

Having Frances back may have been one positive but it was outweighed by the arrival of two new tormentors in the Garenne regime – the Jordans. The Scottish couple, who would later get married, were the kind of sadists that fitted in perfectly at the care home. Morag was a small woman who would pick up children by their hair and taunt them. Anthony was a big man with bad breath who would fondle the girls sexually when he wasn't punching them in the stomach.

Morag would patrol the rooms at night hoping to catch one of the children talking. If she did they could expect a whack with a hairbrush round the head, a twisted arm, a foot stamped on, or a finger bent back. If a child had wet the bed, Morag would rub their face into the urine. And that was just the physical abuse. Morag was a master of humiliation, with a seeming sixth sense for children's weak spots. For Madeleine it was her love for her mother, and Morag would endlessly taunt her about how Madeleine's mum couldn't really love her, leaving her in a home like Garenne. Morag was waiting for the smallest sign of any defiance or back chat. If any of the children were insolent they would be hauled to one of the cells in the cellars where they would be locked in alone. After one incident where Madeleine dared to challenge the warden she was locked, naked, in one of the underground cells for 48 hours.

In July 1971, a man who had terrorised the children of Jersey for over a decade was finally caught. Edward Paisnel, otherwise dubbed 'The Beast of Jersey' had been breaking into people's houses and abducting and raping women and children for 11 years. Like something from a horror film, Paisnel had worn iron-studded wristbands and a hideous rubber mask to conceal his identity when he broke into residents' homes. Once inside, Paisnel would abduct children and threaten to cut their throats before dragging them to nearby woods or fields where he would abuse and rape them.

In 1971, Paisnel was caught almost by accident when he ran a red light and refused to stop when the police tried to pull him over. A dramatic car chase along the coastal roads of the island ensued until Paisnel was apprehended. In his car, police found a rubber mask and pair of studded wristlets which proved him to be the long-sought Beast of Jersey. He was later convicted on 13 separate counts of rape and sodomy and sentenced to 30 years in prison. But to the eleven-year-old Madeleine watching his face on the news, this wasn't the most remarkable thing about Paisnel. The thing that astonished Madeleine most was that she recognised him. To her the Beast of Jersey was 'Uncle Ted', the man who came to Haut de la Garenne at Christmas dressed as Santa Claus.

Incredibly, Paisnel had regularly visited Haut de la Garenne, acting as the resident Santa. Madeleine remembered often being sat on his knee while he stroked her leg and asked if she had been a good girl. Luckily for her the touching went no further than that. Other children later reported being sexually abused by 'Uncle Ted' and some reported waking up at night to see the paedophile leaning over their beds staring at them.

Having a serial rapist as Santa Claus was just part of the festivities at Haut de la Garenne. Volunteers would regularly donate food and gifts for all the children – often handed out by Uncle Ted himself – but after these had been opened and the grateful children had written thank you letters to their benefactors, the wardens would take the gifts away never to be seen again. When Madeleine and the other children asked for their presents back, the wardens would just laugh at them.

When Madeleine was 11 she was diagnosed as having learning difficulties and sent to a special school in England. Her fear of being sent alone to an entirely new place was offset by the elation of leaving Haut de la Garenne behind. Any fears that she might receive similar treatment at her new boarding school were quickly allayed. The place was run by nuns who were friendly and caring and Madeleine soon settled in.

But even moving to the mainland didn't end Madeleine's association with Garenne. After her first term at the new school she was flown back to Jersey for the Christmas holidays. She was expecting to be reunited with her mum but was horrified to find out that she was being sent to the children's home for the duration of the holiday. She was still a ward of court, her social worker informed her, which meant she couldn't return home until she was 16.

On her first night back at Garenne, Mr Tilbrook sent for her. This time the headmaster had a new horror for her. He drew the curtains and locked the door behind her then told her to undress and pushed her against his desk. Madeleine put up a fight, struggling against his powerful arms. He put a hand over her mouth to try to smother her noises of protest, and she tried to bite the nicotine-stained fingers. Tilbrook banged Madeleine's head hard against the desk bringing tears of pain into her eyes. He raped her then on his desk and afterward warned her about the consequences of telling anybody. He gave her a glass of brandy and coke to calm her nerves, which she drank while blood trickled down her legs. Then she was dismissed.

It wasn't the only horror of her brief Christmas sojourn at Haut de la Garenne. Later in the same holiday, Madeleine was woken in the middle of the night along with a number of other girls from her dorm. By torchlight, the wardens led them to the secret door behind the cupboard where their shoes were stored. From here a steep stairway led down to the cellars beneath the floorboards. In the narrow corridor, Madeleine was given a tablet and told to swallow it. From there they were led to an underground room where music and laughter were coming from. The girls were led into the room where men and women were touching and having sex. Madeleine remembered having her pyjama top unbuttoned and hands touching her chest, then her crotch. The next thing she remembered was waking up back in bed with a banging head and a sore body.

In the same holiday, she saw her second dead body. One day a girl came running into the common room shouting that there was a dead boy in the showers. Madeleine followed the rest of the children to the showers where they saw a boy who had hanged himself. Madeleine recognised him as he had arrived a few weeks earlier clinging desperately to his older sister. He was handsome, she remembered, with blond hair and big, sad eyes. He had suffered the same fate as other good-looking boys at Haut de la Garenne: taken to a nearby tower and raped by a male warden. Madeleine and three of her friends had followed when they saw him being led away and heard the sounds of protest and screams of agony as the boy was raped inside the building.

Madeleine was never more glad to get away from Haut de la Garenne than she was that January. She spent the spring term in her new school in England and when the Easter holidays came around she finally had some luck. Returning to Jersey, she was sent by a friendly social worker to a different care home, La Preference, where the staff were kind and, most importantly, didn't abuse the children. But in the summer holidays, the bad news came again. La Preference was full and Madeleine would have to be sent back to Haut de la Garenne. When she heard the news in the social workers car driving her back from the airport, Madeleine couldn't bear what she knew lay ahead. She waited until the car stopped at some traffic lights then threw open the door and sprinted away. She hid before going to the house of one of her mother's friends, then made her way back home when she was sure the police attention had died down.

But back at home, her mother convinced her she had to turn herself in, otherwise there would be recriminations. The police had told her she would be arrested if she harboured Madeleine and she feared that Madeleine's younger brother might even be taken away. Regretfully Madeleine agreed. Her mum made her a quick fry up, then Madeleine left, intending to call children's services from a pay phone. She never even made it to the phone. A police car spotted her and took her to the station. She was picked up by the Jordans. They drove her back to Haut de la Garenne and threw her straight into one of the underground cells to welcome her back.

There was some small ray of light that summer however – Mr Tilbrook had left Haut de la Garenne. Tilbrook had left the island altogether and moved to England where, incredibly, the paedophile headmaster secured himself a new job as a social worker in Dorset, vetting children's homes. With Tilbrook's replacement the regime at Garenne began to change and other, kinder, wardens began to arrive. One of these arranged for Madeleine to start working at a local tea shop that was popular with tourists. The job would get Madeleine away from Garenne as much as possible as well as helping her to become more independent.

Madeleine enjoyed the job and was asked back to work in following summers. The rest of her time at Haut de la Garenne was still tough – the Jordans were still there after all – but was nothing compared to the terrors of Tilbrook's reign. And yet the home had one last horror reserved for Madeleine before it was time to leave. She was 16 years old and on the brink of leaving when she was violently raped by another resident. The boy was 17 years old with a muscular body made large by constant weight training and a barely suppressed rage that made the other children fear him.

Madeleine knew why. When he had been younger and much less tough-looking he had been one of the Garenne boys taken on a yacht ride by the rich men who often visited the school. Like the other boys before him, he came back changed, crying silently with his knuckles pressed hard into his eyes and a tell-tale bloodstain on the back of his shorts. Madeleine had tried to comfort him then but he had ignored her and angrily walked away. Since then he had become the macho anger-fuelled teenager that so scared the other residents.

He had raped Madeleine's friend, Rachael, leaving her covered in cuts and bruises and with bite marks on her breasts. Madeleine had tried to persuade her friend to tell the headmaster but Rachael had refused. Next it was Madeleine's turn.

She had no chance when the older, bigger boy came up behind her and grabbed her by the throat. He pushed his knee into her back, forcing her to the ground. He turned her over and punched her so hard she had to fight to retain consciousness. He raped her then, biting her breasts and covering her mouth with his to muffle the screams. Madeleine was about to lose consciousness when he finally stopped, leaving her a broken and bloody mess on the floor.

Unfortunately, it was Morag who found her. The sadistic Scottish warden patched up her wounds and disinfected the bites but also took the opportunity to dissuade Madeleine from reporting the crime. The warden told her that Madeleine wouldn't be believed and that she wouldn't support Madeleine's claims if she went to the headmaster or the police. Once again, like so many young victims before her, Madeleine stayed silent.

It didn't help her rapist much. He died of a drug overdose before he reached his twenty-first birthday, a victim, ultimately, of his own horrific treatment.

Two days after the rape Madeleine tried to commit suicide. She snuck out of the grounds in the evening and went to a pub in a nearby village where she knocked back drinks, trying to drown out her pain. When she had drunk enough she walked down to the seaside and jumped off the pier.

Fortunately, two local fishermen spotted her and saved her from drowning. She was taken to hospital then transferred to St Saviour's psychiatric unit. There she was diagnosed with depression and given electric shock therapy.

When she was released from psychiatric care, Madeleine was transferred to a girls' hostel that was, mercifully, well-run and kind. From there she was found a job sewing in a local clothes factory. Within a year, her friends from the factory had introduced her to the man who would become her future husband, a Portuguese immigrant. By the time she was 21, Madeleine was married and pregnant and, at last, happy.

Madeleine stayed in Jersey and built a new life for herself and her two children. Haut de la Garenne stopped being a children's home in 1986 and, incongruously, became a set in the TV crime drama, Bergerac. Madeleine managed to forget about her horrific experiences at the children's home – apart from in her nightmares – and live a relatively normal, happy life. But all that changed in 2007 when Haut de la Garenne was forced back into her consciousness. Now the children's home was national news.

When Graham Power became Jersey's new chief of police he was given some advice about the job by an old hand. Lock up some drunks on a Friday night, he was told, catch some burglars, but otherwise mind your own business. When Power heard about the possibility of a paedophile ring operating on the island, he chose not to follow that advice, a brave move that would lead to the exposure of Haut de la Garenne and, ultimately, the loss of his job.

Power's first task as Jersey's new chief of police was to appoint a deputy. He chose an officer called Lenny Harper who had been described by one former colleague as one of the best detectives of his generation. When Harper took up his new post in Jersey he would soon find those detective skills being put to full use. One of his new colleagues, the head of Jersey Police's law department told Harper he was convinced there was a paedophile ring operating on the island. The reason he gave for this was the extreme difficulty in securing any convictions for sex offences against children. Intrigued, Harper began looking into historic child abuse cases and found one name coming up again and again – Haut de la Garenne.

Harper began looking deeper and started speaking to people who had come forward claiming to be victims. He was immediately impressed by the sincerity of their claims and the reality of their fear when speaking about Garenne. At around the same time, Power was approached by Stuart Syvret Jersey's health minister. Syvret told Power that he was aware of multiple historic claims of sex abuse at Haut de la Garenne and that if the police didn't do something about it, he was going to blow the whistle. Syvret was brought into what was now becoming an extensive police investigation – Operation Rectangle.

Rectangle was kept under wraps at the beginning but Syvret was doing his own private investigations, meeting with and speaking to dozens of victims of historic and ongoing child abuse. Syvret had to operate undercover and on his own time because of what he saw as a lack of will to tackle the problem of child abuse in his own department. Increasingly concerned about corruption, Syvret ended up making a public statement saying he had no confidence in his own department to protect the children of Jersey. This did two things – it cost Syvret his position as health minister and it also forced Operation Rectangle to come out into the open.

As soon as the police announced their investigation to the public they were inundated with calls, hundreds within just the first two weeks. One of these was Marina Cremin. The daughter of Irish immigrants, Marina had first been sent to Haut de la Garenne in the 60s as a five year old and had quickly suffered abuse at the hands to the school's headmaster, Colin Tilbrook. Tilbrook would tell her what he wanted her to do, Marina told the police, and that he had a leather belt which he would snap like a whip as a threat. She also told how Tilbrook always had a pillow with him which he would thrust over her face if she tried to scream. Peter Hannaford was another victim, who told the police he was abused almost daily at the children's home, sometimes by staff, sometimes by older boys encouraged by the staff. Another victim, Carl Denning, spoke about being forced to fondle another boy at the sick bay after being threatened with death. Jean Neil was another victim scared into silence by being told she would have her tongue cut out. She also talked about girls getting pregnant and having their babies taken away. Kevin O'Connell was abused at Haut de la Garenne alongside his brother, Michael. Kevin told the police how Michael had hanged himself when he was 14. Another victim told how he was anally raped as an eight year old and left with a bleeding anus that was so bad he had to keep it packed with toilet paper for days before eventually the staff were forced to take him to hospital. Yet another victim told how she was abused almost daily at the age of 14 until one day she could take it no longer and threw boiling water over her attacker. Instead of sympathy from the authorities, she was arrested and charged with attempted murder.

Among the hundreds of terrible stories there were even accounts of children who had been dragged out of their beds, never to be seen again. One account told of a child who was chased around the dormitory by staff and who leapt out of the window, never to be seen again. Another victim spoke about seeing dead bodies buried under the floorboards.

One of the victims the police spoke to was Madeleine Vibert. She first spoke to Jersey Police in 2008 as part of Operation Rectangle and gave information on all the abuse she had suffered at the hands of Tilbrook, the Jordans and other members of staff as well as other children and visitors. She was also interviewed directly by the chief, Graham Power, and was struck by how much more willing he was to believe her than the other officers, who seemed more cynical, sometimes even sneering at her stories.

But the sneering would soon stop. Spurred on by the stories about dead bodies and children disappearing, Power and Harper decided they needed to search Haut de la Garenne for evidence. They took a specialist dog, trained to sniff out cadavers, to the children's home, and soon the canine had identified an area of the building which it reacted to strongly. The team decided to dig beneath the floorboards here and quickly found fragments of human bone, including what the forensic anthropologist described as a piece of a child's skull.

Power had hoped to make the search as discreetly as possible but as soon as the bones were found a media frenzy developed which saw dozens of journalists and camera crews from the national press descend on Jersey. Suddenly, the tiny island that liked to fly under the radar was making headlines in the national news.

As soon as the media spotlight was on the investigation, senior Jersey politicians including the chief minister, Frank Walker, started a backlash against the investigation. The politicians tried to put pressure on Power and Harper to keep the investigation under wraps to protect the reputation and the economy of the island.

Jersey is a not officially a part of the United Kingdom but instead is classified as a crown dependency, meaning it is essentially owned by the crown. This important distinction means it is not governed by the usual UK tax laws, making it an attractive offshore tax haven for investors. Thus offshore investments make up the vast majority of Jersey's economy, seeing billions of pounds a year poured into the tiny nine-mile-long, five-mile-wide island with a population of just over 100,000. With foreign investment being so crucial to its economy, Jersey couldn't afford the kind of scandal that Power and Harper were exposing at Haut de la Garenne. What they needed was a return to what locals called the 'Jersey Way'. This meant turning a blind eye and keeping one's mouth shut, just as Power had been instructed when he took the role as chief of police.

The problem for Frank Walker and his other minsters was that Power and Harper weren't interested in the Jersey Way and weren't ready to play ball. Instead they held public press conferences, keeping a horrified but fascinated nation updated on every new development in the investigation. In one of these conferences, Lenny Harper took the opportunity to defend the witnesses from unwarranted attacks in the press, telling reporters:

"I've seen in some quarters of the media in the last few days some of our victims being harangued and criticised for having criminal offences, and I think that is totally and utterly contemptible and outrageous. Some of these people have got criminal offences because of what happened to them. The fact that they've got criminal offenses is neither here nor there. They have seen fit to come forward and talk to the police. They've spoken to us and told us their experiences and I think it is absolutely disgraceful that they are being labelled and discouraged in this way."

Power and Harper may not have realised it at the time but they had stirred up a powerful hornets' nest which now turned against them. The first sign of trouble came when Sir Philip Bailhache, the bailiff of Jersey – a position appointed directly by the crown – spoke about the investigation in his annual Liberation Day speech. Bailhache said that although child abuse was a scandal wherever it occurred, it was the "unjustified and remorseless denigration of Jersey and her people that was the real scandal".

Bailhache was the same man who as Jersey's attorney general in 1992 had appointed an honorary police officer even though he knew that the man had previously sexually assaulted an underage and disabled girl. In a later inquiry, Bailhache claimed that he felt the officer had been "rehabilitated" and that his crime of putting his hands up the top of a young girl with learning difficulties was "at the lower end of the scale". Despite Bailhache's apparent faith in the officer, the man went on to commit further crimes while in his new role and was convicted of two counts of indecent assault on underage girls in 2000.

Despite Bailhache's critical speech, Power and Harper continued their investigation undeterred. By now they had more than 160 victims on record. They had also found a trapdoor and a cellar under the floorboards of Haut de la Garenne. This was an important corroboration of the testimony of many of the victims, like Madeleine, who had spoken about sexual abuse and punishment occurring in a basement area that was accessed by hidden trapdoors.

Another common theme arising from the stories about Haut de la Garenne was the name of a famous celebrity – Jimmy Savile. One of the victims who had mentioned Savile was Madeleine Vibert. She spoke of how she had always been confused that so many rich and powerful men had visited the children's home under Tilbrook's reign, only realising later in life that Tilbrook was running a high-profile paedophile ring from the building. One of these important visitors, Madeleine remembered, had been Jimmy Savile. She recalled the excitement she and the other children had felt when they heard that the TV star would be visiting their home.

But when Savile arrived, Madeleine said she found him creepy and decided to keep her distance. Thanks to her terrible experiences she already had a nose for predators and Savile distinctly fitted the profile. She watched as Savile posed for photos with the kids, laughing and joking and smoking his trademark cigar. She told the police interviewing her for Operation Rectangle how Savile had tried to grab her bottom when he thought no one was looking. The police had barely been able to suppress their smiles, she said, at the 'ludicrous' allegation.

But the same allegations were being made by several other victims. One of these was Marina Cremin, who told Jersey Police in 2007 that Savile had visited Haut de la Garenne several times. We have also seen how Keri, one of Savile's victims at Duncroft Approved School, had described a trip to Haut de la Garenne in which Jimmy Savile had been the centre of attention. This was the first time Keri had met Savile and she described him laughing, joking and posing for photos with the kids, just as Madeleine did. In her book, *Victim Zero*, Keri recounted how she had had dinner in Haut de la Garenne that night after which she suffered a string of sexual assaults including one by a French man who raped her in a hotel room and one by a boxer who raped and threatened to kill her on a beach.

Keri's account provides powerful corroboration that Savile had indeed visited Haut de la Garenne and that a paedophile ring was operating from the children's home. In 2008, when Savile's name was brought up in press reports about Haut de la Garenne, the aging disc jockey vehemently denied ever visiting Garenne. He was soon to be embarrassed however when a photo emerged which clearly showed him posing with the children outside the care home, just as so many of the victims had testified.

Meanwhile Operation Rectangle was powering ahead and three arrests had been made. More digging was also underway at Haut de la Garenne which was uncovering a network of underground corridors, rooms and spaces, further corroborating the victims' accounts. The complex of underground tunnels and rooms beneath the care home gave a new sinister twist to the name Garenne which meant 'warren' in French.

The investigation was at its height, with new revelations and breakthroughs each day. But it was just at this point that the rug was pulled from under Power and Harper's feet. A sample of the child's skull first discovered in the cellar at Garenne had been sent to Oxford University for DNA testing in March 2008. Soon after a story appeared in *The Daily Mail* saying that the skull had been found to be in fact a piece of wood or coconut shell.

The article was written by a journalist called David Rose who had a history of writing pieces countering claims of institutional child abuse. Rose was also a self-proclaimed sceptic about Jimmy Savile's crimes, saying that many of the victims had made up their stories. Harper later told the BBC's *Storyville* documentary about Haut de la Garenne that their own team of forensic anthropologists had clearly identified the evidence as a fragment of child's skull which contained collagen, a material that is not found in wood or coconut but only in mammals. Harper also revealed that experts handling the evidence had failed to seal it or audit it correctly. The fact that this was not done led the evidence open to tampering. When the fragment was returned by Oxford University the forensic anthropologist who had originally identified it said it had changed completely, writing in her forensic report, "Since I had initially examined the fragment it had dried out considerably and changed in colour, texture and weight."

Once the news about the coconut shell emerged, the press did a U-turn. Where before they had over-sensationalised the horrors at Haut de la Garenne, now they turned their attention to rubbishing every aspect of the inquiry, including personally targeting its two leads, Graham Power and Lenny Harper. In the

BBC documentary about Haut de la Garenne, one of the Jersey officials admitted that a PR team had been brought in to protect the island's image and it seems clear that a massive PR campaign was now launched to discredit the investigation.

Meanwhile behind the scenes, Power was under increasing pressure from Jersey politicians to remove Harper from the investigation. Also under pressure was Wendy Kinnard, the home affairs minister, and the woman in charge of overseeing Jersey Police. Kinnard had been supportive of the investigation and was now asked by colleagues to step aside as overseer of Operation Rectangle and to hand over her powers to her assistant minister, Andrew Lewis.

Digging at Haut de la Garenne abruptly stopped and the press were informed that, given the inconclusiveness of the DNA testing on existing bone fragments, a murder inquiry was extremely unlikely. The investigation had found partial remains of at least five children aged between four and eleven but problems dating the remains made it impossible to be conclusive about when they had died. Given the likely tampering with the "coconut shell" fragment, it seems reasonable to question whether foul play was at work with the dating of the other remains too.

Soon the extreme political pressure took its toll. Lenny Harper was forced into retirement and Graham Power was suspended from his position. An independent inquiry into Power's suspension later found that he had done nothing wrong and that the suspension was unfair. Part of the 'evidence' that had led to Power's suspension, it was later found, came from Wendy Kinnard's successor as home affairs minister, Andrew Lewis. Lewis said he had seen a report from the Met Police which confirmed "gross misconduct" by Power while leading the investigation. Lewis was later found to have lied. He had never seen such a report. However, by then it was much too late. Operation Rectangle had effectively been derailed. Power's replacement, Acting Chief of Police David Warcup, promised to continue to push the investigation forward but it soon became clear that he had no such intention at all.

In a press conference on 12th November 2008, David Warcup and his new lead investigator, Mick Gradwell, told the UK media that of the 170 bone fragments found at Haut de la Garenne, only three fragments were possibly human, the rest were animal. The 65 teeth found beneath the floorboards, Gradwell said, "generally had the appearance of being shed naturally". When asked what had happened to the remains of the five children's bodies previously mentioned in press conferences by Lenny Harper, Warcup could only look confused and apologetic. His implication was clear – Power and Harper's previous investigation had been seriously flawed. No further explanation was given. On top of this, Gradwell claimed the cellars at Haut de la Garenne were too low to have been used as dungeons and were now relabelled "voids". These "voids", where around 30 victims had stated their abuse had taken place, were later measured by citizen journalists from Jersey and found to be four feet eight inches high, enough for the kind of child abuse reported by the victims to have taken place. Furthermore, it was found that the floor had been lowered in the 70s so the original height of the cellars in the 60s, when much of the abuse occurred, was more like six feet.

For the national press, this was clearly enough and the spotlight moved away from Jersey and Haut de la Garenne. At the same time, Operation Rectangle was quietly wound down. Meanwhile the victims of the abuse had lost all confidence that they would ever receive justice. A support group for the victims called an emergency meeting in St Helier, Jersey's capital, which Gradwell attended. At the meeting Gradwell told the victims that they might as well drop their cases. The stunned victims asked him to leave the meeting.

Madeleine Vibert experienced the change in tone of the investigation first hand. Once the handover was made to Warcup and Gradwell the angle of her questioning changed significantly. Now the officers asked if she had heard of false memory syndrome and she found many of her memories being challenged. She was told about the cramped height of the "voids" at Haut de la Garenne and asked if she would retract her statement about the abuse that occurred in the cellars. Madeleine was stunned by the new police approach but could do nothing. She had lived on Jersey too long to be surprised by what was happening.

There was one brave official who tried to continue the investigation, largely off his own back. Bob Hill, the deputy of St Martin's parish, wanted Madeleine to show him where the hidden trapdoors were located that led to the underground spaces, believing this would be hard evidence that could re-start the inquiry. Madeleine agreed to accompany Hill back to Haut de la Garenne but soon this small glimmer of hope was also choked off.

Not long after her conversation with Hill, Madeleine received another call, this time from an unknown person. The voice on the other end of the line warned her that it would be a bad idea for her mental health if she were to accompany Bob Hill on his search of Haut de la Garenne. She had no idea who the person was, how they had got her number, or how they knew about the plan with Hill. In the end it didn't matter. She didn't go back to Garenne with Hill. She had suffered enough at the hands of the Jersey authorities to know what they could do to her.

Some arrests were made as part of Operation Rectangle. However, the new attorney general appointed by the crown was William Bailhache, the brother of Sir Philip Bailhache, the Bailiff who had previously stated that the real scandal was not child abuse but the damage to Jersey's reputation, and the man who had knowingly employed a paedophile as an honorary police officer. The new attorney general decided not to prosecute 12 of the cases of child abuse and these were subsequently dropped.

Operation Rectangle had identified 192 victims and 151 suspects, 30 of whom were already dead. Only eight of these suspects were ever tried in court, of which seven were successfully prosecuted. But these were all low-level perpetrators. Not a single high-ranking, well-off or famous name from the list of suspects faced a court trial.

Colin Tilbrook was one of the names on the list of suspects but, like Jimmy Savile, he had not lived to face his comeuppance, having died in 1992. It is unclear whether Tilbrook would have faced his day in court but his reputation as a serial paedophile was sealed when his foster daughter told the press that he had sexually abused and raped her on a weekly basis in the years after Haut de la Garenne when he had been a child social worker in Dorset.

Madeleine Vibert was present at court to witness one of the trials – that of Morag and Anthony Jordan, the wardens who had made her life hell in Haut de la Garenne. The Jordans were found guilty on eight counts of abuse, ill-treatment and negligence but were acquitted on a further 32. For their years of sustained and sadistic abuse of the children in their care, the couple received prison sentences of just nine months for Morag and six for Anthony. On hearing the sentence, Madeleine lost her cool and started shouting. She was removed from the courtroom.

After the trials, the investigation was closed down. Two citizen journalists, Rico Sorda and Neil McMurray, bravely continued doing investigations of their own, as did Stuart Syvret, the man who originally started the whole thing. Syvret had lost his job as health minister for his troubles and now he was persecuted ruthlessly by the authorities for having the temerity not to keep quiet. He was arrested by Jersey police in 2009 for breaking the data protection law and was jailed for three months. He was later arrested again and imprisoned for a further three months. Syvret maintains that the arrests were designed as an example to other Jersey inhabitants to keep their mouths shut and adhere to the Jersey Way.

Thanks to the perseverance and bravery of people like Syvret, Sorda and McMurray an inquiry was finally launched into the state of Jersey's childcare services in 2014, no less than six years after it was promised. The inquiry found that "a significant number" of children in Jersey care homes suffered physical, sexual and emotional abuse. It condemned the Jersey government for its lack of oversight of the care system and further condemned

Sir Philip Bailhache, the Bailiff, for his public statement about Jersey's reputation being the real scandal. It also noted its concern about Graham Powell's suspension. And it stated that children in Jersey's care homes might still be at risk and weren't always receiving the care and support they required.

The results of the care inquiry were something of a vindication for the victims, but as ever it was too little too late. Some of those who had been affected by the abuse went on to live relatively normal lives. Madeleine Vibert went on to have a son and daughter and co-wrote a memoir of her experiences at Haut de la Garenne called *They Stole my Innocence*. Marina Cremin went on to have a daughter and grandchild. But others weren't so lucky. Many committed suicide and many others died of drink or drug overdoses.

The full extent of the child abuse in Jersey care homes may never be known but a few things seem clear – it was common, wide-ranging, and perhaps even institutionalised, with the full knowledge and, in some cases, sanction of those in positions of authority within the government, judiciary and police.

It also seems clear that Haut de la Garenne during Colin Tilbrook's reign was the base for an organised paedophile ring which offered children for the sexual gratification, not only of its staff, but of visiting guests who, like Jimmy Savile, were often from the well-to-do sections of society. These paedophiles were given free rein to abuse the children on the premises individually and in group orgies, and in some cases were allowed to take the children out on yachts and other day trips to abuse and rape them.

That Savile was intimately connected to Haut de la Garenne, and visited there many times seems indisputable. And given his presence there and his actions at other homes, it seems highly unlikely that he wouldn't have indulged in abuse at Haut de la Garenne himself. We can see from Keri's account that Savile even brought outside children on trips to Haut de la Garenne who were used as 'fresh blood' for paedophiles on the island.

What is less clear is how and why the reports coming out

of Haut de la Garenne weren't picked up and acted on by other police forces, especially Surrey and Sussex who were investigating Savile at the same time as Operation Rectangle was underway. Several victims of Haut de la Garenne had mentioned Savile in their testimony, so why was this not recorded and shared in such a way that it could have been picked up by Surrey and Sussex officers?

The NMIC report into police failings regarding Savile said that in total five victims from Jersey had reported abuse by Savile, but none of these reports, it seems, made their way to the mainland where they might have had an effect on the Duncroft investigation. According to the HMIC report, the Jersey Police had no access to INI, the police national intelligence sharing database at the time of Operation Rectangle, so would have been unaware of ongoing investigations into Savile occurring on the mainland.

But even so, surely some information about Savile would have percolated between Jersey and the mainland police forces. The fact that Savile had lied about never visiting Haut de la Garenne was headline news in 2008. Wouldn't this alone be enough to encourage officers from the Duncroft investigation to make contact with their Jersey counterparts for more information? If they had bothered to do so they would have received crucial corroboration of the kind of behaviour Savile exhibited at Duncroft.

But none of this happened. It is a theme which has become familiar throughout this book. High-profile paedophiles like Savile being ignored, sanctioned and ultimately let off the hook.

CHAPTER 6

SAVILE, SATANISM AND INTELLIGENCE

The 12-year-old girl's curiosity turns to nervousness then fear as she is led ever further away from her hospital bed. The people accompanying her are taking her down into one of the lowest levels of the hospital building, a basement area that she has never seen before.

She is led through a seemingly unending maze of corridors until finally they reach a doorway. Through the door is a dark chamber dimly lit by several dozen candles. The girl is led inside where several figures wait, all wearing robes and sinister masks.

One of the figures speaks and the girl instantly recognises his distinctive northern accent. It's the famous volunteer porter, Jimmy Savile. A glimpse at his face confirms this as wisps of his crazy blond hair have escaped from the side of his mask.

She has no more time for thought as terror takes over. A dark ritual begins in which she recognises the words, "Ave Satanas!", Latin for 'hail Satan'. The girl is sexually molested, raped and beaten before finally being dragged, limp and lifeless, back to her bed.

According to Dr Valerie Sinason a therapist, and director of the Clinic for Dissociative Studies in London, the girl told her about this terrible ordeal during a therapy session in 1992. The ritual abuse occurred in 1975 in Stoke Mandeville where Savile was working as a volunteer porter.

According to Sinason, another victim told her about a similar experience that happened to her in 1980. This woman told Sinason in 1993 that she had been "lent out" as a prostitute to party in a house in London. The party had started off as an orgy but as the night went on more sinister proceedings began to occur. The woman was shepherded into another room and when she was allowed back into the original room, it had been decked out with satanist regalia and there were several figures wearing robes and masks. She instantly recognised Jimmy Savile who, she said, was acting as a kind of master of ceremonies. She also heard Latin chanting and was raped and abused. According to Sinason, both victims told the police after speaking to her but no action was taken.

Following the release of these stories in 2013 by *The Daily Express* in the wake of Savile's exposure, another victim came forward claiming she had been raped by Savile during a black mass in a house in London. The woman said she was 13 years old in 1975 when the attack happened. She said she was taken to a house with the consent of her parents who were well-known satanists. Inside the house she was led to a dark cellar and made to stand in a circle in front of three men wearing robes. The man in the middle, sitting on a throne, dressed in a bright robe, and smoking his trademark cigar, was Jimmy Savile. The 13-year-old girl was then stripped naked and tied to an altar where Jimmy Savile raped her. She said she could smell stale smoke on his breath throughout the act, which made her feel sick.

Another allegation soon followed that Savile had attended satanic ceremonies in a building known as 'The Chamber' in Whitby, a seaside town in North Yorkshire not far from Savile's favourite haunt, Scarborough. According to a report in *The Express*, the room was decorated with pentagrams and goats' heads and had a whipping post in the middle. The article said that North Yorkshire Police were investigating claims about the house but, as with so many investigations concerning Savile, nothing appeared to come of it.

For some people it is hard to square these stories of satanic rituals with Savile's self-professed Catholicism, but Savile was a deeply complex man of many contradictions. Could his Catholicism have cloaked his satanism? Ex-detective and police whistleblower, Jon Wedger, certainly thinks so. "I think this guy was a very sinister individual that had his claws in satanism," Wedger told me on one of our many interviews for my True Crime podcast. "… And as well as the sacrifice of children, they also need children for sexual abuse."

Savile always cultivated a sense of mystery and weirdness about him which led to rumours of strange powers, such as the time (mentioned in Chapter 1) when he was working down the mines and was late for his shift. Hurrying to the lift, Savile was forced to get in still wearing smart clothes. Down in the shaft where he worked alone, Savile then changed into his overalls and kept his clothes scrupulously clean. Just before the end of his shift he used the last remnants of his water bottle to clean his face, leaving his fellow miners stunned when he emerged from the pit wearing the same clothes he had gone down in, and still looking spotless. As Savile told the Parkinson chat show, this led to rumours among the superstitious miners that he was a witch. Then there were his two miraculous escapes from death, one when he was buried in a mine shaft in an accidental explosion, and the other as a baby when a severed muscle in his neck left him unable to close his eyes. Who knows what horrible and disturbing visions the infant Savile saw in those sleepless days and nights? And of course there was his date of birth – 31st October: Halloween.

Some of the occult mysteriousness surrounding Savile may have had some basis in fact. In his Savile biography, Dan Davies recounts how one day in his Scarborough flat Savile told him about his powers of hypnosis. According to Savile, he had learned them from an entertainer called Josef Karma who used hypnosis in his shows. Savile said he met Karma at a DJ event on the Isle of Man and asked him to teach him some of his techniques. Karma agreed and gave Savile lessons over a period of six weeks. Savile picked the skill up quite easily and was soon hypnotising people himself. When he returned to Leeds he said he went to a hypnotherapy clinic where he volunteered to help hypnotise patients and learned more about the skill.

Savile claimed to have used hypnosis during his time volunteering at Leeds General Infirmary. He told Davies about one incident in A & E where he had used hypnosis to calm a boy who was having an asthma attack. On another occasion he said he was with an ambulance crew when they attended the scene of a road traffic accident. On finding a man with shards of windscreen glass sticking out of his eyeball, Savile claimed again to have used hypnosis to calm the man. Davies himself said he found Savile's voice induced a strange drowsiness in him. Savile was certainly charismatic and persuasive. Who knows how much of his charm came from these hidden powers. Even more worryingly, did he use them on his victims?

Another part of Savile's mystique is his possible connection with Britain's intelligence services. Jon Wedger is one of the people who believe that Savile was deeply linked to the clandestine world of spying. "Savile was what they call an 'asset'," Wedger told me, "a paid informant for the intelligence services."

According to Wedger ,this explains Savile's incredible influence in the upper echelons of British society and his untouchable status. He even thinks that Savile's BBC programme, *Jim'll Fix It*, was a sly reference to his role for the spy agencies. "In my opinion 'Fix It' was a double entendre," Wedger told me. "…In the whole hierarchy of the ritualistic world there is a rank called 'the fixer', and their job would be to go out, procure children for this machine, and I think that was his job, and in doing so he knew who was doing what, and that's very powerful information to have." We know that Savile often referred to himself as a fixer and that Lord Mountbatten also referred to him as a fixer who could get anything done.

According to Wedger, the children procured for such purposes were usually obtained from the streets or from care homes. We know already that Savile was intimately connected with Haut de la Garenne, the children's care home in Jersey, and that Haut de la Garenne was the centre of a paedophile ring where young children were pimped out to older men.

Other evidence that Savile was involved in the procuring of children for sexual abuse comes from his own nephew. Guy Marsden was one of Savile's older sisters, Marjorie's 14 children. Marsden told Dan Davies that in his early teens he got into trouble with the law and, with a group of other friends, decided to run away to London in 1967.

Marsden and his friends were hanging around Euston Station one day, (unknowing that it was a well-known pick up point for young boys) when a man approached and offered to buy them food. The boys accompanied the man back to his flat where they stayed for several days. Then one day, to Marsden's complete surprise, his uncle Jimmy turned up. Marsden thought he was in for the scolding of a lifetime but instead Savile moved him and his friends into a house nearby. Over the next five weeks the boys stayed at the house and accompanied Savile to a number of parties where only men and children were present. The children were aged between six and ten and, according to Marsden, they would often disappear into separate rooms with adult males. Many of the parties were held at plush residences and Marsden named several celebrities who he saw there. He maintained that he and his older friends were there to make the younger children feel more comfortable and at home in the surroundings where they were being sexually abused.

Jon Wedger confirmed to me that Euston Station was a notorious child pick up point for paedophiles. Wedger recounted a story from a man who claimed that he and five of his friends had escaped from a children's home. The man told Wedger that one day all five of his friends were picked up at Euston Station and taken to a party, after which his friends were never seen again. Wedger also told me about persistent gossip about a man in a white Rolls Royce who was often seen picking up boys at Euston. Savile of course drove a white Rolls Royce.

Wedger also told me about a woman who had recounted

being at one of these parties when she was a child, along with two friends. The woman said that she had been drugged and had passed out. When she came round people were giving CPR to one of her friends. She said Savile was there and that he said he knew what to do with the body and where to take it. Given his association with several mortuaries this sounds like a credible detail.

We know from several historic cases of organised sexual abuse involving children's homes that the intelligence services are often mixed up in the sordid events that occur there. One such example is the Kincora boys' home in Belfast in Northern Ireland which we have already seen has ties to Louis Mountbatten, Savile's paedophile friend in the royal family.

Kincora was run by William McGrath, the founder of a shadowy far-right group, Tara, and a paedophile who was sentenced to four years in jail in 1981 for sexually abusing boys. As with Haut de la Garenne, boys from Kincora were pimped-out to older men, some of them rich, powerful individuals like Mountbatten.

Kincora was included in the Historical Institutional Abuse Inquiry into child sexual abuse in Northern Ireland between 1922 and 1995, led by former judge Sir Anthony Hart. In his report Hart stated that MI5 consistently obstructed investigations by the Royal Ulster Constabulary police into Kincora. He also said MI5 had destroyed all its files in relation to Kincora. MI5 was also found to have pressurised Thatcher's government into not setting up a full inquiry into Kincora back in the 80s when the scandal first came to light. MI5 also blocked attempts by the Royal Ulster Constabulary to interview any of its agents regarding Kincora. It is thought that the cover-up of the Kincora scandal was instigated by MI5 to veil the fact that McGrath was an MI5 informant.

Given what we know about children's homes and organised sexual abuse, it seems likely that Kincora boys were being used as paedophile 'honey traps' to provide political blackmail for MI5.

It is possible that the satanic ritual abuse of children, organised paedophilia centred around care homes, and the intelligence services are all linked, according to Wedger. The former Scotland Yard detective spoke to one Kincora witness who claimed to have seen Mountbatten at a ritual. And he says he has spoken to several witnesses who have reported seeing Savile at satanic rituals. Wedger believes that Savile was himself a satanist as well as a procurer of children for ritual abuse. So we have a picture building up of Savile as a procurer of children for paedophile rings, for satanic ritual abuse and for the intelligence services. If, as much evidence points to, the intelligence services used paedophilia for political blackmail purposes, is it too much of stretch to suggest they were also involved in satanic ritual abuse for the same purposes?

The nexus of paedophilia, ritual abuse and intelligence-backed blackmail would certainly explain Savile's incredible influence as well as his apparent untouchability. It's useful in this context to consider his friendship with another former prime minister. Savile has been pictured alongside Ted Heath several times laughing and joking. They clearly appear to have had a friendly relationship. But, as with Thatcher's government, there are reports of Heath being a paedophile who sexually assaulted and raped young boys.

Heath was the Conservative prime minister from 1970 to 1974. He died in 2005 and was subsequently investigated for sexual crimes against children by Wiltshire Police. A report by the police found seven allegations against him spanning from 1961 to 1992 including the rape of an 11-year-old boy, the indecent assault of a 10-year-old boy, and the indecent assault of two 15-year-old boys. There was enough evidence, the police said, that had Heath been alive he would have been interviewed under caution.

David Icke has spoken to several victims of Ted Heath and he told me that the likelihood they are telling the truth is confirmed by a corroborating piece of information which they all mentioned. This detail is so weird it would have been impossible for more than one of Heath's victims to have coincidentally made it up. The detail was that Heath used a metal hand to touch his victims when he was abusing them. Icke also claimed that most of

Heath's abuse happened aboard his series of yachts named Morning Cloud and alleged that most of the victims never survived, being thrown overboard afterwards. He also said he has spoken to several witnesses who have seen Heath at satanic rituals.

If Savile were allegedly involved in providing children for paedophile rings and satanic groups that included higher-ups like Louis Mountbatten and Ted Heath, all backed by the intelligence agencies, it would certainly go a long way to explaining how he moved in such rarefied circles and how untouchable he was.

Some evidence has recently emerged of how Savile was directly protected by the intelligence services. Ex-BBC journalist, Tony Gosling, recently mentioned on a podcast that a journalist colleague gave him bombshell information on Savile's links with MI5. Gosling's journalist friend, Chris Hewitt, who worked for *The Coventry Telegraph* in the 70s, told Gosling that he spoke to members of West Midlands Vice Squad about Savile in 1978. Hewitt told Gosling that the detectives he spoke to told him that Savile had already been arrested six or more times by various police forces across the country but that every time he had been released on the orders of MI5.

If true this would certainly explain why Savile was never charged with any crimes during his lifetime. Let's not forget as well the Surrey Police investigation in 2007. The Crown Prosecution Service refused to take on the case, saying there wasn't enough evidence. Could a higher hand have been involved here as well?

If Savile enjoyed this level of protection from MI5, what exactly was he doing for them and the country? Was he really just providing children for political blackmail or could it have been more important? If so it might go some way to explaining why Savile said he worked "deep cover". It might also explain Prince Charles's enigmatic note on the 80th birthday card he sent to Savile. The message read, "Nobody will ever know what you have done for this country, Jimmy." What could this refer to? Obviously, not Savile's charity work as everybody knew about that already. There are some intriguing hints that Savile might have been involved in international relations that benefited UK foreign policy.

Savile had definite links to Northern Ireland and was deeply involved in the peace process. In 1973, he led a march of 20,000 teenagers from across the Catholic-Protestant divide in Belfast. The eight mile sponsored walk raised money to build a new youth centre in Belfast. It traversed sectarian areas of the city and culminated with a pop festival in a disused airfield. There had been 51 terrorist attacks across Northern Ireland and the British mainland the previous year. Whether it was linked to Savile's march or not, there were no more bombs in 1973.

In 1980, Savile sat down for a meeting with the newly-elected Irish prime minister, Charles Haughey. The meeting had been set up because, it was noted, Savile would be an excellent mediator with the British government due to his friendship with Margaret Thatcher. And Savile's friend from Scarborough, Jimmy Corrigan, told The Scarborough News how Savile would often bring famous guests to his family Christmas celebrations, guests which one year included Mairead Corrigan, winner of the Nobel Peace Prize in 1976 for her efforts to restore peace in Northern Ireland.

Savile, by his own admission, also seems to have had close links to the IRA. In one startling rant to a local reporter at Stoke Mandeville about a local man who had died after being mugged, Savile revealed his close links to the Irish terrorist organisation. "I want to know names," Savile raged at the reporter, "and I can have them waking up in hospital with every bone in their body broken. All I have to do is call my friends in the IRA. They'll have someone waking up in hospital the next morning eating their breakfast through a fucking straw."

"I know the IRA," Savile continued, "men from the IRA, and you don't need to ask these guys twice. I'm serious. Don't fucking think I'm not serious. I can get them done – just with a phone call, that's all it takes."

Other hints at diplomatic assignations came from Savile's

1975 trip to Israel. Ostensibly Savile was visiting the Holy Land to fulfil the wish of a guest on his *Jim'll Fix It* Christmas special in which a child had asked to visit the place of Jesus's birth. Savile chose to coincide the filming of the show with a 10-day visit he'd been invited to by the Friends of Israel Educational Trust. But, according to Savile himself, the real reasons for the trip went much deeper. He told *The Jewish Telegraph* newspaper that he had been invited by the Israeli president, Ephraim Katzir, to advise on national security issues.

It sounds like a typical Savile boast but one of Savile's Jewish friends from Manchester told Savile's official biographer, Alison Bellamy, that the trip had been arranged to discuss the possibility of a meeting between Israeli prime minister, Menachem Begin, and Egyptian President, Anwar Sadat. Apparently Savile had been chosen because of his close links with Israel and his friendship with the mother of Sadat's wife.

Savile did meet several Israeli officials during his trip, including the president and several other politicians at a reception in Jerusalem hosted by the city's mayor. Savile told Dan Davies that he spoke at length to the president at the gathering and took the opportunity to chide him on his country being too soft with its foreign policy. Savile claimed president Katzir was so impressed by Savile's advice, he invited him back the next day to speak to members of the Israeli Knesset, who subsequently acted on Savile's suggestions.

How much Savile was involved in secret foreign diplomacy we'll probably never know, as with his links to the UK's intelligence services. But whether Savile worked for MI5 or not, one thing does seem clear, that the intelligence agencies knew he was a paedophile and a rapist and by doing nothing about it, sanctioned his offending.

As several commentators have pointed out, there is no way Savile could have got such intimate access to the royal family without the security services having done close checks on him, which surely would have uncovered enough doubt to have red flagged him. Furthermore, it was revealed in 2018 that MI5 vetted thousands of BBC staff from 1933 to the 1990s, including newsreaders and presenters. Again is it possible that the intelligence agency failed to spot Savile's offending behaviour?

Savile was definitely a man with two distinct halves to his life. One was the public-facing, charity-fundraising, good catholic. The other was the private side that included paedophilia, sexual assault and rape. Did that private side also include working for intelligence agencies, providing children for secret paedophile rings, and even involvement in satanic ritual abuse? We will probably never know, but the hints are certainly there. As ever, the biggest one may have come from Savile's own lips. "I work deep cover," he told Dan Davies. "People don't realise I work deep cover until it's too late."

CHAPTER 7

HE HAD THE POLICE IN THE PALM OF HIS HAND

The closest Jimmy Savile came to being caught in his lifetime was in 2007 when he was 80 years old. The previous year he had made a cameo appearance on Channel 4's *Celebrity Big Brother*, appearing over two days as the housemates' 'fairy godfather'. Savile's re-appearance on the nation's TV screens dredged up some bad memories and provoked one person who had witnessed the real Jimmy Savile to do something about it.

The woman, now in her early forties, had been a Duncroft resident in the late 1970s. Seeing Savile lording it among the other celebrities on TV sparked something in her that made her pick up the phone and report him to Childline, the child protection charity set up by Savile's BBC colleague, Esther Rantzen. "He does paedo stuff under the guise of charity," she told Childline. "It's almost like he's above the law, untouchable."

The Childline advisor told the woman to contact the police, so she called her local force in Dorset and reported the incident, which involved seeing Savile sexually assault one of her friends at Duncroft. The woman's complaint was passed on to Surrey police whose jurisdiction Duncroft fell under. Two days later a female officer from Surrey police's Public Protection Investigation Unit called the woman to take a formal statement.

Her friend had warned her about Savile's behaviour, the ex-Duncroft girl explained, and they had agreed a code phrase so that her friend could warn her if something was happening. The phrase was "Ooh, beef biryani!" which was a line from a TV advert for curries and a popular catchphrase among the girls.

The two girls were watching TV in the TV room at Duncroft one evening, the woman reported, when she suddenly heard her friend say, "Ooh, beef biryani!" Alerted by the code phrase, she turned to see Savile take her friend's hand and force it down onto her crotch, making her squeeze his testicles and penis.

Following the allegation, Surrey police launched an investigation into Savile which it called 'Operation Ornament'. Investigating officers began by contacting Barnardo's, the children's charity that had owned Duncroft at the time of the reported abuse, to see if there had been any other complaints against Savile. They also contacted the woman who had made the original report to Childline and visited her home in Dorset for a face-to-face interview.

Next they needed to find the woman who was reportedly assaulted by Savile. It took the investigators five months before they found an address for her. They sent her a letter explaining that they were investigating events that had happened at Duncroft in the 70s and asked her to get in touch. The woman never responded so later that month, November 2007, a female officer visited her house and left a calling card. Later that day the woman called back and asked if the investigation concerned anyone famous. When the officer asked who she thought it might be, the woman said, "Jimmy Savile".

It turned out the woman was angry at having been put forward as a victim of Savile and just wanted to forget about it. She was persuaded however to give a statement over the phone in which she confirmed that Savile had forced her hand onto his crotch and moved it around until he got an erection. This had happened in 1978, she said, when she was 14 or 15. But apart from giving the statement the woman was adamant that she didn't want to be part of an official investigation, especially if she was the only victim. This would later become an important point in why Operation Ornament failed.

In the meantime, Surrey police continued their enquiries. The investigators had now recorded Savile as an official suspect in the investigation and they contacted West Yorkshire Police, who covered Savile's hometown of Leeds, for records of any crime reports relating to him. West Yorkshire Police replied with the only report it had relating to Jimmy Savile, an incident where his glasses had been jokingly stolen by a student at the Queens Hotel in Leeds. As Savile's home police force ,West Yorkshire Police should have held copies of any crime reports or intelligence concerning Savile from around the country. The fact that it had only one incident in which Savile was the victim pointed at major flaws in the reporting system at best, and corruption at worst.

At the time though Savile was still regarded as the nation's darling. Further evidence that this façade might be crumbling however emerged when another Duncroft girl contacted Surrey police in reply to a letter sent out to several ex-residents whose addresses had been obtained from Barnardo's. This woman said that her sister had been assaulted by Savile during a trip to Stoke Mandeville hospital. When the police contacted the woman she said she had been 14 at the time when she visited the hospital with her choir. When she was about to leave, Savile had rushed over and asked her for a kiss then shoved his tongue down her throat. The woman agreed to give an official statement but, crucially, she was unwilling to take the matter further.

Of the 23 ex-Duncroft girls that Surrey police wrote to from the list Barnardo's had given them, 14 responded with some form of information regarding Savile's behaviour at Duncroft. However, the police still only had two victims and one witness and, crucially, neither of the victims were willing to testify. In a meeting with a Crown Prosecution Service lawyer they were told this would not be enough to launch a prosecution.

However, further evidence soon arrived when another ex-Duncroft girl contacted Surrey police to report an incident concerning Savile in 1977. She told of how Savile would often visit the school and ask the girls to comb his hair and massage his neck. She recalled one specific incident in which the headmistress,

Margaret Jones, told her to accompany Savile to Norman Lodge, a separate building where the 16-to-18-year-old girls lived. Once at the Lodge she said Savile told her he could help get her a job as a nurse at Stoke Mandeville if she gave him oral sex, adding that it would be no problem as he could just slip his tracksuit bottoms down. The woman said she was horrified and made an excuse to go to the toilet, where she hid until Savile left. She also said she got in trouble for doing this.

The woman's report didn't qualify as a crime as she had been over 16 and no actual abuse had taken place, but it did provide important corroboration of the pattern of behaviour that was building up around Savile's abuse. Another important corroboration came from a victim who had spoken to Sussex police in March 2008. Jill from Worthing had already contacted *The Sun* newspaper in 2007 about being abused by Savile. The investigating reporter had urged her to report the crime to the police to encourage more women to come forward but the woman had decided not to go through with it. In March 2008, the same reporter told the woman that the newspaper had evidence connecting Savile with abuse at Haut de la Garenne children's home in Jersey. The reporter encouraged Jill again to contact the police. This time she did so.

In her statement to Sussex police. Jill said that she had been corresponding with Savile for several years when one day out of the blue in 1970 he sent a chauffeur-driven Rolls Royce to her home and had her driven to his caravan in Worthing. Jill, who was 22 at the time, said Savile pushed her onto the bed and groped her breasts. He then grabbed her hand and moved it up and down on his penis.

Unfortunately, the two police officers who interviewed Jill chose to focus on how difficult it would be to press charges against Savile, saying the press would make "mincemeat" of her. Consequently Jill decided not to continue with a formal complaint.

Sussex police decided not to pursue its own investigation of Savile. However, the officers did find documentation of Surrey police's ongoing Savile investigation recorded on the police's national Impact Nominal Index (INI) system. Sussex police shared Jill's report with their colleagues from Surrey, thus providing Operation Ornament with further corroborating evidence.

More than a year had now passed since the beginning of Operation Ornament and Surrey police now had testimony from three victims and a witness. It was time to see if the evidence amounted to enough to prosecute the ageing DJ. In August 2008, Surrey police started putting together a dossier of evidence to be reviewed by the Crime Prosecution Service. This was handed to a CPS lawyer in January 2009. By March 2009, the CPS had returned the file saying that there was insufficient evidence to prosecute Savile.

Despite this, Surrey police decided to interview Savile anyway, both to inform him about the allegations and to get his responses. The senior officer in the North Surrey Child Protection team sent Savile a letter requesting an interview. Savile called back the same day and was informed about the allegations against him. Savile told the officer that he had a friend at West Yorkshire police who "usually deals with this sort of thing". Five days later Surrey police received a call from this officer who said that Savile had lost the letter and gave them the DJ's phone number. He also mentioned that Savile was a personal friend and that the aging celebrity had "so many of these types of complaints".

A telephone conversation with Savile failed to fix a date for an interview and Surrey police waited three months before sending a follow-up letter in September 2009. Savile called back and an interview was finally arranged to take place at Stoke Mandeville hospital on 1st October 2009.

Savile had delayed and used an intermediary from West Yorkshire police. He was now setting his own location for the interview on what was essentially home turf at Stoke Mandeville. The interview hadn't even begun and Savile was already in control. It was perhaps no surprise from a man who had a long and intimate relationship with the police and knew how to handle them.

Dan Davies wrote several articles about Jimmy Savile during his career as a journalist, culminating in a biography of the disgraced DJ a couple of years after his death. Like Meirion Jones of *Newsnight*, Davies was someone who had encountered Savile in childhood and who had been left with a distinctly equivocal feeling about the man, a feeling that had led to a lifelong fascination.

That first meeting was as a nine-year-old boy when Davies's mum had taken him to watch an episode of *Jim'll Fix it* being filmed at the BBC in London. But instead of the magical feeling Davies had expected to experience, he came away from the show with a sense of unexplained foreboding.

"In his gruff manner there seemed to be a suggestion of menace," Davies wrote in his biography, *In Plain Sight: the Life and Lies of Jimmy Savile*, "For someone that we all felt we knew so well, there was something remote and cold and untouchable beyond the façade. I spent the car journey home in silence."

The next time Davies met Savile it was at his Leeds flat in 2004 for an article about the now ageing and largely retired TV star. When Davies buzzed himself in and waited in the foyer of Savile's block of flats, Savile emerged from the lift flanked by two burly men who advanced menacingly on Davies.

"Frisk him!" shouted Savile and the two men pinned Davies up against the wall and patted him down. It was a typical Savile joke, both comical and sinister in equal measure, and which put him firmly in control of the interaction. The frisk itself was only partially for show. One of the men was an ex-West Yorkshire Police officer called Mick Starkey who was a life-long friend of Savile. Later in their conversation, Savile told Davies that he had "high-ranking police officers" in his inner circle of friends and that he'd had a lifelong relationship with the police that still continued.

This wasn't just hyperbole. Savile certainly enjoyed a close relationship with West Yorkshire police on an official level. In 2008, West Yorkshire police used Savile's voice on 'talking signs' in Leeds in a campaign to warn students about burglary. In 1995,

Savile had opened a climbing wall at Killingbeck police station in Leeds. In 1998, he'd been the guest speaker at a police dinner. He'd had lunch with the chief constable at Leeds police headquarters, and he'd made various contributions to West Yorkshire police affiliated charities.

But the relationship went much deeper than the official façade. For over 20 years Savile was known to host what he called 'Friday Morning Clubs' at his flat in Leeds. These social gatherings over tea and biscuits included local businessmen and a handful of West Yorkshire police officers. According to some reports, police officers made up around three quarters of the gathering. Savile was of course the centre of attention and would hold court, acting as a kind of godfather (a name he applied to himself in his autobiography, *As it Happens*) who could 'fix it' for his supplicants.

One of the Friday Morning Club regulars was Mick Starkey, the ex-policeman who had frisked Dan Davies at his first interview with Savile. After joining the police in the 70s, Starkey served most of his career as a plain clothes detective after being seconded onto the Yorkshire Ripper case in the early 80s. He later became the Force Incident Manager in Leeds. Other officers remembered him as being a regular visitor to Savile's Friday Morning Clubs and Savile himself described Starkey as his "bodyguard". The policeman also appears to have doubled as one of Savile's impromptu chauffeurs, often driving the celebrity across the Yorkshire Dales in his Rolls Royce. It is likely that Starkey was the officer who called Surrey police to explain why Savile hadn't responded to their request for an interview, the same man who told them that the ageing star got "so many of these types of complaints". Given that West Yorkshire police had not a single complaint on file against Savile, it is not too far a stretch to imagine that it was also Starkey who was responsible for destroying these complaints for Savile. If that is the case, one wonders what favours the Friday Morning Club invitations elicited from other officers.

Savile himself boasted about reading out his "weirdo" letters to the Friday Morning Club where all present would have a good laugh about them, so it seems that more police officers than just Mick Starkey would have known about the various complaints against Savile, no matter how light-hearted the context. One Friday Morning Club regular, Mathew Appleyard, recalled one letter that went beyond amusing, containing threats to Savile's safety, so much so that those present at the social gathering advised him to hand it over to the police for fingerprinting. Appleyard couldn't however remember any details about the letter.

If there were more sordid goings on at the Friday Morning Clubs than just tea, biscuits and weirdo letters, the clue might come from Savile's earlier relationship with Manchester police when he was a dancehall manager there in the 60s. Stephen Hayes was a policeman who worked the beat in central Manchester during Savile's heyday in the city. Hayes told Davies that he was one of several police officers who would regularly pay Savile social visits at his Manchester flat. Hayes said that he and the other officers would visit Savile because of the "girl element", explaining that Savile always had teenage girls at the flat and that some of the visiting officers would often disappear into the bedrooms with them. He also told Davies that one of the officers was with the drug squad and would bring cannabis along which he would smoke with Savile.

One of Savile's dancehall employees, Tony Calder, said something similar about Savile's flat in Leeds during the 60s which he described as a "shag pad" with three or four bedrooms with couples "shagging in them all night long". Calder, who was mentored as a DJ by Savile in the early 60's, described a typical scene at Savile's Leeds flat to Dan Davies: "There were queues of girls outside waiting to get shagged. He'd share them out. They'd do as they were told."

Calder also remembered Savile keeping a tight relationship with the police in Leeds, often visiting a jazz club on Saturday nights where he would cosy up to high-ranking officers, buying them dinner and paying for their drinks. Calder told Davies about one night when he accompanied Savile to dinner with the chief of police. During the meal he overheard the officer warn Savile, "You've got to cut it out." Calder didn't hear what it was Savile had to cut out but he remembered him being "taken aback".

In 2013, a former Leeds police officer told *The Mirror*, "There wasn't a copper in Leeds who didn't know Savile was a pervert." The officer, speaking anonymously, told the newspaper how he had come across Savile in 1965 parked in his Rolls Royce near Roundhay Golf Club in Leeds. At first the policeman thought the car had been stolen and approached, only to find Savile inside with a young girl. Somewhat starstruck by meeting the famous local DJ, the officer asked what Savile was doing. The celebrity replied, "I'm waiting for midnight. It's her 16th birthday tomorrow."

The policeman said he looked at the girl, who looked young, and asked her if she was alright. The girl smiled but didn't respond, at which point Savile said, "If you want to keep your job I suggest you get on your bike and fuck off."

When he got back to the station the officer told his sergeant about the incident. The more experienced officer told him to leave it alone, adding, "He's got friends in high places." Savile, the man told *The Mirror*, had Leeds police "in the palm of his hand".

Another Leeds police officer told Operation Yewtree that Savile was well-known in the early 60s for taking young girls to his canal boat for parties. This is the boat he lived on while making his way as a manager for the Mecca dancehall in Leeds. Another policeman said he recalled Leeds Vice Squad running an investigation into Savile in the early 80's which involved an assault on two girls. Despite the man's insistence on his story, no records were found of such an investigation. Another police officer who worked for West Yorkshire Police in the 60s and 70s reported how the unit she worked for would often visit Savile's flat when looking for missing girls. Supposedly this was because Savile's club was a favourite haven for teens, but even so, his connection with young teenage girls must have been noted.

One such occasion illustrates the point clearly, as Savile himself recounted in his autobiography. One day a female police officer, new to the area, visited his flat in Leeds to ask about a girl who had gone missing from a remand home. The DJ told the officer he would keep an eye open and if he found the girl, would keep her for one night as his reward. Taken aback, the officer mentioned the incident back at the police station, presumably without much reaction. As it happened, the girl did turn up at Savile's dancehall and he persuaded her to give herself up, but only after she had spent the evening at the disco and gone home with him that night. The next morning Savile took the girl to the police station where the female police officer was "astounded" but dissuaded from taking any action against Savile by her colleagues because "it was well known that if I were to go I would probably take half the station with me".

Perhaps if Surrey police had known this background the officers would have ascribed a more sinister motive to the call from the West Yorkshire police officer who arranged the interview with Savile and told them about his many similar complaints. But, of course, they had checked the databases and asked West Yorkshire police for any files on Savile and received nothing except the half-serious report about his glasses being stolen.

When the time for Surrey police's interview with Savile arrived on 1st October 2009, the scene was set for a classic Jimmy Savile show reminiscent of times gone by. The interview took place in Savile's private office at the National Spinal Injuries Centre at Stoke Mandeville hospital, the centre that he had himself helped to set up. In attendance were two female Surrey police officers who had worked on Operation Ornament, Savile himself, and an unnamed trustee from Stoke Mandeville Charitable Trust who was not a lawyer but who Savile apparently wanted present as a witness. The interview was recorded and the transcription is available with redactions under Section 38 and 40 of the UK's 2000 Freedom of Information act. Section 40 is to protect private information from becoming public. Section 38 is to protect individuals from mental and physical harm and likely included the names of other individuals mentioned in the conversation. It later came out that one of the redacted names was Princess Alexandra, a cousin of the Queen, and one of the celebrity visitors to Duncroft.

The interview began with one of the female police officers introducing herself and asking for Savile's name. The exchange that followed set the tone for the interview – informal, obsequious and with Savile fully in control:

"Police: Ok you said earlier it was OK to call you 'Jimmy'?

Savile: That's me name, yes.

Police: Ok thank you. And Jimmy can you confirm your date of birth for me?

Savile: 31.10.26.

Police: Thank you.

Savile: That makes me 83 and proud that in 83 years I've never, ever done anything wrong.

Police: Okay.

Savile: That doesn't mean to say that in my business you don't get accused of just about everything because people are looking for a bit of blackmail or the papers are looking for a story, so they keep going up but if you've got a clear conscience, which I have, everything's OK.

Police: Lovely, thank you."

The police officer then introduced her colleague and Savile's friend from Stoke Mandeville who was sitting in on the interview. She told the man that he was present as an advisor and to make sure the interview was conducted fairly and to facilitate communication. When asked if he understood, the man replied:

"I understand and if Jim wanted my opinion I would say not to answer any questions without first speaking to a solicitor, but that's entirely up to him of course."

Savile responded breezily:

"I'm quite happy to answer questions, because if you've done nothing wrong then you're okay. If somebody alleges you've done something ... but I've had so much of it in 50 years, it started in the 1950s and its always either someone looking for a few quid, or a story for the paper."

Eager to get the formalities over before Savile continues his rant, the police officer then interrupts him to explain the legal status of the interview:

"Police: What we'll do Jimmy, I'm not being rude stopping you there.

Savile: Right.

Police: I will give you a chance to say, but it's just important that I get the introduction bit done so sorry to interrupt you.

Savile: Right, well get the introduction bit done, you didn't interrupt me.

Police: Just on that point, that important point that [redacted] made, I would be saying to you that this interview is what we call an out-of-custody interview.

Savile: Yes.

Police: So you're not under arrest, Jimmy, and you are free to leave at any time.

Savile: I should hope not.

Police: But you are still entitled to free and independent legal advice, do you understand this?

Savile: Yes.

Police: And did you want to have a solicitor present?

Savile: No, not at all.

Police: Okay, As stated, any time you want this stopped, it stops.

Savile: No, you do your job.

Police: Okay.

Savile: And I'll help you to do your job."

Following another redacted section the police officer explained that the interview was being conducted "under caution". She then read out the caution and explained what it meant:

"Police: You do not have to say anything. But it may harm your defence if you do not mention when questioned something which you later rely on in court, And anything you do say may be given in evidence. What that means is, any question I ask you today you don't have to answer it if you don't want to.

Savile: I'll say everything.

Police: Yeah Okay. Basically, any police investigation has the potential to go to court.

Savile: not everything does.

Police: Sure, but if something should and you didn't answer a question today and you did at court they might say 'why didn't you answer the first time round', and the last part; 'anything you do say may be given in evidence' it's just being tape recorded.

Savile: Sure.

Police: Just to reassure you, at the end these tapes will get sealed up, we'll sign and seal them, and they get stored in a secure place at Staines Police station.

Savile: Oh, what a pity."

The police officer then went on to outline the three main allegations against Savile. The first from the witness from Dorset who saw Savile grab her friend's hand and place it on his crotch in the TV room at Duncroft; the second from the girl who had been asked to show Savile to the Lodge at Duncroft, where he had asked her for oral sex in return for getting her a job as a nurse at Stoke Mandeville; and the third from the girl who Savile had forcibly kissed on a visit to Stoke Mandeville with her choir.

After each allegation Savile exclaimed, "Out of the question!" and, "Not true, none of it."

The police officer then asked Savile if he had any general response to the allegations, to which he responded with a rambling rant about Duncroft:

"Right, the main allegations are completely fictional, in fact they are made up, you can tell they're made up anyway. In your letter, you referred to Duncroft as a children's home, which it wasn't, it was a posh borstal, because what could happen, all the girls who were there, through the courts, and under the circumstances, if a parent could afford, instead of a girl being sent to a borstal, normal borstal, they could actually pay for them to go to this place, and it was an experiment run by Doctor Barnardo's, and of course this was a godsend for the parents because when questioned where their daughter is, (inaudible) she's at school in Staines…"

A redacted section follows which is probably where Savile talked about his first visit to the school on an open day which also involved Princess Alexandra, the Queen's cousin. He then finally got around to refuting the allegations, saying:

"And there's no chance for anything that you described to happen say, cos there's never less than 30, 40 people, all milling around, and so you can't do things like you've just suggested, so that's why I know, A, I wouldn't do anything like that anyway, and, B, it's a made up story, and what can you do with a made up story?"

The police officer then stated that she was going to ask Savile some more focused questions on certain topic areas, starting with his charity work. She asked him what charity work he was doing at the time to which Savile evasively responded that he had been doing charity work for 70 years. The woman tried to pin him down to the specific charity work he'd been doing at the time of the accusations but Savile remained evasive going on a long rambling rant about his childhood and fundraising career:

"I grew up in a charity type family, but my parents, bless 'em, didn't have any money, so they would do whist drives and stuff like that, and anything, a pound for a charity that was the lot. When I got to be well known, it was obvious that it was easier for me to make money, but I quite enjoyed helping people. The reward for helping people is sometimes you get, like a situation like this for instance, when nice, cos you can see the friendly way that I am, and all of a sudden, somebody turns round and bites your leg, and it's the same at Leeds infirmary, it's the same here, so I would be engaged in the day-to-day workings of a lifestyle, because from, I don't reckon up how much I have raised, but the newspapers do, and about three or four years ago, they'd worked out that I'd raised just over 40 million pounds, ain't no big deal, it's just a way of life, and the wages for raising 40 million pounds, it's just something just going to knock you on the head."

Giving up on trying to pin Savile down on his charity work in the late 70s, the officer then changed tack, asking about his television career at the time. Savile responded with another rebuttal of the allegations:

"Yeah, yeah, yeah, yeah, I did 42 years on *Top of the Pops*, did the very first one, and the very last one. I did thirty six years on Radio One, and when you're doing *Top of the Pops* and Radio One, what you don't do, is assault women, they assault you, that's for sure, and you don't have to, because you've got plenty of girls about, and all that, so dealing with something like this, is out of the question and totally wrong. Full stop."

The officer asked if Savile would have been considered a celebrity at the time and he responded with an emphatic "yes", saying he had been on TV since it was black and white, adding incongruously that working on TV was better than down the pit where he had started his working life. The officer then asked him if he was affiliated with Barnardo's to which he responded, "no", going on to explain how his system of charity donations worked, affirming that he never worked with the big charities which he called the "glossies" but concentrated on the smaller ones.

The police officer then focused on Savile's Duncroft visits which he had admitted to earlier in the interview. She asked whether Savile had known that Duncroft was connected to Barnardo's at the time. Savile denied this, saying he didn't even realise it was a borstal, which contradicted his earlier statement that Duncroft was basically a "posh borstal". The officer asked if he could remember the year of his visit and Savile replied that he couldn't. The officer pressed him, asking if it could have been the late 70s and Savile admitted it probably was. She then asked him to confirm his earlier statement that he had visited the school annually after his first visit to which he responded that he just called it an "annual", by which he presumably meant "regular". The officer then asked him how he would have travelled to the school and an exchange followed about Savile's various cars and whether he would have had a chauffeur. Here the police officer was probably trying to tease out information she had received from the victims about Savile taking the girls out in his car.

The woman then asked Savile about his specific role at Duncroft which Savile again responded to with a meandering ramble about his charity work:

"Savile: Yes... Like it is, everywhere. I've done three jobs this week, which I've actually been looking to try, because at 83, you don't take too kindly to rushing about, do you understand? I've done 216 sponsored marathons, which is a lot of marathons, and I've all been toying with the idea of cooling it, unfortunately, nobody else has that idea, because they say, well can you come to so and so? I'll say well it's a bit of a long way – we'll send a car for you. In other words, they've got everything."

Police: Ready set up for you, yeah."

Savile: And the terrible thing is, I actually enjoy it, cos if you're going, there's (inaudible) bring sunshine into people's lives, you get plenty of their own, and when you see some of my patients here, you see this sort of thing I consider to be a skid in the car. Driving along all of a sudden you skid like that right. Now nine times of out of ten, a skid will correct itself and you keep going, but the tenth time it won't, and I've got plenty of patients here, who's skids didn't correct, which means a nothing can turn into a something. So this is why I take this sort of thing very, very seriously, cos it's a nothing (inaudible) it's nothing totally, but it's like a skid, if it goes wrong, it turns into a something and all of a sudden, that's not good. So that's why I take everything seriously and I'll tell you what I've done about it, cos this is what you guys are doing about it, but I've done something already about it, which is a policy of mine, but I'll tell you when you've finished."

This is typical Savile and shows, despite the seemingly random, almost senile ramblings, he is totally in control of the interview.

He portrays himself as an innocent almost doddery old man, but out of the almost unintelligible ramblings about skids comes a sinister reference to his "policy" on matters such as the one at hand, a policy which he mentions he will talk to them about when the questioning has finished. This matter of the "policy" then hangs over the rest of the interview.

The police officer tried to pull Savile's memory back to Duncroft and he pontificated some more about how it was a 'posh borstal" dressed up as a children's home. When she asked him what he did there on his visits he replied breezily:

"Yeah, just what do you do, I mean it's like us, we have a cup of tea down there, you're chat, chat, chat, chat, chat, and then wander about and go and powder your nose or something like that, and then the day goes by."

When the woman asked Savile to describe Duncroft he said:

"Yeah, it was a stately home, it was a small stately home with big, enormous grounds with a wall all the way round, and of course it lent itself to being a lock up, cos you couldn't see it from the road, and it had bars at the windows, bars at the door, the staff used to walk around with bunches of keys, just like we did at Broadmoor."

The officer then asked whether there was a TV in the common room or a separate TV room at Duncroft, presumably trying to tease out confirmation of the witness who had said Savile assaulted her friend while they were watching TV. Savile stated that he didn't think there was a TV because he couldn't remember one. The officer then asked what sort of contact Savile had with the staff or girls at Duncroft, to which Savile replied:

"Talk to 'em, because the staff used to mingle, the girls used to mingle, and it was just talking, they'd be asking me questions about the pop world, and all that sort of stuff, because the staff would be asking me more questions about the pop world than the girls were actually."

The woman asked if Savile ever had any one-to-one contact with the Duncroft girls. To which he replied emphatically, ""No, never, never, never," going on to reiterate his earlier point about there always being 30 or 40 people milling about. It's interesting that Savile used this as his go-to alibi when we know from witness testimony at Broadmoor, Leeds General Infirmary, Stoke Mandeville hospital and the BBC, as well as Duncroft itself, that Savile did indeed conduct many of his assaults in public settings, in full view of others. It makes one wonder if this was one of the reasons he did it – plausible deniability. We know Savile was an intelligent man, perhaps by conducting his assaults in public settings he was staying one step ahead of possible allegations.

Hammering the point home Savile then brought in his experience at Broadmoor, saying:

"You don't do that in lock ups… You've got to make sure that when you're in a lock up, that whatever you've got, is secure. I mean for 50 years I've had a set of keys at Broadmoor, but I never ever forget the rules, never forget the rules. You can if you want but you finish up dead."

After clearing up a point about the dining room at Duncroft the police officer then moved on to questions about the specific allegations, asking if Savile remembered the first victim. He replied that he didn't. She asked if he had ever been in the common room and Savile answered rather incongruously:

"Not on a one-to-one basis, no, and I can specifically say that that's not my nature, and it never happened and it is a fabrication. Why on earth anybody would want a fabrication I don't know, probably cos it's coming up for Christmas, and they're looking for a few quid off a newspaper."

The officer asked if Savile had ever sat next to the first victim in the TV room at Duncroft, which Savile denied. She then mentioned the assault happening under a blanket which the girl had on her lap, to which Savile said, "No, ridiculous. In front of 30, in front of all the people, what are you talking about? Ridiculous." Seemingly forgetting that he wasn't supposed to be in the TV room in the first place.

The police officer then put several of the direct allegations to Savile:

"Police: The way they described it, is they were sort of watching TV in the common room.

Savile: No, not at all.

Police: Okay, then said did you take her hand and place it on your groin area over your clothes?

Savile: No, no.

Police: Did you then move her hand round causing you to become aroused?

Savile: No, not at all, not at all. It's starting to sound like the Mad Hatters tea party this.

Police: Is there any sort of situation you can think of like mucking around or joking where they could have misinterpreted this?

Savile: No, you don't do that in the lock up, and you don't do that with girls like that.

Police: Have to ask you as if it had happened, so if it that had happened, did you get sexual gratification from this girl touching you (inaudible)?

Savile: Out of the question, never happened, that was a non-question."

Moving on to the second allegation, the police officer recounted the victim's statement of escorting Savile to Norman Lodge on the Duncroft grounds where he propositioned her for oral sex. The woman asked if Savile was ever massaged or had his hair combed by the Duncroft girls as the victim had alleged, to which he replied with another of his stock denials about being a celebrity, "No, not at all. Bearing in mind I was in the business where there was a million girls, which was the pop business. You didn't have to go to these people for that sort of thing, it was out of the question."

The woman asked if he had ever offered the girl a job as a nurse or asked for oral sex from her, to which Savile replied, "No, not at all, never," and, "Out of the question." The police officer asked if he was aware that the victim was under 16 years old or if he was aware of the general age of the girls at Duncroft. Savile's reply was revealing:

"I reckon that the girls there, they all came from court, right? How old is a girl when she gets nicked, and finishes up in court, and finishes up with a… custodial sentence? It would be 16, 19, they all looked, (inaudible) because they were unbelievable as a team, and their accents were immaculate, well they all come from wealthy parents, so you didn't really bother whether they were 16, what the hell they were, because they all seemed like adults, and they all acted like adults. And I as I said, I thought that the idea, of putting them somewhere like that, was much better than banging them up in a nick, because you bang them up in the nick, and you're really asking for trouble then, with young people."

It seems like Savile slips up slightly here, especially where he says, "You didn't really bother whether they were 16, what the hell they were, because they all seemed like adults." It's not only incongruous, like many of his answers, but it gives away his point of view as a predator, someone reflecting on the fact that he didn't bother about the exact relationship of their age to the legal age of consent, than someone genuinely answering the question. In any case, it's nonsense to think that he wouldn't know most of the girls were under 16 at an institution which was, after all, a school.

There was then another direct exchange of allegations and denials:

"Police: So did you ask any girl at Duncroft to perform a sexual act?

Savile: Never.

Police: Did you specifically go to Duncroft, knowing it was an all-girls place, to receive sexual gratification?

Savile: No, out of the question, that is a complete flight of fancy, and fantasy and down the corner.

Police: Did you use your TV or radio status to request this?

Savile: No not at all, never. Never done that in my life."

The officer then moved on to the final allegation from the

girl who claimed to have been forcibly kissed by Savile on a trip to Stoke Mandeville. On this allegation Savile changed his tack, this time not denying all memory of the incident. This might have been because the event was so unique that denying memory of it would seem suspicious, or perhaps because he was in the presence of another Stoke Mandeville colleague who might wonder how Savile could have forgotten such an event. In any case Savile chose to recount the incident from his own perspective:

"What happened was, here we get people come, for instance today, there's a little jewellery sale down in the foyer, and people do things, and I walked in here one day, long time ago, and I said, 'Not many people about.' And the lads, the porter lad says, 'No, it's local girls' choir here.' So I said, 'Oh right.' And they were going to sing down in a room at the far end, so I wandered down there, of course, there was much excitement when I walked in because they knew that I worked here as a porter right – 'Oiih! [mock applause] it's Jimmy Savile!' So I had pictures taken with them, but I mean, there was at least 40 of them in the choir, so how on earth anybody's going to kiss somebody on the lips and stick their tongue down their throat, is ridiculous."

Savile had admitted to remembering the incident but in the end it was his same tried and trusted answer – how could anyone get away with anything like that in front of so many people? The woman asked if Savile had messed around with any of the choir girls on the coach and then kissed the girl in question, forcing his tongue into her mouth. Savile answered, "Impossible. Untrue and impossible."

Leaving the specific allegations behind, the police officer then moved onto the last section of her questions which she had marked "anything else". Prefacing the question apologetically by saying she had to ask it due to the nature of the allegations, the officer asked Savile if he was sexually attracted to girls under 16 years of age. Savile replied, ""No. Exactly the opposite." The policewoman asked, "Were you attracted to girls under 16 in the late 1970's, in early 1980's?" Savile answered, again incongruously:

"No, they have nothing to offer, in so far as, they didn't even have much of a conversation, so I'm not socially attracted to them at all, and that's why I never got married anyway, because I wasn't particularly keen on accepting the responsibility of another person, and I enjoyed being on my own anyway."

The officer then repeated the allegations which Savile denied again, seemingly becoming agitated:

"Police: Have you ever sexually assaulted any girl under 16?

Savile: Never, never.

Police: And just in relation to these girls, did you sexually assault [redacted] at age [redacted] at Duncroft?

Savile: First of all, I don't know who you're talking about. Second of all, I've never sexually assaulted anybody, so the answer to that would be no.

Police: And just going through the process of the next one, did you ask [redacted] Duncroft?"

Savile: Oh! Why would anybody do that? The answer to that is no, not at all, and the observation is, where on earth could you actually do it in front of 40 people (inaudible).

Police: And finally, did you sexually assault [redacted] by placing your tongue in her mouth at Stoke Mandeville hospital?

Savile: Not at all, not at all, complete fantasy."

The officer's final question was set up as a chance for Savile to have his own say about why the girls would have made such allegations. As if let off the leash Savile launched into a tirade about how as a celebrity he was the endless target of such allegations from people looking to earn a quick buck or a moment of fame. However, given free rein, he was soon veering off into territory which, in an interview conducted more effectively, might have got him into hot water:

"Well in 50 years in showbiz, we showbiz people get accused of just about everything. One of the reasons is people are looking for money, and they will try blackmail, and they will write letters, saying if you don't send us money, I will say you've done this and you've done that. So that's why, there is a group of people who just like causing trouble, because we get plenty of that anyway, they just like causing trouble. Now that's why I have up in Yorkshire, where I live in Leeds, a collection of senior police persons, who come to see me socially, but I give them all my weirdo letters, and they take them back to the station – 'Oh, have you seen what Jimmy's got today – and' this that and the other. So the answer to the question, why would they want to do it, you'd have... to ask them, and you'd have to get a psychologist to see why they did it. You would be amazed at the depth that they go to, and the intelligence they go to. I got a letter here, (inaudible) from a girl who lived in somewhere down in Devon way, and she said, 'Dear Jimmy, you were very naughty, you left the window open last night, when you got up.' It's (inaudible) I've never been to in my life you see, and so that caused (inaudible). I gave that letter to the girls here, (inaudible). About five, six weeks later, I get a letter, would you believe, from a consultant, a Doctor – 'Can you tell me your intentions, with regards to my patient?' This is a place I've never been to, a person I've never knew. My girls here were furious and they said, "(inaudible) well look, we don't, you know, (inaudible) will you let us answer this letter cos the man's a Doctor is a lunatic?' so I said, 'Yeah.' So the girls here answered, (inaudible) and I've never heard from him since. But it's that sort of thing which is quite, it's quite amazing really. Wearing my Broadmoor hat, I don't find it amazing at all because, wearing the Broadmoor hat, people do strange things, the strangest of strange things, and if they do it, they do it, why they do it is, who the hell knows, even Doctors don't know, and why do they do it? I don't know, but you've got to be prepared that they will do it, and ever since like being on TV and radio, stuff like that, there's always been people who think that you're an easy touch for a few quid."

Incredibly, Savile had actually given his interviewers several more examples of allegations against him. Even more so, he had just admitted that he had a team of "senior police officers" in Leeds who came to see him socially and who dealt with similar "weirdo letters". But even more incredibly the Surrey police officers didn't see fit to ask any follow-up questions about these other allegations. They didn't question the statement that senior police officers in Leeds were regularly dealing with complaints about Savile – however spurious – despite the fact that West Yorkshire Police had told them they held not a single report on file about Savile. This alone should have suggested that complaints against Savile were being regularly destroyed by West Yorkshire Police.

However, instead of asking any questions about these startling admissions, the police officer simply ignored them and, again kowtowing to Savile's agenda, asked if he now wanted to explain his earlier point about his "policy". Savile demurred, saying first the women had a job to do, but was reassured that they had finished with their questions. The tape was then changed and Savile was reminded of the legal caution at the beginning of the recording. In bullish mood following his rant, Savile declared. "I don't accept the fact that I'm under caution 'cause I've not done anything."

The police officer explained that the caution was just the statement that she'd read out to him, not that he had been legally cautioned for an offence. There followed a confused exchange in which Savile appeared to be fencing for high ground while perhaps pretending to be more ignorant of the law than he actually was in order to play the confused-old-man card:

"Savile: It's from your point of view, you have to do a job and you have to say I'm under caution. I legally am not obliged to say I accept to be under caution and I go from a humanist point of view because I've not done anything wrong so therefore I'm not under caution.

Police: It's confusing, all it means is I've read you out the caution, I've told you that you don't have to answer any questions if you don't want to.

Savile: But I'm perfectly happy to answer every questions, every one.

Police: 'Cause there's also, there's another police term called 'the caution', being given a caution, where it's like instead of a conviction, that's not what I'm meaning, I'm meaning I've told you that…

Savile: Yeah good I won't understand either of them anyway.

Police: But you're happy still with the understanding of that?

Savile: Yes, when you've done nothing wrong you're not worried."

The police officer obligingly went on to remind Savile about his "policy". However, given time perhaps for the "weirdo letters" comment to sink in, the other officer suddenly decided to question Savile about his references to complaints being handled by senior police officers in Leeds:

"Police: You mentioned about your weirdo letters, referring to letters that you received of a threatening nature or otherwise?

Savile: Yes.

Police: And that you give those to some police office in Yorkshire?

Savile: Yeah to let them see them.

Police: Who is it that you give those to?"

Savile, probably realising he had gone too far earlier, now switched to the defensive. The officers were finally doing their job, asking some questions which were actually prodding at something rather than just going through the motions:

"Savile: Erm I'm not sure, they've all got nicknames.

Police: Well, what are their nicknames?

Savile: Well one's called [redacted] what's the other one called? He's an inspector… It's something that you just, they say, 'Any more weirdos then Jim?' I said, 'Yes,' and they say, 'Wo-oh, ha-ha, ha-ha.'

Police: When you meet them socially? Where do you meet them?

Savile: My place, yes, yeah they come round and drink tea and that. One of the reasons that I do that is that things happen to people like me that don't happen to normal people who are not normal. And just in case anything happened to somebody like me then the lads would be able to sift through all this weirdo stuff and maybe find somebody that they…

Police: Okay, so your expectation in handing the letters to them is that they're going to investigate them?

Savile: No, no, not investigate them no, not going to do anything with them, but if anything happens to me...

Police: But, store them on your behalf then?

Savile: Well yeah but they don't keep them very long. They pass them round the office, and everybody has a laugh, just like the girls here did when we got the thing from the consultant. You don't have a routine, an office routine with weird stuff, you don't have an office routine, you go, 'Oh this is the latest blah look at this ha-ha, ha-ha.'"

Again, a direct affirmation from Savile that he regularly passed complaints regarding himself to West Yorkshire police despite the fact that the force denied having any complaints regarding Savile on file. But instead of maintaining this line of questioning which seemed to have Savile momentarily on the ropes, the officer then switched tacks, concentrating on letters which might be considered threats to Savile – an assertion which he never himself made. Grateful, presumably for being let off the hook, Savile agreed that he often received threatening letters. The officer then asked him if he ever received a threatening letter from one of the Duncroft girls, which makes one suspect that the whole line of questioning about the "weirdo letters" was done more in the spirit of protecting Savile and exposing the Duncroft victims as frauds than at poking holes in Savile's story.

With that little diversion out of the way, Savile was reminded helpfully again that he wanted to talk about his "policy". Savile accepted the invitation and went on to deliver what amounted to a direct threat to the police officers concerned:

"I take this sort of thing very seriously and have done right from the 1950's when it started because instinct tells me that whereas it's a nothing, I know that a nothing can turn into a something because I've got many patients here at Stoke Mandeville where a nothing, a skid in the car, a slip, a fall, they're paralysed for the rest of their lives, so a nothing can be a something. So all of a sudden somebody comes and makes an allegation. Now I've had five people make allegations that I did something about, because I take them to court, I sue them, and the five I've already sued happen to be newspapers, but they made allegations, and not one of them wanted to finish up in court with me, so they all settled out of court. Now this to me, that's going on today, is exactly one of those things, so I've already told my legal people that somebody were going to come and talk to me, they've got a copy of your letter, and the process or the policy will start because if this disappears, so if it disappears it disappears, if it doesn't disappear for any reason then my policy will swing into action at the same time. But the difference with my policy is that my people who are one of the initials after my name is LOD that's a Doctor of Law right, not an honorary one, a real one, that gives me, how shall we say, friends. And if I was going to sue anybody – which I never actually got round to actually suing because they all run away and say, "Shush, pay him up,' – we go not to the local court, we go to the Old Bailey cos my people can book time in the Old Bailey. So my legal people are ready and waiting, all they need would be a name, and an address, and then the due process from my angle would stop. Because obviously if I'm prepared to take somebody to court and put it in front of a judge then there can't be very much wrong with my policy of behaviour because I've never done anybody any harm in my entire life, cos there's not need to, no need to, no need to chase girls, I've thousands of them on *Top of the Pops*, thousands on Radio One, no need to take liberties with them, out of the question. And anyway it's not my nature because all my life I've been a semi-pro athlete with 216 Marathons, over 300 professional bike races, and when I was fighting, 107 pro fights that I had. So socially, and I don't drink, never taken a drug in my life ever. In fact from a newspaper point of view I'm very boring. They consider me dreadfully boring because I don't do anything, but I have a terrific time, but I don't do anything, I don't drink no booze, no drugs, no kinky carryings on, don't go to brothels or anything like that, didn't even know where one was, so the tabloids consider me very, very boring. But because I take everything seriously I've even now alerted my legal team. They may be doing business, and if we do then you ladies will finish up at the Old Bailey as well as everyone else because we want you there as witnesses. Yeah, only a bit of fun. But nobody ever seems to want to go that far because the prospect of me being one side of the court, and the accuser or the newspaper are on the other side of the court and the man in the middle who happens to be one of us (inaudible). What did I get from *The Sun*? This is actually not dissimilar to, do you remember that thing a few months ago, that house in, the place in Jersey where the dead bodies that never were, so there's something doing with that, I've visited everywhere in the British Isles and so they had a picture of me with about six Jersey councillors standing on the steps of there, like that, right. For a garden fête or something. Headline: "Sir Jimmy in the house of hell", you see so that could be argued in court as malicious, right. They had a sudden rash of conscience, did *The Sun* and they sent a reporter round with a £400-box of cigars, 'Sorry about that, Jim'. So sometimes, the time before I've had them and it cost them like £200,000 because they were out of order and I'm known in the trade as Litigiousness because, which means to say that I'm, willing to pull people into court straight away, no messing, thank you. Now if you're litigious, people get quite nervous actually because for somebody that don't want to go court, I love it. (inaudible) Get into court right, what happened – 'Oh dear (inaudible) I've been wronged your worship, wronged oh, oh dreadful, oh…' – Bang, £200,000 or whatever, whatever. Five times I've done that, I'd rather not, I'd rather not, I'm not a clever-clogs or anything like that. What I'd really like to do is to go out, up the Dales, have a walk, go training, this that and the other but my business won't let you do that. My business there's women looking for a few quid. We always get something like this coming up for Christmas because we want a few quid for Christmas right. And normally you can brush them away like midges and it's not much of a price to pay for the lifestyle that we're getting, you know what I mean? I own this hospital. NHS run it, I own it and that's not bad. Seeing I started off life down the pit, not bad, and when they see the faces and you go in there and suddenly they smile, paralysed and (inaudible), 'Hello Jim, you're here today,' that's worth all the money in, all the tea in China. And one of the reasons that I get, that I take it seriously is because I wouldn't let anything get out of hand to run the risk of spoiling things for my people here. Because if I wasn't here they wouldn't get the quarter of a million pound a year that they need to keep it going. There's nobody these days of that calibre that can do that, so whereas I would like life to retire at 83 I mean how the hell I'm going to keep going on at 80-bleedin'-3, you know, I want to retire but the world won't let you retire…"

It was an extraordinary rant to end an extraordinary interview. Savile had gone from being questioned as the suspect in multiple cases of sexual assault against underage girls, to actively threatening the police officers concerned with being taken to court themselves. Not to mention the extraordinary comment that he "owned" Stoke Mandeville hospital thrown casually into the mix.

However, seemingly unperturbed that they had just been threatened with being taken to court for doing their jobs, the police politely gave Savile one last chance to say any concluding remarks, to which he responded:

"… its complete fantasy, it really, really, really is and neither thing was at a place where you could get away with what they said you've got away with, and I wouldn't want to in the first place anyway, complete fantasy."

And with that the interview was over. Before the end of the same month, on the 28th of October 2009, the three victims and the witness mentioned in the interview were sent letters informing them that the CPS had decided not to prosecute Savile. Operation Ornament was over. None of the extraordinary admissions that Savile had made were followed up on and no further investigations were conducted to check his statements. The interview was basically a complete failure. As Mark Williams-Thomas summed up on my podcast:

"[Savile] did that interview on his terms, when he wanted it, where he wanted it. Surrey police did not advise Stoke Mandeville hospital of allegations, three separate sexual abuse allegations against him while he was working at the hospital. He had access to the hospital and he had access to vulnerable people, young children, at Stoke Mandeville yet he's being investigated for indecent sexual assaults on three people and they didn't bother telling Stoke Mandeville – total failure. They didn't tell Thames Valley police, of whose force area it was, didn't tell them that. And the interview itself provided vital information that, had the police officers bothered to follow up on, would have shown Savile to be lying. But they just simply took what he told them as being true, dismissed everything else."

A later report into police failings regarding Savile by Her Majesty's Inspectorate of Constabulary (HMIC) appropriately titled 'Mistakes were Made', came to the same conclusions as Williams-Thomas. The HMIC report pointed out several failings with Operation Ornament, including the long time scale of 29 months and the long gaps between first contacting and following up with some of the victims (five months in one case). The report also pointed out that the victims should at some point have been made aware of each other. Each of the victims had made it clear that they didn't want to be part of a court case if it only centred on them. Knowing that other victims and witnesses were being interviewed as part of the investigation might have proved crucial in encouraging them to testify in court. Yet Surrey police never informed any of the victims about each other, thus leaving them feeling alone, isolated and unwilling to testify.

The worst case of this was Jill from Worthing who had alleged being sexually assaulted by Savile in his caravan to Sussex police. In her interview the officers from Sussex police showed a "regrettable lack of understanding concerning the law and practice in relation to sexual offences," according to the HMIC report. Jill's interviewers chose to concentrate on the negative consequences of testifying against Savile, telling her that if she were to prosecute, she would be publicly branded a liar, that Savile's lawyers would make "mincemeat" of her, and that her name would be plastered all over the newspapers. Naturally, after being told this, Jill decided she didn't want to take the matter further.

Despite then being made aware of a similar investigation into Savile by Surrey police, neither force made any effort to co-operate with each other on a joint investigation, nor was Jill told about the other victims in the Surrey investigation who could have provided important encouragement to change her mind about testifying. The report went on to point out that, after the decision was taken by Sussex police to shelve any further investigation into Savile, when the Sussex investigators filed their crime report, they initially tried to file it under the reference 'no crime' rather than 'complainant decides not to prosecute'. They also made no attempt to interview Savile to put the allegations to him, a move which was "neither usual nor good police practice," as the HMIC report pointed out.

The way Jill had been interviewed was so one-sided that in 2012, after Savile had finally been exposed, she re-contacted the detectives at Sussex police to say she wanted the investigation re-opened on the basis that she "had been pressurised into not pursuing the case at the time of the original complaint," according to the HMIC report. However, according to the report, Jill couldn't get in contact with the officers who had originally interviewed her. Contact was only made after *The Sun* reporter who had originally interviewed Jill about the Savile allegations back in 2007 called Sussex police to inform them that Jill had been trying to get in touch.

All in all, the HMIC report concluded that investigating police officers from both Surrey and Sussex forces had been too aware of Savile's celebrity status and had made decisions based on how much more difficult (they thought) it would be to bring a successful prosecution against such a celebrity.

Whatever the case, the only police investigation into Savile during his six decades of offending ultimately came to nothing in

2009 when Operation Ornament was shelved. The last chance to catch Savile while he was still alive had been missed. The aging celebrity would die just two years later, unexposed and unpunished and, reportedly, with a smile on his face. No wonder. He had gotten away with it. And whatever the reasons for the police's failings, they had been a large part of the reason why.

CHAPTER 8

PROWLING HOSPITALS AND MORGUES

It was 1977 and a 12-year-old girl was in Stoke Mandeville hospital in Buckinghamshire after having her tonsils removed. For some reason, she had been put in the geriatric ward. She was bored and wandered down to the day room to watch TV in her nightdress.

As she left the ward, the girl noticed a man wearing a long coat, brown tracksuit bottoms and lots of gold jewellery. He had shoulder-length blonde hair and was smoking a large cigar.

The man asked her where she was going and she told him the television room. "I'll show you," he replied, and walked her down the corridor. The man seemed friendly and the girl felt comfortable.

The day room was empty and the girl sat in one of the chairs. The man asked her if she had a boyfriend. She didn't reply. The man then knelt down in front of the girl, positioning himself between her legs. She noticed that the man had pulled his tracksuit bottoms down to reveal his penis. The man then manoeuvred himself forward and penetrated the girl. After a short time, the man made a groaning sound and withdrew. His semen was all over the seat and the girl's thighs. He wiped the semen off with the front of his white coat and, without saying anything, left the room. The door had been open the whole time.

Confused and disoriented, the girl wandered around the corridors, trying to find her way back to the ward. On her way, she bumped into a nurse. She said, "Your porter hurt me." The nurse asked where, and the girl pointed to her vagina. The nurse said, "Don't say anything. I'll get into trouble."

The girl went back to her bed and thought over what had happened. She knew it was wrong and wanted to tell someone. She found a pencil and tore out two pages of her bedside Bible. On one of the pages she wrote, "To the doctor. Your porter hurt me. Please ring my dad," followed by the phone number and address of her father and her own signature. She posted the note in a box that said 'Letterbox' in the corridor outside the ward, thinking it would be read by the doctors.

Later that night in bed, the girl saw the same man come into her ward and head straight for her bed. She pulled the covers over her head but the man put his hand under the sheets and began rubbing her vagina, making sounds of pleasure as he did so. The contact lasted only 10 or 20 seconds, then the hand was withdrawn. The girl peeked her head out of the covers as the man walked away and watched as he jumped on top of an elderly patient, lying face down on top of her. A nurse suddenly appeared and shouted, "You shouldn't be in here, Jimmy." The man got off the woman and left the ward, without anything else being said.

Two years later, aged 14, the girl was watching TV at home when she saw the porter who had raped her. He was on television. She couldn't understand what the porter from Stoke Mandeville was doing on TV. "In time," she declared in her statement, made decades later to lawyers representing dozens of similar victims, "I came to know that the porter was Jimmy Savile."

This account marks a shift in Savile's offending in the 60s and 70s. As the famous DJ got older, his targets shifted from young party-goers at dancehalls or on *Top of the Pops* to even more vulnerable victims at hospitals, care homes, special schools and mental institutions around the country.

It started at Savile's local hospital, Leeds General Infirmary where a childhood friend, Charles Hullighan had been appointed head porter. Hullighan had been serving with the army in India but had been invalided out after being stabbed on duty. On his return to Leeds, he had landed the job as head porter at Leeds General. Hullighan, it seems, was Savile's passport into the hospital. As we shall see there are some hints that Savile's volunteering work at Leeds General may have started as early as the 1950's, but as far as official records go his main connection with the hospital began in 1961. As an increasingly famous local DJ, Savile had offered Hullighan his services with the launch of the hospital's in-house radio station. Savile helped with the radio launch then offered his services as a volunteer porter for a few shifts.

Later in 1968, Savile cemented his association with the hospital during the national 'I'm Backing Britain' campaign. In the late 60s, Britain's economy was in such dire straits that the government endorsed a scheme called 'I'm Backing Britain', whereby staff across the nation volunteered to work extra, non-paid shifts to help prevent businesses going under. Savile saw his opportunity and, in 1968, turned up at Leeds Infirmary in his Rolls Royce Silver Shadow, sporting a Union Jack waistcoat, to work nine shifts as a porter. From then on, Savile became a more or less permanent fixture at the hospital, and the hospital became his permanent hunting ground for victims.

One patient in the neurological ward, June Thornton, described watching in horror as Savile sexually molested a young girl in the bed opposite her. "Jimmy Savile came to a young lady sat in a chair," Thornton told a BBC report in 2012. "Unfortunately this lady, I think, had brain damage because she just sat there, and he kissed her. And I thought he was a visitor coming to see her. And he started rubbing his hands down her arms. And then, I don't know of a nice way to put it, but he molested her. He helped himself, and she just sat there and couldn't do anything about it." When Thornton told a nurse about the assault, the woman "merely shrugged her shoulders," she said.

Another porter was a witness to Savile's abuse in the late 70s when he entered the X-ray department to pick up a patient. "[Savile] was there with this young girl on a trolley with a blanket over her," the porter told an NHS report into Savile's abuse at Leeds General Infirmary, "and he was the only one in X-ray, and she was waiting to be X-rayed ...and as I walked in his hand came from under the blanket very quickly. I would swear blind he was touching her up."

Savile's offending at Leeds General wasn't just confined to women and girls. A male victim spoke about waiting for an X-ray on a hospital bed in 1988 when he was 29 years old. The man said Savile approached him dressed in a staff uniform and started speaking to him in a friendly manner. During the conversation, the man said Savile put his hand on his thigh then brushed his penis with the same hand before walking off.

Another male victim was just 14 years old in 1994 when he was left alone in the X-ray department in a wheelchair wearing just a dressing gown when Savile entered the room. "He came up to me," the man told the NHS report, "... and lent over me and told me to cheer up and said things can't be that bad. He put his hand on my leg, as he said it and then all of a sudden just moved his hand under my gown, because I had a hospital gown on, I just had my dressing gown draped over me, put his hand on my genitals and squeezed them. How long it lasted, I don't know, I can't say. It was five seconds, 10 seconds. It wasn't a long time and then he looked at me and said, 'Now then, I bet that's cheered you up.'"

Neither were Savile's attentions confined solely to the patients. One nurse recalled being assaulted by Savile in 1981 when she was a 21-year-old student nurse doing a placement on the male urological ward. She told the NHS report that she was aware that Savile was having an affair with another nurse on the ward and that one day she saw Savile speaking to the other nurse as she was heading to the linen cupboard. Once inside the cupboard, with her back to the door, the nurse described how Savile had snuck up behind her. "He grabbed me from behind," she said, "grabbing both breasts and then he started pushing his groin into my back and bottom." The woman was saved from further abuse when another student nurse entered the linen cupboard, at which point Savile just laughed and said goodbye.

Incredibly, it seems Savile may even have had his own set of keys to the nurses' accommodation at Leeds General. According to a post on an online Leeds forum by the ex-husband of a student nurse at the hospital in the early 70s, Savile would often enter the nurses' accommodation when they were getting undressed. He would also turn up to "clean" the shower room while the girls were showering. The man said the nurses complained to the hospital's board of directors but nothing was done. He said that the female nurses grew so scared of Savile that he and a friend smuggled themselves into the accommodation one evening to lie in wait for Savile. When Savile duly entered the accommodation using his keys, the man and his friend jumped out on Savile, who turned pale and left. But Savile was soon back with two security guards, threatening that the girls would lose their jobs if they said anything about the incident.

The man also recounted how he and a friend got into a fight with Savile at the student nurses' Christmas ball at Leeds Polytechnic. He said Savile groped then slapped his friend's girlfriend before he and his friend intervened. According to the man, Savile had tried to press charges but there had been too many witnesses to what had really occurred. Again the incident was hushed up.

Another story shows just how complicit some of the Leeds staff were in covering up Savile's offending. A 16-year-old girl called Beth was admitted to Leeds General after suffering a nervous breakdown. She told Dan Davies how Savile first groomed her by taking her to a newsagent outside the hospital and promising to buy her anything she wanted. The next day, a porter came to collect her and took her to a small office stationed off an underground corridor. Savile was waiting inside. He immediately began kissing Beth and stroking her thigh. He asked if she was on the pill and, when she said no, he forced her to masturbate him. When he was done, another man was waiting outside to take her back to the ward. Beth said she tried telling the nurses but, as soon as she mentioned Savile's name, they all laughed and walked away.

Incidents were hushed up and blind eyes were turned, it seems, largely through Savile courting the higher ups in the hospital while keeping the lower staff sweet with a mixture of bribery and threats. As the student nurses found out, Savile was always quick to threaten someone's job if they talked. To add to this stick he had an additional carrot – his various caravans around the country which he would offer for free holidays to his fellow porters and other staff. Meanwhile Savile tightened his hold over the head porter, Charles Hullighan. In 1972 Savile made Hullighan secretary of the firm that oversaw Savile's earnings. Hullighan was on a handsome monthly salary from Savile which amounted to £91,599 in 1981 according to a Telegraph article.

Then there was Savile's relationship with Alan Franey, the man Savile would go on to appoint as the head of his Broadmoor taskforce. Franey was an administrator at Leeds General Infirmary in the early part of his career when the two became friends. Franey became a part of Savile's running club, accompanying him on long weekend runs up into the Yorkshire Dales as well as more formal long-distance events. Franey was also one of the last people to speak to Savile, calling him at his Leeds flat just before his death.

As Savile's influence over the hospital staff grew, so did his access. Savile was increasingly present in the accident and emergency ward, even helping out with the treatment of patients, using hypnosis techniques he had learned from a popular entertainer. Savile told Dan Davies how on one occasion he had helped a boy suffering from a massive asthma attack in A & E. The boy could hardly breathe, according to Savile, until he used some hypnosis on the young lad which promptly cured him. According to Savile this prompted one of the emergency doctors to comment, "Ah Jim, you're doing your black magic again. You know we don't like that." The fact that Savile was able to wander around the emergency department speaking to and even treating patients with unorthodox – to say the least – methods almost beggars belief, but then so much of what he got away with does.

Not content with curing patients in A & E it seems Savile

also attended emergency incidents along with ambulance crews from Leeds General. This was illustrated by another story he told Dan Davies in which he attended a road accident where a man had shards of glass sticking out of his eyeball from a shattered windscreen. Savile said he jumped out of the ambulance and got to the man before the rest of the crew. He said he used a hypnosis technique to calm the man before advising the emergency workers not to mention the glass in order to keep the patient in a relaxed state.

If Savile's access to the various wards and roles at Leeds General Infirmary was shocking, none was more so than his association with the mortuary. Since his childhood experiences at the old people's home, Savile had nurtured a lifelong obsession with death. As a porter, he took particular delight in wheeling corpses to the mortuary, saying in his autobiography that he held it as a "great honour" to be with the bodies after their death. There is only anecdotal evidence of Savile's necrophilia but, as criminologist and author, Christopher Berry-Dee, explained to me, it definitely fitted with Savile's offending behaviour.

"We've got to remember that Savile was a control freak," Berry-Dee told me. "He was an extreme narcissist. He's a sexual predator. And so, if he thought a young girl's laying on a mortuary slab or a woman on a mortuary slab, it's like a sweet shop. The mortuaries became sweet shops for him."

One interesting piece of evidence that Savile was hanging around the mortuary as early as the mid-50s comes from an independent report into Savile's offending at Leeds General Infirmary. A witness interviewed in the report by Leeds Teaching Hospitals NHS Trust recounted that the woman began training as a nurse at Leeds General in 1954. On one of her shifts the ward nurse mentioned that she had forgotten to take the wedding ring off one of the corpses and asked the trainee nurse to go to the mortuary to get them. Before she went the ward nurse added an important warning: "Be careful and come back if the pink-haired man is there."

The student nurse went to the mortuary and did see the pink-haired man. According to the nurse the man didn't seem to be doing anything in particular, merely standing around. Remembering the ward nurse's warning, she promptly turned around and left. The nurse told the report that she subsequently saw the pink-haired man around the hospital doing various odd jobs like cleaning the windows, but she said his main job was as the night porter.

Could the pink-haired man have been Savile? The oddly dyed hair would certainly point to that. We know at this time that Savile had begun dyeing his hair all sorts of weird and wonderful colours including tartan, and black and white. The 50s was a conservative decade when men didn't dye their hair, especially pink, so the likelihood that it was Savile seems quite high. Working as a porter also fits his modus operandi and, of course, that the nurse was warned to stay away from him, indicating that he was known for predatory behaviour.

Most importantly the nurse herself thought it was Savile because she said she later recognised him when she saw him on TV. She told the report, "...There was one occasion when I saw him on a children's TV programme and his hair do was exactly the same as it had been at the LGI, and that's when I thought, gosh that's either a look-a-like or the same man."

Not only does this provide intriguing evidence that Savile was indeed loitering in the mortuary but also ties him to Leeds General Infirmary half a decade before he was previously thought to have started volunteering there. Could Savile's association with Leeds, and his offending there, have started much earlier than was previously thought?

In 1954, Savile would just have started his career with the Mecca Locarno dancehall in Leeds. He was not yet the famous local DJ who attracted hundreds of screaming teens to his revolutionary record-playing dances. Instead he was merely the manager's assistant, dealing with the doors, lost property and other humble tasks. It was about this time that Savile also moved out of his mother's house, sleeping first in the Mecca's cloakroom then moving onto an old lifeboat moored on the canal that ran through Leeds city centre. It was a time when not much is known about Savile's whereabouts or doings but we do know he was on a low wage at the Mecca Locarno so it is certainly possible that he was working the odd shift as a night porter and doing other odd jobs around the hospital to make ends meet.

Another piece of anecdotal evidence came from the NHS and Department of Health report into Savile's offending in hospitals. It interviewed a witness who was a patient at Barnet General Hospital in London in 1983. The witness told the report that she was told by nurses that Savile liked to have sex with corpses. The nurses told the patient that they had spied on him when they had worked at another hospital, which she thought was Stoke Mandeville, and had watched him having sex with a dead body.

Another accusation of necrophilia came from one of Savile's DJ colleagues at Radio One in the 70s. Paul Gambaccini, said in a radio interview in 2012 that Savile's fondness for working in mortuaries was in fact a cover for his necrophilia. It also emerged after Savile's death that British Rail had terminated Savile's £80,000-a-year advertising contract in 1984 after bosses heard rumours that Savile was having sex with corpses. As ever, much of the evidence for Savile's darker pastimes came from his own mouth. In 1972 Savile was quoted in a *Daily Mail* article saying, "I find I've got a great aptitude for dead people. When I'm holding somebody that has just died I'm filled with a tremendous love and envy."

According to the NHS report into Savile's offending, Savile had told witnesses that he removed the glass eyes from dead bodies and that he had two large rings which he'd had made from the glass. And a nurse at Broadmoor told the inquiry that Savile posed with dead bodies for photographs. The report concluded that Savile had easy access to the mortuary at Leeds General because of "a lack of stringent procedures regarding the mortuary at the infirmary until the late 1980s at the earliest". And it went on to detail the astonishing levels of access Savile had to the hospital as a whole including offices, residences and other restricted areas which "remained unchallenged for the entirety of his association with the infirmary," The DJ even had staff to manage his fan mail according to the report.

Savile claimed that he was just doing what the patients wanted. He told one of his friends that many patients who knew that they were dying requested Savile to take their bodies to the mortuary. Another friend told a local newspaper on Savile's death that he had liked to work in the mortuary because he thought it made it easier on the grieving relatives to see him there.

We might not have any concrete proof that Savile engaged in necrophilia but there is enough anecdotal evidence to make a good case. It also fits with his psychological profile. I interviewed CPTSD coach, Richard Grannon, about Savile's necrophilia for my True Crime podcast. Grannon told me that necrophilia would fit perfectly with Savile's profile as a narcissistic psychopath and paedophile as it would enhance his sense of individual power. "Maybe it made him feel a certain way, like powerful or God-like," Grannon told me. "It's very taboo, it's boundary breaking to do that. That person is as helpless as a human being can be… But it seems like he could have had a proclivity towards power as most paedophiles do. It's the point of the experience that you hold all the power."

Grannon believes that Savile suffered from Narcissistic Personality Disorder, a medical condition that leads to an unhealthy sense of one's own importance. According to Grannon, this could have been brought on by the experiences of Savile's childhood, like being treated as a miracle child by his family. "To create someone with real Narcissistic Personality Disorder," Grannon told me, "… you need quite extreme immersive experiences from childhood. So being told that you should have died but you survived because you're special – perfect for Narcissistic Personality Disorder."

Another immersive experience from his childhood could explain Savile's unhealthy fascination with corpses. When he was a boy, Savile used to spend much of his time at St Joseph's Home for the Aged, an old people's home just across the street from the family home in Leeds. The young Savile would wander the corridors of the institution that his father was a trustee of and do errands for the nurses. When residents died, Savile told Dan Davies, the nurses would encourage him to go down to the mortuary to "say goodbye". Savile would kiss the corpses and would even ride on the hearse during the funeral procession.

It was the beginning of a lifelong obsession with death, perhaps indeed a love of death, which Savile himself admitted in his book, *God'll Fix it*. In the chapter, 'What Happens when I die?' Savile wrote that death was something he was looking forward to "with quite considerable excitement".

Savile had faced death twice, once as a baby and once in his accident down the mines. His mother had saved him from that first brush with death with the help of some divine intervention and his mother appears to have been intimately connected with Savile's morbid fascination.

The first indication of Savile's strange infatuation with his mother, Agnes, came in 2000 with the Louis Theroux documentary, *When Louis Met Jimmy*. Theroux specialised in spending lots of time to get to know his interviewees, hanging out with them at their houses and favourite haunts. This along with his Colombo-style pretence at being somewhat naïve and bungling often lulled his interviewees into a false sense of security that caused their façade to slip. Theroux never got an admission of paedophilia out of Savile but he did pull back the curtain on the darker side of Savile's relationship with his mother, especially in the scene where Savile shows Theroux his mother's bedroom at his flat in Scarborough.

Savile had kept the bedroom exactly as it was when Agnes, or 'the Duchess' as he called her, was still alive and the wardrobe was still full of her clothes. In the scene, Theroux asks if Savile could remove one of the dresses and Savile, suddenly edgy, refuses. Theroux suggests that perhaps the subject is too emotional for

Savile who reacts defensively by saying that no emotions are involved. "It's not emotional, it's a friendly thing," Savile insists. "Nothing emotional about it." He goes on, seemingly unable to stop himself, "Nooooo, it's friendship. Friendship's not emotional. Friendship is happy, lovely, wonderful." Savile then explains how every morning when he walks past the door he pops his head in and says, "Alright darling," to the Duchess. Then he adds again, unnecessarily, "So it's a friendly thing, not morbid."

Savile then tries to leave the room but Theroux calls him back, asking why he's becoming passive aggressive. Savile insists he was just thinking of the time factor and reclines on the bed trying to look relaxed but looking anything but. He says the dresses give him "great pleasure" and insists again, "They don't give me any morbidity." To which Theroux responds, "I didn't even bring up morbidity, so why are you bringing it up?" "It's the way your face looks," replies Savile in a rare spasm of anger as the mask slips momentarily.

Did Savile's defensiveness in the documentary cover necrophiliac tendencies centred around his mother? This might not be as far-fetched as it sounds, especially considering his own words concerning the five days he spent with his mum's corpse. Agnes Savile died suddenly in 1972 at the age of 85. The Duchess's body was kept in state for five days at Savile's sister's house in Filey where the family gathered to mourn. While staying there Savile would sit up at night alone with the body. In an interview with *The Telegraph* two years later Savile called the time he spent alone with his mother's corpse "the best five days of my life". And in a radio interview in 1992 called 'In the Psychiatrist's Chair', he went on to explain, "Once upon a time I had to share her with other people. We had marvellous times. But when she was dead she was all mine, for me."

There are also indications that Savile's weird relationship with his mother may not have been limited to the afterlife. "I think that we will never know what was going on in that relationship with his mum," said Mark Williams-Thomas, the investigator who first blew the lid on Savile in the ITV documentary, *The Other Side of Jimmy Savile*. "But I think it would be fair to say – and people will draw their own conclusions – that it was unhealthy at best."

As usual some of the most telling clues came from Savile's own mouth. He called Agnes "the only true love" of his life and said their relationship was "a complete association". Perhaps the most telling thing he mentioned about his relationship with his mother – and perhaps the most disturbing thing he ever said on record – was when he described the holidays he would take with Agnes to Torquay and Rome. In his autobiography, *As it Happens*, Savile described how on such occasions Agnes had "the energy of a teenager and could pleasure all night as often as the opportunity arose."

For Agnes's part there seems to be a suggestion that she knew what Savile was getting up to with young girls. In a previously unpublished interview with *The People* that was released in 2016 Savile gave some revealing quotes about his mother's attitude to him. He told the paper, "My mother never got round to being proud. If anyone said, 'What is Jimmy like?' she would say, 'I don't know what he's up to, but he's up to something.' She never trusted me as she thought I was going to get nicked and end up in the pokey."

In 1969, flushed no doubt with his success at Leeds General Infirmary, Savile began volunteering at Stoke Mandeville hospital in Buckinghamshire. The story was familiar, according to the NHS inquiry that followed Savile's exposure – starstruck managers gave the DJ unrestricted access to the hospital grounds. The warning signs were immediate with junior staff reporting feeling "annoyance and distress" at Savile's constant sexual innuendo. But the ears of the upper management were closed to such complaints and Savile was given free rein of the hospital. He soon made the most of the opportunity, sexually assaulting patients, visitors, fundraisers and volunteers with apparent impunity.

One victim was just eight years old when Savile first attacked her. The young girl was visiting the hospital where her relatives worked when Savile raped her in a fairly public part of the hospital. When the girl cried and complained about the pain, Savile told her to stop crying and not tell anyone. She said Savile went on to rape her on 10 separate occasions.

Another victim was a 16-year-old girl who had been in a serious and disfiguring car accident. Savile sexually assaulted her twice and on the second occasion told her, "Now then, you will be beautiful again."

Just as at Leeds, the staff weren't immune to Savile's attentions. One woman in her early 20s reported running into Savile in the porters' lodge where he promptly grabbed her face and stuck his tongue down her throat. She said she had been warned by staff that Savile was a "dirty old man" but she was told not to report the incident because the "paraplegic centre" might be shut down.

One 11-year-old girl was repeatedly sexually assaulted by Savile during mass at the hospital's catholic chapel where her family regularly worshipped. Samantha Dearan used to hand around the collection plate and described how she would have to enter a separate room to get the item, where Savile would invariably be waiting. "I knew what was going to happen before I walked through the door," Dearan told *The Sun*. "I just tried to get in and out as quickly as possible. It was so blatant." According to Dearan, Savile liked to keep the door open so he could see the priest while he was groping the 11-year-old girl. These attacks went on for three of four years before Dearan eventually gave up on going to church.

Many of Savile's child victims at Stoke Mandeville reported being attacked in the wards or corridors when they were wearing dressing gowns which made them vulnerable to his wandering hands. Savile seemed to revel in committing assaults in public areas where lots of people were milling about but the victim couldn't draw attention to what was happening. We have seen the same modus operandi at work in his attacks at Broadmoor, the BBC and other hospitals where he volunteered.

That most staff at Stoke Mandeville knew about Savile's

behaviour seems undeniable. The stories of victims nearly always include accounts of how staff told them they would get in trouble or repercussions would happen that would harm the hospital. Several accounts tell how nurses instructed patients to pretend to be asleep if Savile was around. There is even some evidence that staff told the police about their concerns.

A detective constable with Thames Valley Police, John Lindsay, told *The Guardian* that he had received a complaint about Savile's behaviour at Stoke Mandeville in the late 70s. Lindsay told the Guardian that a nurse had approached him saying the staff were concerned about Savile because he was touching little girls in the hospital inappropriately. Lindsay says he passed on the report to a senior officer but that he was told to leave it alone. "Jimmy Savile is a high-profile man," the senior officer said, according to Lindsay, "He must be okay. He could not be doing anything irregular. Don't worry about it." Nothing more was done and the complaint went no further. It's a story we have heard many times when it comes to the police's handling of Savile complaints.

Savile's hold over Stoke Mandeville tightened in 1979 when he began his appeal to rebuild the hospital's critically important National Spinal Injuries Centre (NSIC). The NSIC was renowned for its pioneering treatments of patients with spinal injuries and paralysis but it was housed in wooden Nissen huts that dated back to 1944 and were crumbling into disrepair. Some were so badly damaged that the ceilings were beginning to fall in and rainwater was dripping into the interior. The new Conservative government under Margaret Thatcher had refused funding to rebuild the centre as part of its policy of defunding the NHS so, barring a miracle, imminent closure threatened. The staff staged a sit-in strike which garnered publicity but still no funding was forthcoming. The stage was set for Mr Fix It, Jimmy Savile.

Savile had a meeting with the health minister, Gerard Vaughan, at the House of Commons in which he secured a deal that would see him try to raise the six to ten million pounds required to rebuild the centre. In a press conference held to launch the campaign, Savile explained that a £5 donation would buy a brick, a £50,000 sum would pay for a bed, and £250,000 would provide a ward. The conference ended with the first donation to the appeal from a retired businessman from Buckinghamshire who handed over a cheque for £150,000.

Savile's charm worked on the public and corporate worlds alike and soon the money was pouring in, with big companies like Ski Yoghurt, Quaker Oats and BUPA all chipping in, not to mention royals like Charles and Diana. By 1983, Savile had raised £10 million and the new NSIC was proudly opened with Chares and Diana cutting the ribbon. It was a monumental achievement and one that would eventually earn Savile a knighthood, with a lot of help from his new friend Margaret Thatcher.

Savile had first met Thatcher in 1976 at a Young Conservatives conference in Scarborough, when she was leader of the opposition. The two felt an instant attraction, perhaps because of their working-class, outsider status, and went on to form a life-long friendship. Thatcher finally secured Savile the knighthood he coveted in 1990. She had first nominated him in 1981 and had done so every year following. Tellingly though, officials had always demurred due to Savile's self-confessed promiscuous lifestyle and background as a 'godfather' in the club scene. Like the British Rail officials, could they also have heard the darker rumours that surrounded Savile?

By 1990, however, they finally caved in and Savile was invited to Buckingham Palace to collect the honour. In the television footage of the event, Savile looks proud as he flaunts the medal to the press, alongside his usual Cheshire grin and outsize cigar. But a remark he made in an interview with *The Independent* gave a hint at the deeper motives behind his pleasure. The status conferred by the knighthood, he told the newspaper, had let him "off the hook." Savile, it now seemed, truly was untouchable.

Savile's heroic salvation of the NSIC meant his star was higher at Stoke Mandeville than ever. As part of the fundraising drive he had been provided with a suite of offices and rooms at the hospital. Anyone who challenged him or threatened to tell was now met with blunt threats about funding being pulled. Requests had now changed to demands and Savile got pretty much anything he wanted according to Christine McFarlane, the director of nursing and patient care at Stoke Mandeville at the time. She added that Savile had the freedom to go wherever he wanted whenever he wanted within the hospital. And he did, often prowling the wards at night looking for sleepless patients to chat to and, if he got the chance, worse. Savile was even known to call the hospital his "country club".

Savile's association with Stoke Mandeville lasted until his death. In 2007, he still had an office on the premises and still felt at home enough to host his interview there with Surrey Police following their Duncroft investigation. "I own this hospital," Savile told the officers while threatening them with legal action for daring to investigate a complaint against him. "NHS run it, I own it."

Stoke Mandeville and Leeds General Infirmary were the two hospitals Savile was most closely associated with, but it would be a mistake to think his offending was limited to those two institutions. Savile was an opportunistic predator who struck wherever and whenever the opportunity arose as is evidenced by the reports from over 40 hospitals around the country. At Moss Side, a high-security mental hospital in Liverpool similar to Broadmoor, two female patients reported Savile sexually abusing them in a ward, and a third male patient reported seeing Savile stroking a female patient's breast at a hospital social event. One of the female patients described how she was encouraged to sit on Savile's knee for a photograph during his visit. Savile put his hand on her thigh, according to the report, then moved it up towards her "intimate area". The patient screamed at this and was subsequently isolated by staff when she tried to explain what had happened.

At Digby hospital in Exeter a female patient said Savile lured her to his motorhome where he raped her. At St Catharine's Hospital in Birkenhead a female patient reported that Savile had jumped into bed with her and touched her inappropriately. At Royal Hospital in Portsmouth a cleaner told a patient that Savile had abused him while he was unconscious. At Staincliffe Hospital in Wakefield a 15-year-old girl reported how Savile had lain on top of her in bed and French kissed her. At Booth Hall Hospital in Manchester a female patient who was just eight or nine at the time said Savile sexually abused her with the complicity of her father. These are just a few of over 100 reports of sexual abuse from the 41 hospitals where Savile offended.

In 1997 Savile would, for a change, find the roles reversed. This time he was a patient at Killingbeck Hospital in Leeds. He was in for a quadruple bypass to save him from the fate that had killed his mother and two of his sisters. He had first been told he had blocked arteries in 1970 but had gone nearly three decades before his body finally told him it was time to get the operation done. Savile was wheeled into the operating theatre wearing his Royal Marines green beret. The procedure was successful and its effect on his health seemed almost immediate. As soon as he came round to find a nurse whispering in his ear if he was alright, he reached up and groped her breast. Clearly everything was back to normal.

With the help of the quadruple bypass Savile survived another 14 years, but in October 2011, aged 84, he found himself back in Leeds General Infirmary, this time on the wrong side of the staff-patient divide. In September Savile had embarked on a cruise around Britain on the Queen Elizabeth's maiden voyage. But he had fallen ill and was forced to leave the ship at Liverpool. He was taken to hospital where he was diagnosed with pneumonia. Four of his major organs were found to be failing. A few days before he died Savile checked himself out of hospital and returned to his flat in Roundhay, Leeds. He had time for one last interview with a reporter from *The Yorkshire Evening Post* and a last trip out into the Yorkshire Dales with his friend from West Yorkshire Police, Mick Starkey, driving. Savile's old NHS pal, Alan Franey, was one of the last people to speak to Savile. Franey called Savile at his flat and found him "Mentally alert but resigned to his fate". Franey said Savile had told him, "I'm coming to the end of the tunnel."

Savile cancelled his Friday Morning Club meeting that week. The last person to see him alive was his heart specialist, Alistair Hall. Hall dropped by on Friday evening to try to persuade Savile to go back to hospital but the ailing DJ demurred. It seems clear Savile knew the end was at hand. The next morning, after several people had tried unsuccessfully to call Savile, he was found dead by the caretaker of the flats. The man later reported that Savile had been lying in bed with an unfinished Cuban cigar in the ashtray and with his fingers crossed.

Savile, like his mother, had nominally been a devout Catholic throughout his life. He often spoke about having a debit and credit side to his life and deeds and expressed his hope of getting into heaven. "When I stand in front of the table and St Peter's there," Savile told a chat show audience, "and he says, 'You are not coming in, I'll say well, 'Why not?' And he'll say, 'Because you're a villain.' And he'll show me the debit side, and I'll say, 'Hang about,' and I'll show him the credit side. 'Does that mean anything?'" He added with typical flippant humour, "And if he says, 'That means nothing,' then I'll threaten to break his fingers."

In his lifetime, Savile raised £45 million for charity, much of which went to the NHS and a quarter to Stoke Mandeville alone. Over the same period, he assaulted 177 known victims across 41 NHS hospitals, 60 of whom were at Leeds General Infirmary and 60 at Stoke Mandeville.

It was quite a tally on both the debit and credit side. At the end, when Savile knew he was about to meet his maker, did he think the credit side was enough to outweigh the debit side, or would he have to threaten to break St Peter's fingers? We will never know, but the fact that Savile's corpse had its fingers crossed gives some indication that there was at least a little doubt in his mind.

CHAPTER 9

EX COP'S STRUGGLE TO EXPOSE SAVILE

The first link in the chain of events that led to Savile's exposure was a chance remark between two journalists on a trip to Europe. It was July 2011, Mark Williams-Thomas, a former police officer turned crime journalist and his producer, Meirion Jones, were travelling back from Interpol headquarters in Lyon, France after filming a piece about catching child abusers for the BBC's current affairs programme, *Newsnight*.

"It was on the way back where my producer said to me, 'Have you ever heard anything about Savile being a nonce and a weirdo?'" Williams-Thomas told me in an interview for my True Crime podcast. Williams-Thomas told Jones that he thought Savile was a bit weird and wouldn't want to spend any time with him but that he had never heard any rumours about Savile being connected with child abuse.

Jones seemed surprised. He told Williams-Thomas that Surrey police had investigated Savile for child abuse claims at some point in the past but the investigation hadn't gotten anywhere. Now Williams-Thomas's curiosity was peaked. He had worked as a child abuse investigator for Surrey police before he left to pursue a career in television. How could he not have heard about such a high profile investigation within his own force, and in his own specialisation?

Williams-Thomas filed the conversation in his memory, determined to make some investigations of his own. When he got back to the UK, Williams-Thomas called a former high-ranking officer at Surrey police to ask him about the rumoured investigation.

The man confirmed that Surrey police had indeed investigated Savile but the investigation had gone nowhere. Williams-Thomas reported back to Jones, confirming the rumours of the investigation and Jones told him that *Newsnight* were going to run an investigation on Savile.

Not long after, Jones called Williams-Thomas back to tell him *Newsnight* had cancelled the investigation. Apparently the programme's producer was looking for a story about police incompetence in failing to investigate Savile, but hadn't found enough material to run with the story which centred around allegations from ex-pupils at Duncroft, an approved school in Surrey for girls with behavioural problems. Williams-Thomas was shocked and non-plussed by the news. "I said, 'I think you're missing the point,'" Williams-Thomas recalled saying to Jones. "The story is surely that he's been interviewed in relation to child abuse.'"

Jones was adamant that the *Newsnight* producers weren't going to run with the story so Williams-Thomas asked Jones if he could carry on the investigation for his own programme, *Exposure*, which ran on the BBC's rival channel, ITV. Jones gave Williams-Thomas his blessing and Williams-Thomas immediately went about persuading his own producers that the investigation was worth pursuing. They agreed, and the first domino that would lead to Savile's ultimate demise was toppled.

The hunt was on.

Mark Williams-Thomas was the right man for the case. A dogged investigator, he had tracked down and caught paedophiles and murderers in a long career both as a police detective and an investigative journalist. Some of his high-profile cases already included exposing the murderer of Tia Sharp, a 12-year-old girl who had gone missing from her home in London; and the police investigation of DJ and record producer, Jonathan King, for child sexual abuse charges. As an investigative journalist he had taken the skills he had learned in the police and applied them to exposing criminals who had previously evaded justice. "I'm very passionate about what I do," Williams-Thomas told me. "I set out to help people. I try to shine light into the darkest of corners and bring justice to those people who have been let down by the authorities." Now, with Jimmy Savile, he would face the toughest case of his career.

Williams-Thomas had always been watchful. As a child he didn't speak a word until he was six years old. His parents sent him to a speech therapist but it turned out he was just shy. The young Williams-Thomas preferred to sit back and observe than to get involved. It was a habit that would serve him well when he joined the police service straight out of school at age 19 in 1989.

Police college brought Williams-Thomas out of his shell and he was soon an outspoken and pro-active member of the force. As a police officer, he enjoyed solving crimes and seeking justice for families who had suffered at the hands of criminals. But the job also exposed him to horrors he would never forget – seeing the bodies of murdered children, attending critical accidents, and facing up to the reality of child abuse. It also introduced him to the underside of humanity, a debased element within people that he had to learn to come to terms with. "The depravity of which human beings will stoop to is the worst you could possibly imagine," Williams-Thomas told me. "So whatever you can imagine, it's worse than that. That's what people are. And I often think of the saying, 'believe the unbelievable,' and that really is the role of a police officer, to believe the unbelievable."

One of Williams-Thomas's toughest moments as a police officer was attending his first post-mortem, which was on the body of a child. "If you've never smelt the smell of death it is unique," he told me. "And while you're there, some people will faint, some people will be sick, some people walk away, and some people cope with it fine. And I remember thinking to myself that I need to manage this, I need to get through this."

Williams-Thomas's way to get through it was by asking the pathologist to explain everything they were doing. By taking a professional interest in the procedure, he was able to adopt a more clinical and less personal approach to the grisly task. He came away from the post-mortem thinking it was one of the toughest things he'd yet to experience. But there were still many experiences left to add to that list, particularly when he joined Surrey Police's child protection unit. As part of his work uncovering child abuse, Williams-Thomas was forced to listen to detailed accounts of child sexual abuse and to watch explicit videos of child abuse and child porn. He explained that, with the advent of the internet, the cases of child abuse have skyrocketed in modern times, so much so that police forces around the world don't have the resources to keep up with it.

As a child protection officer, Williams-Thomas was fighting a losing battle, but he had to persevere, scrolling through hours of child abuse material that has left a permanent effect on him. "They'll never leave me," Williams-Thomas said about some of the images he had to witness. "They're in my head and I see them – really horrible stuff and particularly when you can see childs' faces who are in trauma and real pain, having been or being abused."

One video he remembers particularly well is one in which the child was abused so brutally that the kid died, or at least appeared to. The officers would never know the truth, but the child in question was never found so the chances were that the kid really had been killed in what amounted to a child snuff video.

Yet the gruesome hours of watching such horrific material could have its payback. Williams-Thomas points out an example in his book, *Hunting Killers*, where detectives were forced to sit through footage of two men working at a nursery in Spain who filmed themselves abusing the babies in their care. One of the reviewers of the footage spotted a train ticket in the background of one of the shots. This ticket was then traced to a specific metro station in France on a specific day. Another detail was a unique logo on one abuser's top. The motif was traced to a garage near the metro station where, it turned out, the abuser's partner worked. This intelligence was sent to Interpol and the international crime agency was able to make arrests.

In Williams-Thomas's case the hours of horrific groundwork paid off in 1997 when he was involved in the high-profile arrest of schoolteacher Adrian Stark for possession of child pornography. Williams-Thomas's team had received specific information that Stark, while on holiday in Prague, had had two children brought to his apartment. Williams-Thomas and the team arranged for Stark to be stopped at the airport when he returned to the UK but unfortunately the suspect didn't have anything incriminating on him. The team then arranged for Stark's house in Leatherhead to be searched where they found an old lock-up box full of child porn magazines and videos. Stark himself, who was the director of music at the prestigious St John's private boarding school in Leatherhead, committed suicide shortly after his arrest.

Williams-Thomas left the police in 2000 after 12 years of service. He had originally planned to be a police officer until he retired but he found himself becoming increasingly restless. "I've done everything I really wanted to do in the police force," he told me. "I dealt with all the major crimes, I'd been exposed to some incredible cases and the time had come really to move on and look for new opportunities."

Williams-Thomas started looking into setting up his own business, but part of his heart was still in investigating crimes. One day when he was looking through a police magazine he saw an advert for a police advisor for a TV production team. He went to meet the team and outlined some of the media work he had already done, and soon they asked him to advise on one of their shows, a crime drama on Channel 5 called *Murder Prevention*. From there he got similar roles in other crime drama series including *Waking the Dead*, *Wire in the Blood*, and *The Inspector Lynley Mysteries*. After a while he became frustrated with the way production teams would use unrealistic police procedures despite his advice. He began to seek out the script writers and told them to come to him for an overview of police procedures before they wrote the script. In that way they could ensure a more realistic final product that retained all the drama of a good crime show. It seemed to work and Williams-Thomas began working more closely with the writers, particularly on *Waking the Dead* where he worked for six years. The attention to detail on the show was partly due to Williams-Thomas's input and some of the storylines even came from real-life cases that he had worked on.

From crime dramas, Williams-Thomas's career moved on to working with Sky News and ITV News, providing them with advice on how they reported major crime stories as well as supplying them with leads. He began working as a kind of liaison between the news desks and police forces around the country, ensuring that the police and the news teams got out important stories to the public and that the reporting was done accurately.

It was from one of his police contacts that Williams-Thomas heard about a case that would land him his big break in TV. He'd heard about a paedophile priest in Germany who was grooming a child in Wales, except that the child was actually an undercover police officer trying to entrap the man. Williams-Thomas went to the producer of ITV's current affairs programme, *Tonight,* and suggested that they take a camera team to Germany and confront the priest.

The producer loved the idea but was less keen when Williams-Thomas suggested himself as the reporter. He had never done anything in front of camera, and the producer required a safe pair of hands and a recognisable face. Undeterred, Williams-Thomas joined the team as one of the production crew and headed for Germany. The team found the priest and began surveilling him, and soon got their chance to confront him. One day, the priest left his house and drove to a nearby internet café where he began using one of the computers. The reporter who was supposed to be presenting the piece was still working on another story in a different country and hadn't joined the team yet, but this seemed an ideal opportunity to confront the man and catch him on camera. A decision had to be made and Williams-Thomas stepped forward to say he would be more than happy to interview the man. The producers decided to go with it, and within minutes a full camera crew was barging into the internet café to corner the priest.

The man was shocked of course but Williams-Thomas managed to use his long experience of interviewing suspects to make the man focus on him and ignore the cameras. Williams-Thomas explained that they knew about the child the priest had been grooming and also revealed that the child was really an undercover cop. Williams-Thomas ended up getting a lengthy interview with the priest, who admitted to being sexually interested in children, even detailing what ages he was interested in and attempting to explain his behaviour. As a piece of investigative crime reporting, it was a real scoop.

It was Williams-Thomas's first time in front of the camera but it wouldn't be his last. He was soon a regular presenter for *Tonight*, and it was while working on this show that he got his biggest scoop before the Jimmy Savile case.

Tia Sharp was a 12-year-old schoolgirl who went missing from her South London home on 3rd August 2012. She had been visiting her grandmother and her grandmother's boyfriend on a deprived housing estate near Croydon where Tia often stayed when her mother was working. The nation's media descended on the estate to report on what they thought was a missing person case. But with Williams-Thomas's police background he was aware that most crimes are committed by someone close to the victim – usually a friend or family member. He began to wonder why no one was looking closer to home and he started looking into the background of Stuart Hazell, Tia's grandmother's partner.

It soon became clear that Hazell had been the last person to see Tia alive. Some digging into Hazell's past found that he had previously been with Tia's mother, Natalie, and had a history of petty crime. When interviewing Tia's uncle for a news piece, Williams-Thomas had met Hazell briefly, and the impression he got was distinctly negative. Williams-Thomas's suspicions were raised and he decided he needed to get an interview with the man Tia had called granddad.

That wasn't easy as Hazell had not given any press interviews and was staying in the background. Williams-Thomas made approaches through Tia's uncle who he'd already interviewed and formed a rapport with. He decided to pose less as an intrusive press reporter and more as a confidante, someone Hazell could trust and open up to. It was a technique Williams-Thomas had learned from interviewing suspects for the police, where he found that making interviewees feel comfortable often relaxed them enough to open up and give away vital information.

His approach worked and Tia's uncle soon reported back to Williams-Thomas that Hazell was ready to do an interview. Williams-Thomas turned up at the house and left the camera crew outside while he went in to speak privately with Hazell. This was to relax the interviewee and show him that Williams-Thomas was on his side and not out to trip him up. Hazell asked to see the questions Williams-Thomas would ask beforehand but Williams-Thomas refused, explaining that he wanted the interview to flow naturally like a normal conversation. Hazell seemed to accept this and the interview was set to go.

When the cameras and crew were set up, Williams-Thomas began by asking Hazell simple questions about Tia's life and personality. This put Hazell further at ease and he soon began to open up about the last time he had seen Tia just before she had disappeared, describing how she had left the house, what she was wearing, and the conversation they'd had. Williams-Thomas strove to keep Hazell talking, probing him gently on details of the case, knowing that the more he spoke the more he could give away a detail that might trip him up further down the line.

The interview was a scoop and made it onto that evening's ITV six o'clock news. At face value it was another chat with a worried relative culminating with an appeal for Tia's whereabouts. But Williams-Thomas knew differently. He was already convinced that Hazell was the murderer and was sure that his interview would form the basis of a murder investigation. When the police contacted ITN to request tapes of the interview, Williams-Thomas's predictions began to be validated. But the biggest corroboration came the next day when, on the way to a show with his daughters, Williams-Thomas's phone started to go mad. It turned out that Hazell had gone on the run. The police had searched the house again and found Tia's body hidden in the loft.

Williams-Thomas was worried that Hazell would commit suicide before the police could find him, and angry that the police had allowed a prime suspect to escape. Fortunately, Hazell was captured later that day, just 12 miles away, and was arrested and charged with Tia's murder. Williams-Thomas's hunch about his interview with Hazell was confirmed when Hazell's case went to trial at the Old Bailey. On the way to court he was stopped by a police officer who told him the police had found the interview crucially helpful for their investigation and would be using it as evidence in the trial.

The interview was used by the prosecution to point out lies in Hazell's testimony. Further evidence from Hazell's phone showed sexualised images he had taken of Tia and of teen porn searches on his phone. The weight of the evidence forced Hazell to change his plea to guilty and he was subsequently convicted and sentenced to a minimum of 38 years in prison. It seems like a long sentence for a single murder but, according to Williams-Thomas, the barbarity and totality of the offence, which included a sexual assault, more than justified the harsh sentence.

As the reporter who had obtained an exclusive interview with the killer just before he had been arrested, Williams-Thomas's star had never been higher. He had used his insider police knowledge about how murderers work to identify the prime suspect, then utilised all his police interview techniques to gain the man's trust, pin him down for an interview, and extract enough information to use as evidence against him. Williams-Thomas was at the peak of his career and on top of his game.

He would need to be because his next case would be the biggest challenge of his career, and indeed his whole life – Jimmy Savile.

In fact Williams-Thomas was already investigating Savile when the Tia Sharp Case hit the news. Following the news that

Newsnight was dropping its own investigation, Williams-Thomas had gotten the go ahead from the producers of ITV's *Exposure* programme and had begun his investigation in earnest. From the beginning Williams-Thomas was in his element – because the case was so high-profile and delicate he ran it like a police investigation, obtaining good evidence and credible witnesses and ensuring that all the witnesses corroborated each other. The security around the investigation was also similar to a police one, perhaps even more so. Much of the evidence was kept on paper files only to keep the identities of interviewees secret. Even ITV was kept out of the loop, with no regular updates and very limited feedback. Nothing about who Williams-Thomas and his producer Lesley Gardiner were talking to or what they uncovered was shared with other ITV staff, and everything about the investigation was kept off the ITV intranet.

The first person Williams-Thomas spoke to was one of the Duncroft victims that Meirion Jones had originally lined up for the *Newsnight* investigation. Despite Savile's death this woman was still very frightened about speaking out. She was a good starting point to kick off the investigation but it soon became clear that the *Exposure* team would have to cast their net further afield. "I was very clear that we need to find victims away from Duncroft," Williams-Thomas told me. "Quite simply it's very easy for the public to be critical of people who are in approved homes, who are in social services' care. What we needed to do is get people away from that environment who were much more likely – wrongly – but much more likely to be believed in the first instance."

In order to find other victims and evidence Williams-Thomas used an investigation technique that hasn't changed despite the advent of the internet – he hit the phones. He would find the numbers of possible witnesses and victims then call them and introduce himself. From them he would get other names until he had a pool of 20 or 30 contacts. Approaching the investigation as a police officer, Williams-Thomas was looking for evidence that would stack up credibly enough to form a prosecutable case. That meant finding similarities between victims' accounts of Savile's behaviour, the things he did and said to them, and the ways he groomed them. He was also looking for independent victims who didn't know each or have ways of sharing information before the case came to light.

It would take Williams-Thomas almost a year of investigating before he had enough evidence and testimonies to make a compelling case. In the meantime he managed to speak to two more girls who claimed they had been abused by Savile at Duncroft. Williams-Thomas and the crew found the Duncroft girls' testimonies shocking and there was still a lot of fear despite Savile no longer being around. However, they managed to persuade two of the girls to tell their stories on camera, which was a huge step forward in terms of making a programme.

Then came the thing Williams-Thomas had been hoping for – the first testimony outside of Duncroft. He managed to track down a witness who had seen Savile committing a sexual assault on a 14-year-old girl in 1978 in Leeds. Sue Thompson was a newsroom assistant at BBC Leeds who helped out on the regional show, Jimmy Savile's Yorkshire Speakeasy. One of Thompson's jobs was to provide the rider for Savile's dressing room, which included Dandelion and Burdock and his usual cigars. One day she was just popping into the dressing room to check it was tidy when she caught Saville with a young member of the Speakeasy audience.

"Savile was sat in the chair with the right side of his body facing me," Thompson said in her interview for the *Exposure* programme, "and there was a girl of about 14 with long brown hair sat on his knee. He had his left arm up her skirt and he was kissing her. But what I distinctly remember, and that's the image that sticks in my mind, was the fact, as I opened the door he turned his head, and it was just his tongue that was just sort of coming out of her mouth, that stuck in my mind."

Thompson said she was shocked and disorientated by what

she had seen. She sought out a colleague and told them about the incident but her friend just laughed it off.

That night the Speakeasy team went to the cinema in Leeds. Savile, who was 51 at the time, was due to visit Leeds General Infirmary that evening but he tagged along to the cinema and made a point of sitting next to Thompson. After just 10 or 15 minutes of watching the film, Savile abruptly left the cinema. Thompson said she thought this strange behaviour was because Savile was checking her out, making sure she wasn't someone who was going to make a fuss over what she had seen. Thompson said she never spoke out about the incident because she had never seen or heard a bad piece of publicity about Savile and felt like she would be a lone voice against millions of others. It is a feeling of loneliness and helplessness that many of Savile's victims must have felt.

Some of the women Williams-Thomas spoke to in the course of his enquiries took weeks, even months to feel comfortable enough to speak to him about their experiences with Savile, so great was the fear. Again Williams-Thomas's career with the police came in helpful. He was experienced at interviewing women and children who were victims of sexual abuse and was able to put the interviewees at ease, avoiding triggering them and, crucially, offering them a path forward. "The only way that people can move on with their life is to deal with what's happened in the past," Williams-Thomas told me, "and that applies to so many environments... In terms of child sexual abuse it's about acknowledging what's happening to you, not blaming yourself, putting the responsibility back to the offender, and understanding that actually there is a way through this by dialogue, by communication, and for some that is about justice. And justice serves itself in many forms. Justice is not just about an element of punitive effect... but justice by being believed. For so many people simply being heard and being believed in terms of what you're saying has the most amazing effect on people."

Meanwhile the investigation was expanding and moving

on to one of Savile's longest-running vehicles – *Top of the Pops*. Williams-Thomas tracked down a BBC producer who worked with Savile at around the time he started on TOTP in the mid-60s. Wilfred De'Ath was the producer of a BBC Radio talk show called *Teen Scene* and was due to work with Savile on an upcoming show. De'Ath said he had heard the rumours about Savile and young girls but didn't know whether to believe them or not, until he turned up for a pre-production meeting with the DJ at a Chinese restaurant in central London.

"He was sitting on a banquette with this very young girl," De-Ath told Williams-Thomas. "I would guess she was 12 if you'd asked me to guess. It could be that she was 13, 14 but I would have said 12. I asked him where he had found her. I said that to him – 'Where did you pick her up?' And he said, 'Oh, *Top of the Pops*' ... I remember saying, 'Is that your happy hunting ground?' And he said, 'Yes.'"

The next evening De'Ath called Savile in his room at the Ascot Hotel to find that Savile was in bed with the same girl. De'Ath is certain of this because Savile insisted De'Ath speak to the girl on the phone. When Williams-Thomas asked De'Ath why he didn't tell anyone about this, he said something very revealing: "Everybody knew that he was constantly in the company of underage girls so it wasn't really very remarkable." De'Ath also said that as a young man and junior producer for the BBC he was intimidated by Savile's status as well as his physical presence: "I wasn't a very strong person. He was a beefy guy. He was brawny. He'd been a coal miner. He was a wrestler. If he'd found out that I was grassing him up to the top in the BBC he – I wouldn't say he would have killed me – but he would have knocked me out."

Next Williams-Thomas managed to get in contact with a group of women who had been sexually abused by Savile on *Top of the Pops*. Two of these women agreed to be interviewed on camera but their fear was still so great that they only agreed on condition of complete anonymity. Both had been sexually abused by Savile at age 15 and subsequently raped by him, one at age 15 and the other 16. Despite Williams-Thomas's long experience of interviewing victims of child sexual abuse, he said the accounts of these women were particularly harrowing, so much so that he and his producer, Lesley Gardiner decided to offer counselling support to the rest of the crew.

After almost a year of investigating, Williams-Thomas now had five Savile victims who had all been interviewed on camera and were all willing to go public with their stories. The victims' testimonies corroborated each other and built up a clear pattern of offending behaviour. But Williams-Thomas was still approaching this like a crime investigation. To be sure his evidence would have been strong enough to result in an arrest and criminal charges, he consulted a top criminal barrister, Ian Glen QC. Glen reviewed the evidence and concluded that it established a clear pattern of offending behaviour, that there was satisfactory independence between two of the groups of victims, and that there were independent witnesses to back up their claims. In short, it was enough to arrest and charge Savile had he still been alive.

And yet the higher-ups at ITV still weren't satisfied. They wanted more victims before they felt the show was ready to go on air. Williams-Thomas disagreed, and he put his foot down. "I said, I've only got an hour," Williams-Thomas told me. "... We can't do them justice if we have any more than five victims. And what I'm not going to do is go and get more victims that I can't tell their story, because that's a massive impact. I take great care in the people that I work with, and when I do go and speak to people, and when I interview them, what you don't want to do is bring all this trauma up and then not deal with it. So there's a real responsibility we have as programme makers."

To his surprise and delight, after listening to his arguments, the channel bosses decided to go with the programme as it was, with five victims and an assortment of corroborating witnesses. Still, the battle to get the go ahead for the programme is one that Williams-Thomas describes as "the hardest thing that I've ever done and will ever do, I'm sure, in the rest of my life".

With the go-ahead from the higher-ups the show was prepared for air and a broadcast date was scheduled – 3rd October 2012. As the show prepared to air tensions began to ramp up among the production team as they realised just what a Goliath they were going up against. Savile may have been dead nearly a year but his reputation was just as strong as ever. Williams-Thomas got an insight into this when he saw a story in the press about how Savile's belongings had been auctioned for charity and fetched staggering sums of money. Savile's reputation was so strong and the public opinion of him so high that it seemed anyone going up against his memory would be hung out to dry. In the run up to the broadcast, after an initial screening of the programme in front of ITV's top executives, he remembers his producer Lesley Gardiner, saying to him, "We'll either work in television for a long time or we'll never work again."

Williams-Thomas got a firsthand experience of this possibility when a story broke in the press that ITV were about to launch a programme investigating Savile's private life. Hearing the news, BBC Radio Leeds, who were supportive of Savile due to his close connection to the city, hosted a listener phone-in. Williams-Thomas tuned in in the hope of finding someone else with allegations about Savile. Instead all he heard was a stream of invective against him that left him shocked and even more worried about the subsequent broadcast.

On the weekend before the show was due to air, ITV prepared some material to give to the national newspapers to drum up publicity. Williams-Thomas gave a full interview about the upcoming show for *The Mail on Sunday*. Yet despite the shocking allegations against one of the country's most adored celebrities, the press still didn't seem capable of appreciating the full scale of the story. Williams-Thomas said he was called by a *Mail* reporter on the Saturday before the broadcast, while he was watching his son's football match, asking him for more details. When Williams-Thomas told the reporter he had already given *The Mail* the full story, he was shocked by the reply that the editors didn't think it was big enough for a front page headline. Instead *The Mail on Sunday* ran the Savile story on page five.

"I'll never forget that," Williams-Thomas told me, "because I think that's a really significant moment in terms of not understanding the gravity of the story. That story then ran on the front pages for a consecutive 41 days – the Jimmy Savile story – so that tells you how massive this was, not just in terms of the UK, but internationally and worldwide."

After the articles appeared in the Sunday papers, Williams-Thomas felt the momentum begin to shift. Other papers began to run their own stories and by the time the *Exposure* episode aired on Wednesday, the tide of public opinion had turned.

It was hard to argue with the evidence that *Exposure: The Other Side of Jimmy Savile* presented. The show began with an overview of Savile's astonishingly successful career before switching gears quickly with Sue Thompson's account of how she had stumbled across Savile with his tongue in the mouth of a 14-year-old girl in his dressing room at BBC Leeds. A brief biography of Savile's early career up to *Top of the Pops* followed, which led to the testimony of Wilfred De'Ath, the BBC producer who had seen Savile with a 12-year-old girl from *Top of the Pops*. This was followed by an account of how Savile was always seen with a young girl on his arms in the 60s, particularly around the Top Ten Club in Manchester. Then came an interview with Alan Leeke, a local Manchester reporter who had interviewed Savile several times.

Leeke told how Savile would regularly disappear with teenage girls in his Rolls Royce or Jaguar, before recounting a bizarre and disturbing story about interviewing Savile in his Manchester home. Leeke was chatting with Savile, he said, when a teenage girl turned up at the flat. Savile put the interview on hold while he took the girl into his bedroom. "He was only in there 10 minutes," Leeke told Williams-Thomas. "When he came out on his own, he proceeded, without any bashfulness or anything, to wash himself off in the in the sink, which I thought was quite an unusual thing to do."

Now the programme switched gears again and introduced the first of Savile's victims, two women he had met and groomed on *Top of the Pops* during the late 60s. Both women were still so frightened of Savile and his reputation that they were interviewed wearing wigs, and both had their names changed and voices disguised. The first victim, 'Val', told of how she had been introduced to Savile in 1969 at the age of 15 on a trip to the BBC, and had soon become one of a select band of teenage girls who regularly visited his dressing room after *Top of the Pops* shows.

Val recounted her first experience of abuse at the hands of Savile in an alcove in his dressing room where he pinned her up against the wall and put his hand up her skirt. She said that this abuse happened regularly, with Savile pinning her up against a wall and touching her whenever and wherever he got a chance. Val went on to tell how she lost her virginity, aged 16, to Savile in his motorhome. "I didn't realise that's what was happening. It sounds really stupid but I didn't realise – again, naive girl – and he promised me he wasn't going all the way but he did and there was no foreplay, no romance, no taking off clothes," she told Williams-Thomas, going on to say, "I remember it being a struggle, with me trying to push him off and him again pinning me down with his body weight. And then the deed was over."

Val told the programme that, with hindsight, she considered the act to have been rape.

A second victim, 'Angie', told the show she had met Savile in 1968 outside the offices of Radio Luxembourg. She was 15 years old and was bowled over by Savile's celebrity. She said that a couple of weeks later Savile invited her to his hotel room and before she knew it he had her on the bed and was having sex with her. Angie told how Savile would regularly have sex with her in his BBC dressing room, making her lie down on the couch while no one was around, or pressing her up against the wall. She told of the menacing and controlling nature of Savile's relationship with her, including a message he wrote to her in a signed copy of his autobiography that said, "No escape" and was signed her "keeper".

Both women said that Savile stopped the relationship when they were in their early 20s and both said they caught a sexually transmitted disease from him.

The programme moved on to another victim of Savile's abuse. In 1973 'Sarah' was 14 years old when she wrote a letter to Savile's *Clunk Click* programme about her choir which was about to perform at Stoke Mandeville, the children's hospital which he patronised. An actress spoke Sarah's words, telling Williams-Thomas about how she got home one day to find that Savile had responded to her letter by calling her house and speaking to her mum. Savile had promised he would attend the choir's performance at the children's hospital. Sarah told Williams-Thomas how, true to his word, Savile was in the audience for the performance and how, after the show, she had rushed over to tell him she was the girl who had sent him the letter. "Before I knew what happened he'd stuck his tongue into my mouth," Sarah told the *Exposure* programme. "It didn't seem to bother him that other people could have seen what he was doing. I was just so shocked, I pulled away and dashed onto the coach. I couldn't believe what had happened."

The narrative then switched to Duncroft, the approved school for girls where the very first victims had come forward. The programme told how Savile had originally been invited to visit the school to raise its profile but had soon made himself a permanent fixture, parking his mobile home in the grounds and taking the girls off on trips in his Rolls Royce. Charlotte was a 14-year-old girl at Duncroft in 1974 when she said she was abused by Savile. Charlotte told Williams-Thomas that Savile's abuse of the girls was widespread and regularly talked about in a resigned kind of way, almost like "having a cup of tea".

Charlotte told how one day she was selected among a group of girls invited to Savile's caravan parked in the school grounds to make a recording that he promised to play on the BBC. "I do remember that I sat on his lap," She told the programme, "and then the next thing I felt this hand go up my jumper and sort of on my breast like this. I jumped up. I absolutely freaked out and started swearing."

Charlotte said she was dragged forcefully from the caravan by Duncroft staff. She said she was locked in the isolation room – a padded cell – for two or three days until she agreed to retract the "filthy" accusations she had made against Savile. Charlotte said she eventually agreed and kept her mouth shut from then on because she didn't want to be thrown back into the isolation room.

Fiona was another 14-year-old student at Duncroft who suffered abuse at Savile's hands. Fiona was one of the many Duncroft girls that Savile would manipulate and groom with trips in his Rolls Royce. She told Williams-Thomas how Savile would make himself at home in the girls' common room and make his selection of which girls to offer rides. Fiona said it was exciting for the girls to be chosen because it was two or three hours of escape from the school, but that most of the girls knew what was expected of them in return. She said the first time Savile assaulted her was in the back of the Rolls Royce while it was parked in the school grounds. The other girls had left the car but Savile instructed her to stay behind. She said she instantly knew what he expected but was still shocked by the severity of the assault, which involved fumbling with her breasts and with his hands up her skirt. "I was expected to masturbate him," Fiona told Williams-Thomas, "and it sounds very odd, and I'm still not sure why, but he wanted me to put my finger into his anus."

Fiona said she was sexually assaulted on two further trips in Savile's Rolls Royce and during a trip to the BBC studios where he would invite the Duncroft girls to be audience members on *Clunk Click*. Fiona described the familiar alcove in Savile's dressing room that several of his victims mentioned. The nook was partitioned by a curtain and, Fiona said, Savile took her behind it and fumbled with her breasts while she was forced to masturbate him.

The *Exposure* programme showed a clip of *Clunk Click* in which Savile invited another subsequently exposed paedophile, the rock star Gary Glitter, to sit down with the audience. The clip shows the two men putting their arms around the girls in a predatory manner. Glitter says appreciatively "I get two?" while smiling like a kid in a sweetshop. The programme went on to quote an interview featuring Savile near the end of his life in which he defended the actions of the by-then exposed Glitter. It then detailed the events of the 2007 Surrey police investigation involving some of the Duncroft girls and how the investigation had been dropped.

The programme finished with an interview with Esther Rantzen, a BBC journalist and a presenter who had worked alongside Savile. Rantzen was invited to view the interview footage with the Savile victims and provide her reaction. Looking visibly shaken, Rantzen, who launched the child protection charity, Childline, told Williams-Thomas, "Before I watched these I had absolutely decided that I would not make up my mind because he's not here to defend himself, it seems utterly unfair. But I must say that what these women say is so matter-of-fact, they corroborate each other, the style of the abuse and the attack on them was absolutely consistent one with each other, and I'm afraid the jury isn't out anymore."

Rantzen admitted to having heard rumours about Savile but, like so many of the people who had worked with or around Savile, she did nothing to investigate them herself despite being a journalist and child protection advocate. "I feel that we in television, in his world, in some way colluded with him as a child abuser," she admitted to Williams-Thomas, "because I now believe that's what he was."

It was a powerful ending to a ground-breaking documentary and it set the tone of contrition and self-reflection that would soon follow among some of the biggest institutions in the UK that had harboured Savile and provided rich hunting grounds for his serial child sexual abuse.

In the wake of the *Exposure* documentary, the flood gates that had been held shut for six decades were suddenly flung wide open.

The press now began to investigate Savile in ways it had singularly failed to do for the past 60 years, keeping the story running on the front pages for several weeks. And still the vast scale of Savile's abuse was only hinted at. However, Williams-Thomas with his extensive police experience of child abuse profiles had an insight into how large Savile's case might become. He remembers being contacted a week after the programme was aired by a high-ranking police officer connected to what would become Operation Yew Tree, the Metropolitan police's massive investigation into child sexual abuse that was sparked by the Savile allegations.

When they arranged to meet, the high-ranking officer told Williams-Thomas, "I reckon there's probably around 20 to 30 victims." Williams-Thomas recalled his reply: "I said, 'There are 500.' And he looked at me and he went, 'Really?' And I went, 'I can tell you, I've been doing this for a long time now, I reckon there's 500 victims.'"

Williams-Thomas's estimate would eventually be borne out by the dozens of reports and inquiries that were already being launched among the various organisations Savile was involved with, including the BBC, the NHS and the police. One of the first organisations thrown into chaos was the BBC, whose own *Newsnight* programme had originally investigated the Savile story and failed to pursue it. Williams-Thomas had asked the director general of the BBC, George Entwistle, for an interview regarding the Savile allegations for his *Exposure* documentary but, according to Williams-Thomas, Entwistle not only refused an interview but dismissed the allegations out of hand. He would soon live to rue his decision. Entwistle was forced to resign the following month in the wake of the Savile scandal and other mishandled child abuse investigations that highlighted "unacceptable journalistic standards" at the BBC.

For Williams-Thomas, the BBC's knee-jerk reaction to the Savile allegations summed up the arrogance and wilful blindness that allowed Savile to perpetrate his crimes for so long in the midst of some of the country's biggest and most respected institutions.

"This is a massive learn for any organisation that's facing these problems," Williams-Thomas told me. "They should have said, 'Listen, it's not on my watch, it's happened a long time ago. We take these allegations really seriously. We will now launch an investigation to find out what's gone on.' That's what they should have said but they didn't. They buried their head, they came up with a very arrogant attitude and actually then that manifests itself and just became worse because what you ended up with was the BBC then having to almost go full circle."

Entwistle's resignation was one of the moments when Williams-Thomas said the scale of what the *Exposure* programme had achieved was really brought home. The other was just a week after the programme's airing, when Savile's extravagant headstone was removed from Scarborough's Woodlands Cemetery where his grave looked out over the sea.

Williams-Thomas's exposure of Savile would go on to spur dozens of separate inquiries and an ongoing police operation that would lead to hundreds of more arrests, including such high-profile names as PR mogul, Max Clifford, and musician and entertainer, Rolf Harris

But not every consequence of the programme was positive. As soon as the *Exposure* show was aired Williams-Thomas says he started receiving hate mail and death threats and even had a petrol bomb sent to him. One correspondent sent Williams-Thomas material of himself sexually abusing children along with a note that effectively said, "catch me if you can." Williams-Thomas left the case to the police who tracked the paedophile to an internet café in London, but unfortunately the premises didn't have CCTV and the police were unable to catch the man. "I was really annoyed," Williams-Thomas told me, "because I wish I'd have pursued that, because I think I would have found him."

Despite the personal hardships, Williams-Thomas saw his TV career and reputation for investigative reporting go from strength to strength in the wake of the *Exposure* documentary. He went on to produce several more ground-breaking crime documentaries, including a follow-up programme on the Savile case. In 2016, he managed to secure an exclusive interview with the South African athlete, Oscar Pistorius, who was convicted of murdering his girlfriend. Williams-Thomas went on have his own series on ITV and Netflix called *The Investigator* in which he followed live investigations to crack previously unsolved crimes. He has also written a book about his experiences called *Hunting Killers*. Williams-Thomas is still motivated to solve crimes and bring perpetrators to justice and he still has a particular interest in preventing child sexual abuse which, despite the recent high-profile arrests of people like Savile, Nygard and Epstein, is, Williams-Thomas says, more prevalent than ever.

But despite his ongoing investigations and his media success, Williams-Thomas is convinced he will never pursue anything as large, as difficult or with as much impact as the Savile story. "Savile led to thousands of people being saved," he told me, "hundreds of offenders being arrested just in the space of a one-hour programme... There was a piece written in *The Guardian* the following day saying never had television defined a moment any more. And I think it's true... In terms of changing attitudes, changing public opinion, I don't think there's been a programme that's done that, and I'm incredibly proud to be part of that."

CHAPTER 10

NO ACCOUNTABILITY ESTABLISHMENT CLOSES RANKS

After the release of ITV's *Exposure* documentary things moved swiftly, as if a dam that had been creaking for several years suddenly cracked and broke. Over the next weeks, dozens of similar stories began to appear in the newspapers from victims who had suffered sexual abuse at the hands of Savile.

Public opinion, which had previously been in Savile's favour, now took a dramatic U-turn. A commemorative plaque placed outside Savile's home in Scarborough was defaced and quickly taken down, as was a road sign named after him. Similar things happened all over the country, with a statue of Savile in a shopping centre in Glasgow quietly removed. The most notable incident was the removal of the headstone from Savile's grave in Woodlands cemetery in Scarborough.

The huge three-piece black granite and steel block costing several thousand pounds was inlaid with gold and inscribed with a list of charities Savile had donated to, as well as tributes by friends, and finished with a typical Savile one-liner: "It was good while it lasted". Placed at a 45-degree angle so it could look over the sea, the headstone became the target of attacks soon after the news started coming out about Savile's true nature.

After a quick consultation with concerned relatives of nearby graves, Scarborough council decided to have the headstone removed. Such was the media attention around the disgraced celebrity that this operation was performed at night under the cover of darkness to escape the media circus and possible seekers of revenge. When the sun came up on the day of the 10th of October Savile's headstone had disappeared and all that remained was an unmarked grave.

As the scale of Savile's crimes became apparent other more constructive, if overdue, action began to be taken. The Metropolitan Police launched an investigation with the help of the NSPCC, called Operation Yewtree. Since the dam had broken allegations were flooding in and the Met Police assigned an initial 10-person team alongside specially trained staff from the NSPCC to handle the complaints and deal with the rapidly expanding lines of enquiry. These already included two rape allegations and six of indecent assault varying across a wide range of settings including the BBC, the NHS and several care homes. The Met's head of Specialist Crime Investigations confirmed that Savile's abuse appeared to be on a national scale. Even he couldn't have guessed the full extent of what the investigation would uncover.

When the report of the investigation, 'Giving Victims a Voice' was published in January 2013, the results were stark and shocking. Since Operation Yewtree had begun, just three months earlier, 600 people had come forward with information, 450 of which related to Savile. Of these, 214 amounted to criminal offences spanning 28 police force areas and 54 years. The earliest incident was in 1955 in Manchester when Savile was 29 years old, and the latest in 2009 when he was 83. Of the crimes reported, 126 were indecent acts and 34 involved rape or penetration. The victims ranged in age from eight years old to 47 with the majority under 18. The main age range of Savile's victims was 13 to 16 and the majority were female although a considerable proportion – 18% – were male. Most of the offending occurred in Savile's home town of Leeds or in London and centred around his places of work or volunteering activities. Offences were recorded at the BBC between 1965 and 2006, at Leeds General Infirmary between 1965 and 1995, at Stoke Mandeville Hospital between 1965 and 1988 and at Duncroft school between 1970 and 1978. The vast majority of the victims hadn't come forward before, they told the inquiry, because they did not think they would be believed or didn't trust the legal system.

Yewtree also led to the arrest of 12 other media stars and six convictions. These included British rock star, Gary Glitter, who was charged with attempted rape, four counts of indecent assault and sex with a girl under 13. Glitter was imprisoned for 16 years. Glitter, as we have seen, had been associated with Savile by some of the Duncroft victims, one of whom claimed to have seen him having sex with another Duncroft pupil in a recess in Savile's dressing room at the BBC. Another DJ from Savile's period, Ray Teret, also went down, convicted on 18 counts of indecent assault and rape, one of which included Savile as an accomplice. Teret was sentenced to 25 years in prison where he died in 2021. Another presenter, Stuart Hall, was imprisoned for 15 months for sexual assaults on several women. In 2014, he was joined by the publicist Max Clifford, who was imprisoned for eight years. Another minor celebrity to join the list was the *This Morning* weather presenter, Fred Talbot, aka 'Fred The Weatherman'. Talbot was imprisoned for five years in 2015 for 11 sexual offences including those against underage boys, dating back to his time as a grammar school teacher. And finally there was Rolf Harris, a singer, artist, TV presenter and children's entertainer who was almost as familiar to the British public as Savile himself. Harris was convicted of 12 counts of indecent assault ranging from 1968 to 1986, including one on an eight-year-old autograph hunter, and two on fans in their early teens. Harris was sentenced to five years and nine months in jail in 2014.

But Yewtree's impressive-sounding list of statistics glossed over a stark underlying truth. Despite the hundreds of accusations now coming forward against Savile, there were only a handful recorded in police files during his lifetime. This shocking disparity was revealed in the March 2013 report by Her Majesty's Inspectorate of Constabularies (HMIC), entitled 'Mistakes Were Made'. The HMIC's report into the performance of the police during Savile's lifetime found a grand total of just five recorded allegations against Savile across the entirety of the UK's police forces during his lifetime.

The allegations kept on record included an intelligence ledger held by the Metropolitan Police's paedophile unit dated from 1964 which linked Savile to an underage brothel in London; an anonymous letter received by the Metropolitan Police in 1998 accusing Savile of being a paedophile; a 2003 crime report based on a complaint of sexual assault by Savile in the 70s; the three Duncroft victims recorded by Surrey police in 2007; and Jill from Worthing who had come forward to Sussex Police in 2008.

We have already looked in depth at the Surrey and Sussex investigations, but the other three recorded pieces of intelligence provide fascinating insights into what the police already knew about Savile. The first of these records dated back to 1964 and was a ledger found by the Metropolitan Police during Operation Yewtree in 2012. It recorded the existence of a house on Battersea Bridge Road in London where four girls and a younger boy all lived. The girls, according to the ledger, were all absconders from Duncroft Approved School in Surrey. A second part to the ledger recorded that a vice ring operated from the house and that three "coloured" men had been arrested for living off the immoral earnings of two of the girls. One of the men was sentenced to two years in prison, another failed to appear at court, and the third was found not guilty. By far the most interesting part of the ledger however was the mention of the name "Jimmy Savile" who was recorded as being a regular visitor to the house. However, as the HMIC report pointed out, there was no record of Savile ever being investigated or questioned in relation to the underage vice ring.

The ledger is interesting because it not only proves that Savile's name was known by police to be connected to underage girls as early as 1964, but also it linked him with Duncroft half a decade before he supposedly started visiting the school. If this intelligence had been properly recorded and kept up to date it might have provided crucial corroboration for Surrey Police's 2007 investigation.

The second piece of intelligence was an anonymous letter sent to the Vice Squad at New Scotland Yard on the 13th of July 1998. The message read:

"I supply here information which if looked into by one of your officers will yield a secret life not unlike that of [name].

"I cannot give you my name as I am too closely involved and do not wish to be in the limelight and have the finger pointed at myself. If you think this is not a genuine letter, then it is your loss.

"The image that JIMMY SAVILE has tried to portray over the years is someone who is deeply concerned with his fellow man; however, the thrust of this is entirely the opposite. His fund-raising activities are not out of altruistic motives, but purely for selfish advancement and an easy living. He has slimed his way in wherever possible. He has tried to hide his homosexuality, which in any event is an open secret with those who know; but did you know that he is also a deeply committed paedophile, and involved in buggery with young children.

"An incident that happened some years ago (not that long) was when he was involved with a young 'rent boy'. This rent boy followed him to [place]. JIMMY SAVILE foolishly gave this rent boy his Leeds telephone number [set out in the text] which he has now subsequently changed; this was because he was having threatening calls from this rent boy, who was going to go to the press and expose him for his paedophilia, if he did not give him more money. I know at the time he was extremely angry and frightened. How it ended, I really do not know. What cannot be acceptable and must be stopped is JIMMY SAVILE's paedophilia. I know he has pornography, but do not know which of his houses it is in. Regularly, he runs for the 'Life' charity in Roundhay Park in Leeds, he would say 'Now I've had a run, I feel like some bum'. And would then later in the evening go where the rent boys hang out.

"He thinks he is untouchable because of the people he mixes

with, and again I know from personal experience, that they find him amusing and the butt of many jokes. There are many more things I could tell you, but they are trivial in comparison to the main issue.

"Sickened. Please, do not let him get away with this perversion and that he feels immune because of the people he mixes with. There are too many of his perverted type around – don't let him continue to think he is untouchable, or that his secret is too well hidden. [Name] made a mistake – don't let JIMMY SAVILE get away with it either.

"When JIMMY SAVILE falls, and sooner or later he will, a lot of well-known personalities and past politicians are going to fall with him. I have done my duty, my conscience is clear, you have the power, time, and resources at Scotland Yard to wheedle him out, and expose him for what he really is. If you think this is a hoax, or a crank letter, think again. It is not I who suffer if you do nothing, but the children."

The letter was a remarkably detailed set of accusations that links closely to what we now know Jimmy Savile was up to. Despite this, according to the HMIC report, the letter wasn't acted upon and was recorded in such a way that access was denied to police forces outside of its originating agency. A copy of the letter was forwarded to West Yorkshire Police in Leeds, according to the record, however no mention of the letter was found in the West Yorkshire Police archives, illustrating that it must have been ignored or destroyed. That meant West Yorkshire Police would have known in 1998 that Savile had been the target of blackmail and, more importantly, had been associated with paedophilia, and yet failed to even record the intelligence. As the HMIC report stated:

"We would expect that, as a result, West Yorkshire Police would have created an intelligence file about Savile (if one did not already exist) so that local officers might evaluate the incoming intelligence from the MPS, alongside any locally known information, and take a decision how best to proceed."

The third police record of allegations against Savile was filed by the Metropolitan Police in 2003. It was a complaint from a woman who alleged that Savile sexually assaulted her on the set of *Top of the Pops* in 1973 when she was just 15 years old. The woman said that Savile had approached her on the set and put his hand on her bottom. The woman said she told Savile to stop and moved away, but Savile followed her and repeated the act. When she told him to stop again he said, "I thought that's what you came here for."

The woman said she was happy to provide a statement but didn't want to press charges. Crucially however, like the victims interviewed by Surrey and Sussex police, she stated that she might reconsider her position if other victims came forward. Her testimony might have been crucial in corroborating the later claims from the Duncroft victims but again the report was filed in such a way that made it invisible to Surrey officers. The Metropolitan Police filed the report as "restricted", presumably because of Savile's celebrity status, which meant it was invisible to officers from other forces. So in 2007, when Surrey Police searched for other allegations against Savile on the police's national intelligence archive, the Impact Nominal Index (INI), they would not have found this piece of corroborating evidence.

As we have seen, the Surrey Police investigation into Savile was a marked failure but Surrey officers did at least, according to the HMIC report, file the details on INI thus making them available to other forces around the country. This is what enabled Sussex Police to liaise with the Surrey investigation after Jill from Worthing came forward with her complaint. But, as we have seen, Surrey and Sussex police failed to cooperate effectively and both investigations were ultimately dropped.

On top of the meagre amount of intelligence about Savile recorded by the police, the HMIC report uncovered disturbing evidence of complainants being ignored, told to go away, or even threatened. HMIC found eight cases where Savile victims alleged they tried to report him to police but were ignored. One of these dated as far back as 1963 when a man reported a rape by Savile to his local police station the day after it occurred. The man was told by the police officer receiving the complaint to "forget about it" and "move on". The officer didn't even bother to record the complaint.

A similar incident happened at the Vine Street police station in London when a man tried to report a sexual assault on his girlfriend by Savile during the filming of an episode of *Top of the Pops*. Not only was the man's complaint ignored, he was told that he himself "could be arrested for making such allegations".

Because of the way complaints about Savile were handled the HMIC report concluded that we will never know how many similar allegations were simply ignored by police. On top of this there is the untold number of reports that were destroyed, either wilfully, as seems to be the case with West Yorkshire Police, or accidentally when police databases became computerised. As well as the untold number of complaints that were turned away by police, the HMIC report noted that there were records of at least six police officers stating that they knew about Savile's behaviour.

The report concluded damningly, "It is therefore clear that, since 1964 and on more than one occasion, police forces knew or suspected that Savile was a sexual offender." It stated that forces failed to work together and were hampered by their fear of Savile's media reputation. The HMIC report was particularly damning of West Yorkshire Police, pointing out that Operation Yewtree had uncovered 40 Savile victims from the Leeds and West Yorkshire area, as well as two local police officers who claimed to have knowledge of Savile's offending. The report also mentioned a newspaper story which stated that Savile had been interviewed by West Yorkshire Police in 1958 and that he had been due to appear in court facing allegations of sexual offences against young girls. And yet, despite all this, West Yorkshire Police had not a single complaint against Savile on record.

The stage was thus set for Operation Newgreen, West Yorkshire Police's own investigation into its shortcomings relating to Jimmy

Savile. The results, needless to say, were hardly earth-shattering.

Operation Newgreen was conducted concurrently with operation Yewtree and the results were shared with the Metropolitan Police. During the investigation West Yorkshire police received a total of 118 separate pieces of information concerning Savile from members of the public and its own staff which led to the recording of 76 crimes committed by Savile in the West Yorkshire area and 68 victims. Eight of these crimes were rapes, four against men and four against women.

The Newgreen report reads like an exercise in blame-dodging and misdirection, repeatedly concentrating on the force's modern improvements without fully taking responsibility – or apologising – for its past failings. The report looked at each of the Savile allegations that were received by the police during his lifetime and sought to explain why West Yorkshire Police had no record of them. As Savile's home police force, West Yorkshire Police should have received copies of all complaints recorded against him so it could build up a profile of allegations. So the fact that none of the five extant complaints could be found in its archives was, to say the least, concerning.

Regarding the 1964 Metropolitan Police ledger about the vice ring on Battersea Bridge Road, the report found there was no information relating to West Yorkshire Police within the ledger and no evidence of its having been shared with them. Whether it was or not we will never know because in 1992 when West Yorkshire Police introduced digital recording systems many such historical paper records were not converted and were simply destroyed.

The case of the 1998 anonymous letter was more difficult to explain away. The Newgreen team managed to find the Metropolitan Police officer who had handled the original report and he insisted that he had recorded the letter and faxed a copy to West Yorkshire Police. Despite this, the force couldn't find a copy of the letter anywhere in its archives. The police officer concerned went on to say that he had received a number of these letters about

Savile which he believed to be by the same author and that he had sent several of them to West Yorkshire Police. The man went on to add that it was common knowledge among his colleagues that Savile was a paedophile. He also claimed that another member of his team had been investigating Savile in 1989.

The investigation then found an officer who had worked in West Yorkshire Police's Intelligence Bureau on the specialist sexual offences intelligence desk who claimed to remember receiving a report about Savile from New Scotland Yard's Paedophile Unit around the period of 1998, but he couldn't remember exactly what the report contained. This officer told the investigation he also remembered the information including a discussion about a possible joint investigation of Savile involving a number of different police forces. However, instead of recording the information on any of West Yorkshire Police's databases, the officer handed it to one of his superiors. He said that this officer then took the information off him and when he later asked him what was happening with it, his superior merely replied that it was "in hand". No records of any of this could be found and, as we know, no investigation into Savile was conducted. The mysterious superior who took the information from the officer died in 2002.

The absence of recorded information didn't stop former members of West Yorkshire Police coming forward to report their knowledge and concerns about Savile. One former member of Leeds Vice Squad told the investigation he remembered his unit conducting an investigation into Savile in 1989, which involved an indecent assault on two girls. Newgreen could find no records of the investigation and said it had interviewed several other officers who served on the unit at that time, none of whom could remember such an investigation.

The Newgreen report claimed it never received any information from the Metropolitan Police regarding the 2003 allegation from the woman who claimed to have been sexually assaulted by Savile on *Top of the Pops* in the 1970s. It also claimed not to have received an intelligence report from Surrey Police regarding the Duncroft allegations in 2007.

The investigation also tried to tackle the claim that Savile had been due to appear in court in Leeds in 1958 facing allegations of sexual assault against young girls. This story had surfaced in 2012 in a newspaper interview with a former employee at Savile's Mecca Locarno club in Leeds. The ex-employee told the paper that Savile had turned up to work one day in a sullen mood and that when he had asked other employees what the problem was, they had told him that Savile was due to appear in court for "interfering with young girls". According to the interview, when the employee noticed a few days later that Savile was in a brighter mood he was told that Savile had "paid them (the police) off".

The Newgreen report tracked down the ex-employee from the newspaper interview and discovered that the newspaper in question had misquoted him, making it appear that he had meant Savile had paid the police off when in fact he had meant Savile had paid the victims' families off. This may have set the record straight on the issue of Savile paying West Yorkshire Police off, but it seemed to miss the point of the larger picture – that Savile had been due to appear in court over sexual assault allegations against young girls, and that West Yorkshire Police had no records of it. Operation Newgreen once again trawled the West Yorkshire Police archives and, of course, found no records of the allegations – another victim of the switch to computerised databases no doubt. For good measure the investigation searched local court archives for records of the alleged court case involving Savile, but, it reported laconically, those appeared to have been destroyed too.

The investigation also looked into the claim Savile made in his autobiography about returning an absconder to the police after spending the night with the young teenager. The report said investigators had looked through Savile's diaries to confirm the story, but said it had found no records of the incident in West Yorkshire Police archives. It did however find confirmation from an ex-officer who said he had accompanied a female officer from the Police Women's Unit to Savile's address in Leeds to enquire about a missing girl at around the same time. However, the man couldn't recall the exact details of the incident.

One of the most embarrassing elements for West Yorkshire Police were the claims – often from Savile himself – of close ties with high-ranking police officers in Leeds, and his regular liaison with Leeds police in his now-famous Friday Morning Club. The Newgreen report attempted to tackle these claims head on by identifying all the people who regularly attended the Friday meetings and interviewing more than 40 of them. One of these was Sergeant Matthew Appleyard who told the investigation he had first met Savile when working in the Roundhay Park area of Leeds. Savile had invited him in for a coffee, Appleyard told the inquiry, and he had agreed, pointing out in his defence that, at the time, officers were encouraged to have more interaction with the local community. Appleyard became a regular at the Friday Morning Clubs and would even go into Savile's flat for a coffee when Savile wasn't there, he told the inquiry.

When questioned about the so-called "weirdo letters" which Savile had claimed he passed around for a laugh at these meetings, Appleyard stated he couldn't remember seeing any letters that involved accusations of sexual assault or any other crimes against Savile. He did however remember one letter which he said involved serious threats to Savile's life, and that one of the officers present had advised Savile to hand it to the police for fingerprinting. Appleyard claimed that one of the officers had then notified their Detective Chief Inspector about the letter. When the investigation questioned the DCI however he couldn't recall anything about the letter. The DCI in question did though remember an occasion when he visited Savile's flat at the request of the divisional commander to give him advice after Savile had expressed concerns for his safety. The Newgreen investigation was unable to establish if this was linked to the threatening letter that Appleyard mentioned or was another separate incident.

One of the regular attendees of the Friday Morning Club was Mick Starkey, the officer who had reportedly informed Surrey Police that Savile had misplaced their letter and told them he received "so many of these types of complaints". The report voluntarily passed the Starkey issue on to the police watchdog, the Independent Police Complaints Commission (IPCC), which later exonerated Starkey. However in 2013 *The Daily Mail* published an interview with a businessman who had been present at one of the Friday Morning Clubs. The man told the newspaper he remembered hearing Savile tell Starkey about losing the Surrey Police letter and asking him to contact the Surrey officers on his behalf. The businessman told *The Daily Mail* that officers from West Yorkshire Police had interviewed him for over two hours about the conversation in the presence of his daughter. However this interview is not mentioned at all in the Operation Newgreen report, or referred to by the IPCC in their decision to exonerate Starkey.

A later report by the IPCC found that no wrongdoing had occurred at Savile's Friday Morning Club. Yet it – and the Newgreen report – seemed to miss the point that the meetings themselves evinced an unhealthily close relationship between Savile and the police, irrespective of whether wrongdoing occurred or not. This misdirection and defensiveness summed up the Newgreen report as a whole which, throughout its 54 pages, seemed more concerned with exonerating West Yorkshire Police form any wrongdoing than taking an honest look at the errors that were made and ways of fixing them.

But despite West Yorkshire Police's poor showing, it might not have been the worst force in the country regarding the cover-up of links to Savile. That title would fall to North Yorkshire Police, whose town of Scarborough became one of Savile's favourite hunting grounds, and the place where he chose to be buried.

Scarborough was one of Savile's lifelong favourite haunts. He had a flat there overlooking the sea and a caravan just outside of town where he took girls he managed to pick up. Despite Savile having a decades-long association with the town however, North Yorkshire Police manged to evade inclusion in the HMIC report by simply declaring that the celebrity paedophile had "no local connection" with the area.

This claim was quickly challenged in late October 2012 when *The Sunday Express* ran a story about a 2003 police investigation into a possible paedophile ring run from Scarborough seafront in the 1980s. According to the article Savile's name had been connected to the ring along with seafront amusement arcade owner, Jimmy Corrigan, and local politician and ice cream shop owner, Peter Jaconelli. According to *The Express* article Savile's name had featured prominently in the investigation, but despite this, North Yorkshire Police doubled down on their assertion that they held no records of Savile being connected with the case.

As Operation Yewtree creaked into action Savile victims from Scarborough started coming forward, including a woman who claimed to have been sexually abused by Savile in the town in the 1960s, and one in the 1980s. Two other women spoke to the local press confirming that they had been interviewed by police in the 2003 investigation and, contrary to NYP's claims, Savile's name had come up in the questioning.

At the same time victims of Jaconelli started coming forward to the local press which, knowing of Jaconelli and Savile's close relationship, understandably started to press for the connection to be investigated by North Yorkshire Police. Peter Jaconelli was literally a larger-than-life character, weighing in at 21 stone and with a 50-inch waistline. He was the self-styled 'Ice Cream King' of Scarborough and owned an ice cream shop and restaurant on the seafront. Jaconelli had been born in Glasgow, but had moved with his parents to the North Yorkshire seaside town at the age of seven. Jaconelli quickly grew into a local celebrity, becoming mayor of the town and serving as a councillor for almost 30 years before his death in 1999. Savile had mentioned his friendship with Jaconelli in his autobiography, and part of his excursions with the Rampton hospital patients was to visit Jaconelli's ice cream parlour. Savile had also featured Jaconelli on one of his TV shows, *Savile's Travels*, where he had wrestled with the 21-stone giant at Jaconelli's Scarborough Judo studio, which he had owned since its opening in 1955.

In February 2013 one of Jaconelli's judo club members and an employee at his ice cream parlour wrote to Scarborough council to demand that Jaconelli be stripped of his title of Alderman of the Borough because, according to the man, Jaconelli was "a predatory paedophile who preyed on local children". A member of the council, Geoff Evans, then came forward to claim that he had been sexually assaulted by Jaconelli at the age of 14. Evans stated that Jaconelli had repeatedly escaped prosecution because of his close connections with the Conservative Party and the police. Other allegations surfaced claiming that Jaconelli, Corrigan and Savile had all been members of something called 'The Club', a local paedophile ring which organised sex parties during which underage children were sexually abused and raped.

All the information that was gathered by the local press was handed to Operation Yewtree, which in turn passed it to North Yorkshire Police. Yet the local force still failed to find any local connection to Savile after another trawl of its archives. The only link to Savile that this review threw up was that North Yorkshire Police had invited Savile as guest of honour to an awards ceremony at a local 'Community Idol' scheme hosted in Selby Abbey in 2008. According to the record a North Yorkshire Police vehicle and driver had been provided to drive Savile to the ceremony from his hometown of Leeds.

Despite local journalists continuing to press for an independent investigation into North Yorkshire Police, the IPCC declared in November 2013 that, after a short review of the evidence presented by the force, it would not be conducting any further investigations. More pressure soon developed however when the BBC's regional current affairs programme, *Inside Out*, picked up on the story. *Inside Out* featured a series of interviews with witnesses to Jaconelli's abuse. It also revealed that North Yorkshire Police hadn't bothered to interview a single one of the people who had come forward to local press with allegations against Jaconelli.

The attention from the BBC report was enough to prompt North Yorkshire Police to undertake a third internal review, after which it voluntarily referred itself to the IPCC for investigation about the way it had responded to allegations about Savile and Jaconelli.

In 2015, the IPCC released the findings of its investigation into North Yorkshire Police's handling of the Savile and Jaconelli allegations. These centred around a single detective based in Scarborough who had dealt with two separate allegations, one against Savile in 2002 and one against Jaconelli in 2009. According to the IPCC report the North Yorkshire Police detective had received allegations in 2002 of a sexual assault by Savile on a 15-year-old girl. The woman told the detective that she had visited Savile's Scarborough flat as a 16 year old alongside her 15-year-old friend and that she had witnessed "sexual contact" between Savile and her friend.

According to the detective the woman told him her friend refused to make a complaint against Savile. He stated that the woman then re-contacted him following Savile's death and told him she had lied in her previous statement. This time she told the detective that it had been just her in the flat with Savile and that she had been underage at the time. The detective said in a statement, "I asked her if she now wanted to make a formal complaint about what had happened with Savile, and she refused to do so."

The same detective handled a 2009 allegation of child abuse against Jaconelli. This one came from a convicted sex offender who was serving a lengthy prison sentence at the time. According to the IPCC report, the prisoner told the detective that Jaconelli had befriended him when he was a teenager living in Scarborough in the 1970s. The man said he had been recruited by Jaconelli to drive him and his young victims to parties in Leeds and Wakefield where the boys would be sexually abused. He said the young boys would be picked up off the streets and drugged prior to being taken to the parties.

The IPCC report completely cleared the detective of any wrongdoing or negligence even though he had failed to record any of the allegations against Savile or Jaconelli. This was extraordinary given that, if the detective had recorded the 2002 allegation against Savile – as he should have done – it would have provided crucial corroboration for the Surrey Police investigation in 2007.

In the meantime further investigations had brought up a litany of complaints against Savile and Jaconelli which completely belied its earlier claims of "no local connection". According to North Yorkshire Police, 35 people had now come forward with allegations against Savile and Jaconelli. Thirty two allegations of child abuse had been made against Jaconelli dating from 1958 to 1998, including sexual assault and rape. Five of the allegations were against Savile, dating from 1979 to 1998 and also included sexual assault and rape. Crucially two of the allegations were against both men, which provides important evidence that the two had colluded in their sexual crimes against children.

What emerges from all the police inquiries is a reticence during Savile's lifetime to investigate him, record any intelligence of allegations against him, or even to listen to those with complaints against him. We will never know for sure but from the mounting body of testimonies it seems almost inconceivable that several police forces, including the Metropolitan Police, West Yorkshire Police and North Yorkshire Police, didn't know about Savile's offending behaviour.

As Mark Williams-Thomas, the *Exposure* journalist and former Surrey Police detective told me, "Prior to our story in 2012, which obviously broke [the story], the police were fully aware of Savile's offending behaviour, albeit in silos. So not all that information had been shared across different police forces. But had they made the necessary inquiries they could have done it."

Boris Coster, the Broadmoor researcher, went further. "Money talks," he told me. "… We've all seen the TV programmes, we all know the story about the backhanders, the people in the Met Police, Surrey Police and so on, you name it, it's a backhander. It was that culture at the time."

The police weren't the only organisation facing tough questions. Savile's universal presence and offending behaviour meant that several British institutions came under investigation following his outing by ITV's *Exposure* documentary. The BBC was one of the main organisations connected to Savile and one where, it was rapidly emerging, much of his abuse took place. So in October 2012, the same month that *Exposure* first aired, the BBC appointed the High Court judge, Dame Janet Smith, to conduct a review.

It took until February 2016 for the findings of the review to be published but when they were the results were damning. The report identified 76 separate victims of sexual abuse by Savile at the BBC including eight rapes. Fifty seven of these victims were women or girls and 15 were boys. Twenty one of the female victims were under 16. The youngest girl Savile raped was 13 and the youngest boy just 10 years old.

The earliest of Savile's BBC crimes was the rape of a 13-year-old girl at Lime Grove Studios in London in 1959. His last was on the final performance of *Top of the Pops* in 2006 when he inappropriately touched a female member of the audience. The report found that sexual misconduct by powerful stars within the BBC was normalised and that there was a culture where complaints about misconduct were discouraged by the fear of losing one's career or the chance to get ahead. The review found that in Savile's five decades of offending at the institution, not a single complaint about him was made to the BBC's duty office which was the official channel for such complaints.

The review did find that eight complaints against Savile were made via other, unofficial channels. The first of these was made in the late 60s and concerned Savile kissing a telephone operator in Manchester on the lips. The woman told her supervisor but said she did not expect her supervisor to do anything about it. In 1969 Savile grabbed the breasts of a studio manager. The woman told her supervisors about the attack and one of them responded that it would have been more surprising if Savile had not tried to touch her. The complaint went no further. Again in 1969 a complaint was received about a 15-year-old girl who had been sexually assaulted by Savile on *Top of the Pops*. The girl had complained to a member of the floor staff who had summoned a member of security and had her escorted off the premises. In the mid-70s a sound engineer complained to his supervisor that Savile had made sexual advances towards his trainee, another young male. The report of this complaint merely "fizzled out" according to the review. In 1976 a girl complained about being sexually assaulted by Savile during a piece to camera. She was told by a member of staff not to worry, it was "just Jimmy Savile mucking about". She was then told to move out of the way as they were trying to move the camera. In 1979 a waitress was invited to meet Savile at a social event by his Radio 1 producer, Ted Beston. At the event Savile sexually assaulted the woman who subsequently complained about it to Beston. According to the report Beston treated her "as if she was being silly". In the mid-1980s two members of staff reported Savile for the use of inappropriate language which amounted to sexual harassment of a female member of staff. No action was taken. In 1988 or 89 a young female member of staff complained to her supervisor about a sexual assault by Savile. She was told to "keep [her] mouth shut, he is a VIP".

It seems clear from these few incidents alone that knowledge of Savile's behaviour was widespread and well-known throughout the BBC but was merely ignored because he was such a big name. Nobody, it seemed, wanted to rock the boat for fear of losing their job or their next chance at a promotion. Yet despite the seemingly open secret about Savile at the BBC nothing was done about it. No heads rolled. No one was held to account. The Dame Janet Smith review found no evidence that any senior member of staff knew about Savile's offending and no evidence that the BBC as a corporate body was aware of Savile's conduct.

Despite the seeming thoroughness of the Dame Janet Smith review, questions have been asked about how far it went or was willing to go. One of these comes from Mark Williams-Thomas, the journalist who initially exposed Savile with his *Exposure* documentary. In October 2012 when the Dame Janet Smith review started, there was arguably no one else in the world who knew more about Savile's offending than Mark Williams-Thomas. Yet Williams-Thomas was surprised to find himself ignored by the review. "I wait and think, oh someone will contact me from the inquiry," Williams-Thomas told me. "Nobody did. So I wrote to Dame Janet Smith's team and said, 'Do you not want to interview me?' And they came back and said, 'Well we don't know if you've got anything relevant to tell us.' And I went, 'Well that's up to you to decide, isn't it? ... But you won't know unless you ask me.'"

Williams-Thomas did eventually get his interview with Dame Janet Smith, along with an apology, but he was shocked at how the inquiry could overlook someone with so much knowledge to share about Savile. As he told me, "I've never done an investigation where I haven't spoken to as many people as possible." The same thoroughness didn't hold true, evidently, for the Dame Janet Smith review team.

If there was one institution where Savile's offending exceeded the BBC, it was the NHS. Subsequently there was a scramble to investigate the scope of his crimes as soon as the *Exposure* documentary aired. Forty-four NHS investigations were conducted over a total of 41 hospitals where Savile's offending was found to have taken place. The worst of these was Stoke Mandeville, Savile's charity project where, like Broadmoor, he seemed to have a total run of the place.

The report on Stoke Mandeville found that Savile had abused victims there for more than 20 years, abusing more than 60 staff, patients and visitors to the hospital, almost half of whom were under 16. The victims ranged from an eight-year-old patient, to a pregnant mother, to a 19-year-old paralysed woman in a wheelchair. According to the report Savile's reputation as a "sex pest" was an "open secret" among staff and management at the hospital, yet he was given a room in the accommodation block used by female students. As with the BBC, it was found that a number of informal complaints had been made about Savile but none had been "taken seriously or escalated to senior management".

Leeds General infirmary, Savile's other long-standing base, provided another 60 victims according to its report. The total number of reported victims across the NHS came to a staggering 177 victims across 41 separate hospitals ranging in age from five to 75. Overall the NHS missed 10 opportunities to stop Savile's behaviour when complaints were missed or ignored. One staff member who reported Savile's abuse at Stoke Mandeville said she was "severely reprimanded" by her bosses and made to drop the complaint. Another told investigators, "We have to tolerate him because he makes so much money.'

Again, despite the seemingly thorough nature of the various NHS reports, they all exonerated higher management whom, they said, had no knowledge of Savile's offending behaviour. As with the BBC and the police, no one was held accountable, and no heads rolled.

Perhaps the best chance at rooting out the systemic failures that allowed Savile to offend so gratuitously over a range of national institutions would have come from a single over-arching report, something with real teeth that could pinpoint those who were truly accountable for the seemingly paedophile-friendly nature of some of the UK's most important institutions. Such a report was called for in November 2012 but it took two years for then-home secretary, Theresa May, to announce the launch of the Independent Inquiry into Child Sexual Abuse (IICSA), which would comprise 13 initial investigations looking into allegations against local authorities, religious organisations, the armed forces, public and private institutions and people in the public eye.

The Independent Inquiry into Child Sexual Abuse (IICSA) was announced in July 2014 and was to be headed by retired judge, Elizabeth Butler-Sloss. However Butler-Sloss was forced to resign within days of her appointment when it was pointed out that her late brother, Sir Michael Havers, had been attorney general in the 1980s during Thatcher's government. It soon came out that during his time in office Havers had tried to persuade a Tory MP not to reveal the name an alleged paedophile in the

House of Commons. Clearly, having a brother who covered up for paedophiles was not a great endorsement to be the head of a child sexual abuse inquiry.

After Butler-Sloss's embarrassing resignation it took until September before another chair was announced. This was former corporate lawyer, Fiona Woolf. But by the end of October she too had been forced to resign when it emerged that she had social links with another of Thatcher's cabinet, Leon Brittan. Brittan himself has faced allegations of paedophilia and also of conveniently losing a dossier containing a list of names of Westminster paedophiles when he was home secretary. Woolf was a close neighbour of Brittan and was said to have dined with him several times. It also emerged that Woolf, with the help of the home office, had re-written a letter to Theresa May no less than seven times downplaying her links to Brittan.

With two resignations before the inquiry had even started, the whole affair was already looking like a shambles. It wasn't until February 2015 that a satisfactory chair was found in Justice Lowell Goddard, a judge from New Zealand. By then three years had already elapsed since the allegations against Savile had first been revealed. According to David Icke this was no coincidence.

"When Theresa May was home secretary," Icke told me, "she had this inquiry, because she's forced into it by public opinion basically, into elite paedophilia. She names someone that's clearly unacceptable and had to stand down because she wasn't. She then names another person who's clearly unacceptable and had to stand down because she wasn't. And what they're doing is they're putting time between the uproar in the public and the point where anything happens."

In August 2016, Goddard also quit the inquiry, later stating that she had been unable to appoint her own staff. Instead, she claimed, the government had appointed its own civil servants whose approach Goddard said was overly "bureaucratic", adding, "The inquiry's progress has been impeded by a lack of adequate systems and personnel, leading to critical delays." She went on to say, "I felt, as chair, handicapped by not being given a free hand to recruit staff of the type that I judged to be essential."

The appointment of government staff who slowed down the inquiry lends credence to Icke's claim that the review was never intended to be successful.

Following Goddard's resignation a 500-strong survivors' group also pulled out of the inquiry saying it had doubts about the independence of the process. In 2017, another survivors' group withdrew from the inquiry stating that survivors of sexual abuse had been "totally marginalised" by the process and that the report had descended into a "very costly academic report-writing and literature review exercise".

The IICSA final report was eventually published in October 2022. It contained a number of recommendations for the government to crack down on child sex abuse in public and private institutions. Crucially though it found no one culpable of covering up or enabling historical child sex abuse in the institutions it had been investigating. The report appeared a full decade after the Savile allegations first surfaced and by then there was little press interest in its findings. The report's publication barely made a headline.

If, as David Icke claims, the true purpose of the investigation was to take the heat out of the story and kick the can down the road, it could hardly have been more successful.

CONCLUSION

Over 500 people have alleged sexual abuse by Jimmy Savile and there are probably hundreds more who never came forward. The ones strong-willed enough to report the crimes were located all over the country, from Jersey to Scotland, from Scarborough to Belfast. When the crimes were committed, they ranged in age from eight to 47 years. They covered adult men and women and underage boys and girls, most of them ranging between 13 and 16 years of age. The assaults occurred over more than six decades of offending, the earliest known happening in 1955 and the last in 2009. They happened at various BBC studios around the country from London to Manchester to Leeds. they happened at over 40 hospitals across the land from Liverpool to Exeter, and included top security mental institutions like Broadmoor, Rampton and Moss Side. They happened in children's homes like Haut de la Garenne and in special educational facilities like Duncroft. They happened in the nightclubs Savile managed in Leeds, Manchester and London. They happened in his various properties and caravans. They happened in his motorhomes that toured the country looking for victims, and they happened in the back of his Rolls-Royces and top-range sports cars.

The numbers and the scale of Savile's abuse is staggering. Yet what we know might just be scratching the surface. Many of Savile's victims were probably already dead or unable to come forward by the time he was finally exposed. Many more were probably too badly affected by the abuse to want to re-open old wounds. Still more would have felt too ashamed or embarrassed to talk publicly about something they wanted kept firmly in the past.

We will probably never know the full extent of Savile's abuse. But the numbers are only part of the story. Savile's life was like an iceberg where the part on public display was dwarfed by what was going on beneath the surface. There were the shadowy links to the intelligence services. There was the possibility of satanic ritual abuse that extended into the highest echelons of society. There were the organised paedophile networks running out of children's homes like Haut de la Garenne and Kincora. There were the links to prime ministers like Ted Heath and Margaret Thatcher, and there was the notorious Westminster paedophile scandal that potentially involved many of the figures in Thatcher's government in a top-level paedophile ring. There are still so many questions left unanswered, like why the press never managed to expose Savile during his lifetime, or how deeply his influence went at the BBC, where no one was ever held accountable for sanctioning four decades of his abuse. There is the question of Savile's involvement with the royals and how deeply it went. Likewise with the police. There is the question of his necrophilia. There is the question of how much his family was involved and of his bizarre relationship with his mother. And there is the question of his links to secret societies such as the Freemasons.

All in all there is still so much to be uncovered that this will not be a standalone book, as I first intended, but the first volume of a series on Jimmy Savile, which I hope will go some way to unravelling the mysteries listed above.

Who was Jimmy Savile? More than anything he was a list of contradictions. He was a practising Catholic who raped young boys and girls and had sex with corpses. He was a God-fearing believer who participated in Satanic rituals. He was an unprecedentedly generous charity fundraiser who was too tight to buy his own meals. He was a friend of princes and dukes who ate bacon sandwiches at his local greasy spoon. He was a peace activist who tied up troublemakers in his nightclubs and had them brutally beaten. He was a fairy godfather who hated children.

Savile was an enigma and his life reads like a riddle whose solution might expose a hidden and secretive world the scale of which is hardly imaginable. I hope that my forthcoming Savile series will go some way to revealing that dark underworld and at least partially unravelling the riddle that was Jimmy Savile.

Of all the many questions which Savile brings up, one of the most common – and the one that troubles me most – is whether it is possible for there to be another Jimmy Savile. I'm sorry to say that there is a definitive answer to that question, and the answer is yes.

Mark Williams-Thomas and Jon Wedger, both ex-detectives who have worked all their lives to expose child abuse, have stated that there is a high-level paedophile still walking amongst us who is just as famous as Savile and just as untouchable.

Williams-Thomas told a newspaper in 2022, "There are still people out there who are untouchable. There is one very significant person who I have done everything to try and get prosecuted because he is clearly a child sex offender." But Williams-Thomas said the Crown Prosecution Service has refused to prosecute the celebrity paedophile on several occasions. He added, "The police and I have tried really hard to get there. He will die in due course and then the floodgates will open in the same way they did with Savile. That's not right. But justice takes many different forms."

And Jon Wedger agrees. He also told me about a celebrity paedophile at large who is a household name and who has never been exposed despite the police being fully aware of his offending. Wedger told me that he was made aware of this celebrity paedophile when he worked for the Metropolitan Police and that his name is well-known to police forces around the country. Wedger confirmed that this man is a household name, so well-known in fact that people dress up like him at fancy dress parties.

This man is now in his old age so, as Williams-Thomas mentioned, it won't be long before he is dead. When that happens we will face another series of exposures that might rival Savile's for their scale and horror, and which, like Savile's, happened in plain sight.

So there *can* be other Saviles. Indeed, there is one walking around freely right at this moment. No doubt there are still more in other countries and there doubtless will be others in the future. This is why we must remain vigilant and do everything we can to explore the life and crimes of people like Jimmy Savile. Because what we find might go some way to preventing it happening in the future.

In book 2 of this Jimmy Savile series, I interview a Duncroft School Savile survivor and Savile biographer, Dan Davies. I probe deeper into the intelligence, masonic and satanic paedophile networks. I examine the links between Savile and the Yorkshire Ripper, including why Savile became a suspect in the Ripper case and how the investigation was manipulated to protect Savile. It seems likely that Savile knew Sutcliffe before his arrest and may have even met the Moors Murderers, who killed kids and recorded the torture.

If you enjoyed this book, there are lengthy interviews with many of the contributors on the podcast platforms, including my YouTube channel. It would help my career tremendously if you would be so kind as to leave an Amazon review. I also cover Jimmy Savile in my previous book: *Elite Predators: From Jimmy Savile and Lord Mountbatten to Jeffrey Epstein and Ghislaine Maxwell*

SOCIAL-MEDIA LINKS

Email: attwood.shaun@hotmail.co.uk
YouTube: Shaun Attwood
Blog: Jon's Jail Journal
Website: shaunattwood.com
Instagram: @shaunattwood
Twitter: @shaunattwood
LinkedIn: Shaun Attwood
Goodreads: Shaun Attwood
Facebook: Shaun Attwood, Jon's Jail Journal,
T-Bone Appreciation Society

Shaun welcomes feedback on any of his
books and YouTube videos.

Thank you for the Amazon and Goodreads reviews and to all of
the people who have subscribed to Shaun's YouTube channel!

OTHER BOOKS BY GADFLY PRESS

By Shaun Attwood:
English Shaun Trilogy
Party Time
Hard Time
Prison Time

War on Drugs Series
Pablo Escobar: Beyond Narcos
American Made: Who Killed Barry Seal? Pablo Escobar or George HW Bush
The Cali Cartel: Beyond Narcos
Clinton Bush and CIA Conspiracies: From the Boys on the Tracks to Jeffrey Epstein
Who Killed Epstein? Prince Andrew or Bill Clinton
Elite Predators: From Jimmy Savile and Lord Mountbatten to Jeffrey Epstein and Ghislaine Maxwell

Un-Making a Murderer: The Framing of Steven Avery and Brendan Dassey
The Mafia Philosopher: Two Tonys
Life Lessons

Pablo Escobar's Story (3-book series)

By John G Sutton:
HMP Manchester Prison Officer: I Survived Terrorists, Murderers, Rapists and Freemason Officer Attacks in Strangeways and Wormwood Scrubs

By Lee Marvin Hitchman:
How I Survived Shootings, Stabbings, Prison, Crack Addiction, Manchester Gangs and Dog Attacks

By William Rodríguez Abadía:
Son of the Cali Cartel: The Narcos Who Wiped Out Pablo Escobar and the Medellín Cartel

By Chet Sandhu:
Self-Made, Dues Paid: An Asian Kid Who Became an International Drug-Smuggling Gangster

By Kaz B:
Confessions of a Dominatrix: My Secret BDSM Life

By Peter McAleese:
Killing Escobar and Soldier Stories

By Joe Egan:
Big Joe Egan: The Toughest White Man on the Planet

By Anthony Valentine:
Britain's No. 1 Art Forger Max Brandrett: The Life of a Cheeky Faker

By Johnnyboy Steele:
Scotland's Johnnyboy: The Bird That Never Flew

By Ian 'Blink' MacDonald:
Scotland's Wildest Bank Robber: Guns, Bombs and Mayhem in Glasgow's Gangland

By Michael Sheridan:
The Murder of Sophie: How I Hunted and Haunted the West Cork Killer

By Steve Wraith:
The Krays' Final Years: My Time with London's Most Iconic Gangsters

By Natalie Welsh:
Escape from Venezuela's Deadliest Prison

By Johnnyboy Steele:

Scotland's Johnnyboy: The Bird That Never Flew

"A cross between *Shawshank Redemption* and *Escape from Alcatraz*!" – Shaun Attwood, YouTuber and Author

All his life, 'Johnnyboy' Steele has been running. Firstly, from an abusive father, then from the rigours of an approved school and a young offenders jail, and, finally, from the harshness of adult prison. This book details how the Steele brothers staged the most daring breakout that Glasgow's Barlinnie prison had ever seen and recounts what happened when their younger brother, Joseph, was falsely accused of the greatest mass murder in Scottish legal history.

If Johnnyboy had wings, he would have flown to help his family, but he would have to wait for freedom to use his expertise to publicise young Joe's miscarriage of justice.

This is a compelling, often shocking and uncompromisingly honest account of how the human spirit can survive against almost crushing odds. It is a story of family love, friendship and, ultimately, a desire for justice.

By Ian 'Blink' MacDonald:

Scotland's Wildest Bank Robber: Guns, Bombs and Mayhem in Glasgow's Gangland

As a young man in Glasgow's underworld, Ian 'Blink' MacDonald earned a reputation for fighting and stabbing his enemies. After refusing to work for Arthur "The Godfather" Thompson, he attempted to steal £6 million in a high-risk armed bank robbery. While serving 16 years, Blink met the torture-gang boss Eddie Richardson, the serial killer Archie Hall, notorious lifer Charles Bronson and members of the Krays.

After his release, his drug-fuelled violent lifestyle created conflict with the police and rival gangsters. Rearrested several times, he was the target of a gruesome assassination attempt. During filming for Danny Dyer's Deadliest Men, a bomb was discovered under Blink's car and the terrified camera crew members fled from Scotland.

In *Scotland's Wildest Bank Robber*, Blink provides an eye-opening account of how he survived gangland warfare, prisons, stabbings and bombs.

By Michael Sheridan:

The Murder of Sophie: How I Hunted and Haunted the West Cork Killer

Just before Christmas, 1996, a beautiful French woman – the wife of a movie mogul – was brutally murdered outside of her holiday home in a remote region of West Cork, Ireland. The crime was reported by a local journalist, Ian Bailey, who was at the forefront of the case until he became the prime murder suspect. Arrested twice, he was released without charge.

This was the start of a saga lasting decades with twists and turns and a battle for justice in two countries, which culminated in the 2019 conviction of Bailey – in his absence – by the French Criminal court in Paris. But it was up to the Irish courts to decide whether he would be extradited to serve a 25-year prison sentence.

With the unrivalled co-operation of major investigation sources and the backing of the victim's family, the author unravels the shocking facts of a unique murder case.

By Steve Wraith:

The Krays' Final Years: My Time with London's Most Iconic Gangsters

Britain's most notorious twins – Ron and Reg Kray – ascended the underworld to become the most feared and legendary gangsters in London. Their escalating mayhem culminated in murder, for which they received life sentences in 1969.

While incarcerated, they received letters from a schoolboy from Tyneside, Steve Wraith, who was mesmerised by their story. Eventually, Steve visited them in prison and a friendship formed. The Twins hired Steve as an unofficial advisor, which brought him into contact with other members of their crime family. At Ron's funeral, Steve was Charlie Kray's right-hand man.

Steve documents Ron's time in Broadmoor – a high-security

psychiatric hospital – where he was battling insanity and heavily medicated. Steve details visiting Reg, who served almost 30 years in a variety of prisons, where the gangster was treated with the utmost respect by the staff and the inmates.

By Natalie Welsh:

Escape from Venezuela's Deadliest Prison

After getting arrested at a Venezuelan airport with a suitcase of cocaine, Natalie was clueless about the danger she was facing. Sentenced to 10 years, she arrived at a prison with armed men on the roof, whom she mistakenly believed were the guards, only to find out they were homicidal gang members. Immediately, she was plunged into a world of unimaginable horror and escalating violence, where murder, rape and all-out gang warfare were carried out with the complicity of corrupt guards. Male prisoners often entered the women's housing area, bringing gunfire with them and leaving corpses behind. After 4.5 years, Natalie risked everything to escape and flee through Colombia, with the help of a guard who had fallen deeply in love with her.

By Shaun Attwood:

Pablo Escobar: Beyond Narcos

War on Drugs Series Book 1

The mind-blowing true story of Pablo Escobar and the Medellín Cartel, beyond their portrayal on Netflix.

Colombian drug lord Pablo Escobar was a devoted family man and a psychopathic killer; a terrible enemy, yet a wonderful friend. While donating millions to the poor, he bombed and tortured his enemies – some had their eyeballs removed with hot spoons. Through ruthless cunning and America's insatiable appetite for cocaine, he became a multi-billionaire, who lived in a $100-million house with its own zoo.

Pablo Escobar: Beyond Narcos demolishes the standard good versus evil telling of his story. The authorities were not hunting Pablo down to stop his cocaine business. They were taking it over.

American Made: Who Killed Barry Seal? Pablo Escobar or George HW Bush

War on Drugs Series Book 2

Set in a world where crime and government coexist, *American Made* is the jaw-dropping true story of CIA pilot Barry Seal that the Hollywood movie starring Tom Cruise is afraid to tell.

Barry Seal flew cocaine and weapons worth billions of dollars into and out of America in the 1980s. After he became a government informant, Pablo Escobar's Medellin Cartel offered a million for him alive and half a million dead. But his real trouble began after he threatened to expose the dirty dealings of George HW Bush.

American Made rips the roof off Bush and Clinton's complicity in cocaine trafficking in Mena, Arkansas.

"A conspiracy of the grandest magnitude." Congressman Bill Alexander on the Mena affair.

The Cali Cartel: Beyond Narcos

War on Drugs Series Book 3

An electrifying account of the Cali Cartel, beyond its portrayal on Netflix.

From the ashes of Pablo Escobar's empire rose an even bigger and more malevolent cartel. A new breed of sophisticated mobsters became the kings of cocaine. Their leader was Gilberto Rodríguez Orejuela – known as the Chess Player, due to his foresight and calculated cunning.

Gilberto and his terrifying brother, Miguel, ran a multi-billion-dollar drug empire like a corporation. They employed a politically astute brand of thuggery and spent $10 million to put a president in power. Although the godfathers from Cali preferred bribery over violence, their many loyal torturers and hitmen were never idle.

Clinton, Bush and CIA Conspiracies: From the Boys on the Tracks to Jeffrey Epstein

War on Drugs Series Book 4

In the 1980s, George HW Bush imported cocaine to finance an illegal war in Nicaragua. Governor Bill Clinton's Arkansas state police provided security for the drug drops. For assisting the CIA, the Clinton Crime Family was awarded the White House. The #clintonbodycount continues to this day, with the deceased including Jeffrey Epstein.

This book features harrowing true stories that reveal the insanity of the drug war. A mother receives the worst news about her son. A journalist gets a tip that endangers his life. An unemployed man becomes California's biggest crack dealer. A DEA agent in Mexico is sacrificed for going after the big players.

The lives of Linda Ives, Gary Webb, Freeway Rick Ross and Kiki Camarena are shattered by brutal experiences. Not all of them will survive.

Pablo Escobar's Story (4-book series)

"Finally, the definitive book about Escobar, original and up-to-date." – UNILAD

"The most comprehensive account ever written." – True Geordie

Pablo Escobar was a mama's boy, who cherished his family and sang in the shower, yet he bombed a passenger plane and formed a death squad that used genital electrocution.

Most Escobar biographies only provide a few pieces of the puzzle, but this action-packed 1000-page book reveals everything about the king of cocaine.

Mostly translated from Spanish, Part 1 contains stories untold in the English-speaking world, including:

The tragic death of his youngest brother, Fernando.

The fate of his pregnant mistress.

The shocking details of his affair with a TV celebrity.

The presidential candidate who encouraged him to eliminate their rivals.

The Mafia Philosopher

"A fast-paced true-crime memoir with all of the action of Goodfellas." – UNILAD

"Sopranos v Sons of Anarchy with an Alaskan-snow backdrop." – True Geordie Podcast

Breaking bones, burying bodies and planting bombs became second nature to Two Tonys, while working for the Bonanno

Crime Family, whose exploits inspired The Godfather.

After a dispute with an outlaw motorcycle club, Two Tonys left a trail of corpses from Arizona to Alaska. On the run, he was pursued by bikers and a neo-Nazi gang, blood-thirsty for revenge, while a homicide detective launched a nationwide manhunt.

As the mist from his smoking gun fades, readers are left with an unexpected portrait of a stoic philosopher with a wealth of charm, a glorious turn of phrase and a fanatical devotion to his daughter.

Party Time

An action-packed roller-coaster account of a life spiralling out of control, featuring wild women, gangsters and a mountain of drugs.

Shaun Attwood arrived in Phoenix, Arizona, a penniless business graduate from a small industrial town in England. Within a decade, he became a stock-market millionaire. But he was leading a double life.

After taking his first ecstasy pill at a rave in Manchester as a shy student, Shaun became intoxicated by the party lifestyle that would change his fortune. Years later, in the Arizona desert, he became submerged in a criminal underworld, throwing parties for thousands of ravers and running an ecstasy ring in competition with the Mafia mass murderer, Sammy 'The Bull' Gravano.

As greed and excess tore through his life, Shaun had eye-watering encounters with Mafia hitmen and crystal-meth addicts, enjoyed extravagant debauchery with superstar DJs and glitter girls, and ingested enough drugs to kill a herd of elephants. This is his story.

Hard Time

"Makes the Shawshank Redemption look like a holiday camp."
– NOTW

After a SWAT team smashed down stock-market millionaire Shaun Attwood's door, he found himself inside Arizona's deadliest jail and locked into a brutal struggle for survival.

Shaun's hope of living the American Dream turned into a nightmare of violence and chaos, when he had a run-in with Sammy "the Bull" Gravano, an Italian Mafia mass murderer.

In jail, Shaun was forced to endure cockroaches crawling in his ears at night, dead rats in the food and the sound of skulls getting cracked against toilets. He meticulously documented the conditions and smuggled out his message.

Join Shaun on a harrowing voyage into the darkest recesses of human existence.

Hard Time provides a revealing glimpse into the tragedy, brutality, dark comedy and eccentricity of prison life.

Featured worldwide on Nat Geo Channel's Locked-Up/ Banged-Up Abroad Raving Arizona.

Prison Time

Sentenced to 9½ years in Arizona's state prison for distributing ecstasy, Shaun finds himself living among gang members, sexual predators and drug-crazed psychopaths. After being attacked by a Californian biker, in for stabbing a girlfriend, Shaun writes about the prisoners who befriend, protect and inspire him. They include T-Bone, a massive African American ex-Marine, who risks his life saving vulnerable inmates from rape, and Two Tonys, an old-school Mafia murderer, who left the corpses of his rivals from Arizona to Alaska. They teach Shaun how to turn incarceration to his advantage, and to learn from his mistakes.

Shaun is no stranger to love and lust in the heterosexual world, but the tables are turned on him inside. Sexual advances come at him from all directions, some cleverly disguised, others more sinister – making Shaun question his sexual identity.

Resigned to living alongside violent, mentally ill and drug-addicted inmates, Shaun immerses himself in psychology and philosophy, to try to make sense of his past behaviour, and begins applying what he learns, as he adapts to prison life. Encouraged by Two Tonys to explore fiction as well, Shaun reads over 1000 books which, with support from a brilliant psychotherapist, Dr Owen, speed along his personal development. As his ability to deflect daily threats improves, Shaun begins to look forward to his release with optimism and a new love waiting for him. Yet the words of Aristotle from one of Shaun's books will prove prophetic: "We cannot learn without pain."

Un-Making a Murderer: The Framing of Steven Avery and Brendan Dassey

Innocent people do go to jail. Sometimes mistakes are made. But even more terrifying is when the authorities conspire to frame them. That's what happened to Steven Avery and Brendan Dassey, who were convicted of murder and are serving life sentences.

Un-Making a Murderer is an explosive book, which uncovers the illegal, devious and covert tactics used by Wisconsin officials, including:

– Concealing Other Suspects

– Paying Expert Witnesses to Lie

– Planting Evidence

– Jury Tampering

The art of framing innocent people has been in practice for centuries and will continue until the perpetrators are held accountable.

Turning conventional assumptions and beliefs in the justice system upside down, *Un-Making a Murderer* takes you on that journey.

HARD TIME BY SHAUN ATTWOOD

CHAPTER 1

Sleep deprived and scanning for danger, I enter a dark cell on the second floor of the maximum-security Madison Street jail in Phoenix, Arizona, where guards and gang members are murdering prisoners. Behind me, the metal door slams heavily. Light slants into the cell through oblong gaps in the door, illuminating a prisoner cocooned in a white sheet, snoring lightly on the top bunk about two thirds of the way up the back wall. Relieved there is no immediate threat, I place my mattress on the grimy floor. Desperate to rest, I notice movement on the cement-block walls. *Am I hallucinating?* I blink several times. The walls appear to ripple. Stepping closer, I see the walls are alive with insects. I flinch. So many are swarming, I wonder if they're a colony of ants on the move. To get a better look, I put my eyes right up to them. They are mostly the size of almonds and have antennae. American cockroaches. I've seen them in the holding cells downstairs in smaller numbers, but nothing like this. A chill spread over my body. I back away.

Something alive falls from the ceiling and bounces off the base of my neck. I jump. With my night vision improving, I spot cockroaches weaving in and out of the base of the fluorescent strip light. Every so often one drops onto the concrete and resumes crawling. Examining the bottom bunk, I realise why my cellmate is sleeping at a higher elevation: cockroaches are pouring from gaps in the decrepit wall at the level of my bunk. The area is thick with them. Placing my mattress on the bottom bunk scatters them. I walk towards the toilet, crunching a few under my shower sandals. I urinate and grab the toilet roll. A cockroach darts from the centre of the roll onto my hand, tickling my fingers. My arm jerks as if it has a mind of its own, losing the cockroach and the toilet roll. Using a towel, I wipe the bulk of them off the bottom bunk, stopping only to shake the odd one off my hand. I unroll my mattress. They begin to regroup and inhabit my mattress. My adrenaline is pumping so much, I lose my fatigue.

Nauseated, I sit on a tiny metal stool bolted to the wall. *How will I sleep? How's my cellmate sleeping through the infestation and my arrival?* Copying his technique, I cocoon myself in a sheet and lie down, crushing more cockroaches. The only way they can access me now is through the breathing hole I've left in the sheet by the lower half of my face. Inhaling their strange musty odour, I close my eyes. I can't sleep. I feel them crawling on the sheet around my feet. *Am I imagining things?* Frightened of them infiltrating my breathing hole, I keep opening my eyes. Cramps cause me to rotate onto my other side. Facing the wall, I'm repulsed by so many of them just inches away. I return to my original side.

The sheet traps the heat of the Sonoran Desert to my body, soaking me in sweat. Sweat tickles my body, tricking my mind into thinking the cockroaches are infiltrating and crawling on me. The trapped heat aggravates my bleeding skin infections and bedsores. I want to scratch myself, but I know better. The outer layers of my skin have turned soggy from sweating constantly in this concrete oven. Squirming on the bunk fails to stop the relentless itchiness of my skin. Eventually, I scratch myself. Clumps of moist skin detach under my nails. Every now and then I become so uncomfortable, I must open my cocoon to waft the heat out, which allows the cockroaches in. It takes hours to drift to sleep. I only manage a few hours. I awake stuck to the soaked sheet, disgusted by the cockroach carcasses compressed against the mattress.

The cockroaches plague my new home until dawn appears at the dots in the metal grid over a begrimed strip of four-inch-thick bullet-proof glass at the top of the back wall – the cell's only source of outdoor light. They disappear into the cracks in the walls, like vampire mist retreating from sunlight. But not all of them. There were so many on the night shift that even their vastly reduced number is too many to dispose of. And they act like they know it. They roam around my feet with attitude, as if to make it clear that I'm trespassing on their turf.

My next set of challenges will arise not from the insect world, but from my neighbours. I'm the new arrival, subject to scrutiny about my charges just like when I'd run into the Aryan Brotherhood prison gang on my first day at the medium-security Towers jail a year ago. I wish my cellmate would wake up, brief me on the mood of the locals and introduce me to the head of the white gang. No such luck. Chow is announced over a speaker system in a crackly robotic voice, but he doesn't stir.

I emerge into the day room for breakfast. Prisoners in black-and-white bee-striped uniforms gather under the metal-grid stairs and tip dead cockroaches into a trash bin from plastic peanut-butter containers they'd set as traps during the night. All eyes are on me in the chow line. Watching who sits where, I hold my head up, put on a solid stare and pretend to be as at home in this environment as the cockroaches. It's all an act. I'm lonely and afraid. I loathe having to explain myself to the head of the white race, who I assume is the toughest murderer. I've been in jail long enough to know that taking my breakfast to my cell will imply that I have something to hide.

The gang punishes criminals with certain charges. The most serious are sex offenders, who are KOS: Kill On Sight. Other charges are punishable by SOS – Smash On Sight – such as drive-by shootings because women and kids sometimes get killed. It's called convict justice. Gang members are constantly looking for people to beat up because that's how they earn their reputations and tattoos. The most serious acts of violence earn the highest-ranking tattoos. To be a full gang member requires murder. I've observed the body language and techniques inmates trying to integrate employ. An inmate with a spring in his step and an air of confidence is likely to be accepted. A person who avoids eye contact and fails to introduce himself to the gang is likely to be preyed on. Some of the failed attempts I saw ended up with heads getting cracked against toilets, a sound I've grown familiar with. I've seen prisoners being extracted on stretchers who looked dead – one had yellow fluid leaking from his head. The constant violence gives me nightmares, but the reality is that I put myself in here, so I force myself to accept it as a part of my punishment.

It's time to apply my knowledge. With a self-assured stride, I take my breakfast bag to the table of white inmates covered in neo-Nazi tattoos, allowing them to question me.

"Mind if I sit with you guys?" I ask, glad exhaustion has deepened my voice.

"These seats are taken. But you can stand at the corner of the table."

The man who answered is probably the head of the gang. I size him up. Cropped brown hair. A dangerous glint in Nordic-blue eyes. Tiny pupils that suggest he's on heroin. Weightlifter-type veins bulging from a sturdy neck. Political ink on arms crisscrossed with scars. About the same age as me, thirty-three.

"Thanks. I'm Shaun from England." I volunteer my origin to show I'm different from them but not in a way that might get me smashed.

"I'm Bullet, the head of the whites." He offers me his fist to bump. "Where you roll in from, wood?"

Addressing me as wood is a good sign. It's what white gang members on a friendly basis call each other.

"Towers jail. They increased my bond and re-classified me to maximum security."

"What's your bond at?"

"I've got two $750,000 bonds," I say in a monotone. This is no place to brag about bonds.

"How many people you kill, brother?" His eyes drill into mine, checking whether my body language supports my story. My body language so far is spot on.

"None. I threw rave parties. They got us talking about drugs on wiretaps." Discussing drugs on the phone does not warrant a $1.5 million bond. I know and beat him to his next question. "Here's my charges." I show him my charge sheet, which includes conspiracy and leading a crime syndicate – both from running an Ecstasy ring.

Bullet snatches the paper and scrutinises it. Attempting to pre-empt his verdict, the other whites study his face. On edge, I wait for him to respond. Whatever he says next will determine whether I'll be accepted or victimised.

"Are you some kind of jailhouse attorney?" Bullet asks. "I want someone to read through my case paperwork." During our few minutes of conversation, Bullet has seen through my act and concluded that I'm educated – a possible resource to him.

I appreciate that he'll accept me if I take the time to read his case. "I'm no jailhouse attorney, but I'll look through it and help you however I can."

"Good. I'll stop by your cell later on, wood."

After breakfast, I seal as many of the cracks in the walls as I can with toothpaste. The cell smells minty, but the cockroaches still find their way in. Their day shift appears to be collecting information on the brown paper bags under my bunk, containing a few items of food that I purchased from the commissary; bags that I tied off with rubber bands in the hope of keeping the cockroaches out. Relentlessly, the cockroaches explore the bags for entry points, pausing over and probing the most worn and vulnerable regions. *Will the nightly swarm eat right through the paper?* I read all morning, wondering whether my cellmate has died in his cocoon, his occasional breathing sounds reassuring me.

Bullet stops by late afternoon and drops his case paperwork off. He's been charged with Class 3 felonies and less, not serious crimes, but is facing a double-digit sentence because of his prior convictions and Security Threat Group status in the prison system. The proposed sentencing range seems disproportionate.

I'll advise him to reject the plea bargain – on the assumption he already knows to do so, but is just seeking the comfort of a second opinion, like many un-sentenced inmates. When he returns for his paperwork, our conversation disturbs my cellmate – the cocoon shuffles – so we go upstairs to his cell. I tell Bullet what I think. He is excitable, a different man from earlier, his pupils almost non-existent.

"This case ain't shit. But my prosecutor knows I done other shit, all kinds of heavy shit, but can't prove it. I'd do anything to get that sorry bitch off my fucking ass. She's asking for something bad to happen to her. Man, if I ever get bonded out, I'm gonna chop that bitch into pieces. Kill her slowly though. Like to work her over with a blowtorch."

Such talk can get us both charged with conspiring to murder a prosecutor, so I try to steer him elsewhere. "It's crazy how they can catch you doing one thing, yet try to sentence you for all of the things they think you've ever done."

"Done plenty. Shot some dude in the stomach once. Rolled him up in a blanket and threw him in a dumpster."

Discussing past murders is as unsettling as future ones. "So, what's all your tattoos mean, Bullet? Like that eagle on your chest?"

"Why you wanna know?" Bullet's eyes probe mine.

My eyes hold their ground. "Just curious."

"It's a war bird. The AB patch."

"AB patch?"

"What the Aryan Brotherhood gives you when you've put enough work in."

"How long does it take to earn a patch?"

"Depends how quickly you put your work in. You have to earn your lightning bolts first."

"Why you got red and black lightning bolts?"

"You get SS bolts for beating someone down or for being an enforcer for the family. Red lightning bolts for killing someone. I was sent down as a youngster. They gave me steel and told me who to handle and I handled it. You don't ask questions. You just get blood on your steel. Dudes who get these tats without putting work in are told to cover them up or leave the yard."

"What if they refuse?"

"They're held down and we carve the ink off them."

Imagining them carving a chunk of flesh to remove a tattoo, I cringe. He's really enjoying telling me this now. His volatile nature is clear and frightening. *He's accepted me too much. He's trying to impress me before making demands.*

At night, I'm unable to sleep. Cocooned in heat, surrounded by cockroaches, I hear the swamp-cooler vent – a metal grid at the top of a wall – hissing out tepid air. Giving up on sleep, I put my earphones on and tune into National Public Radio. Listening to a Vivaldi violin concerto, I close my eyes and press my tailbone down to straighten my back as if I'm doing a yogic relaxation. The playful allegro thrills me, lifting my spirits, but the wistful adagio provokes sad emotions and tears. I open my eyes and gaze into the gloom. Due to lack of sleep, I start hallucinating and hearing voices over the music whispering threats. I'm at breaking point. Although I have accepted that I committed crimes and deserve to be punished, no one should have to live like this. I'm furious at myself for making the series of reckless decisions that put me in here and for losing absolutely everything. As violins crescendo in my ears, I remember what my life used to be like.

ABOUT THE AUTHOR

Shaun Attwood is a former stock-market millionaire and Ecstasy trafficker turned YouTuber, public speaker, author and activist, who is banned from America for life. His story was featured worldwide on National Geographic Channel as an episode of Locked Up/Banged Up Abroad called Raving Arizona.

Shaun's writing – smuggled out of the jail with the highest death rate in America run by Sheriff Joe Arpaio – attracted international media attention to the human rights violations: murders by guards and gang members, dead rats in the food, cockroach infestations...

While incarcerated, Shaun was forced to reappraise his life. He read over 1,000 books in just under six years. By studying original texts in psychology and philosophy, he sought to better understand himself and his past behaviour. He credits books as being the lifeblood of his rehabilitation.

Shaun tells his story to schools to dissuade young people from drugs and crime. He campaigns against injustice via his books and blog, Jon's Jail Journal. He has appeared on the BBC, Sky News and TV worldwide to talk about issues affecting human rights.

As a best-selling true-crime author, Shaun has written a series of action-packed books exposing the War on Drugs, which feature the CIA, Pablo Escobar and the cocaine Mafia. He has also written the longest ever Escobar biography: *Pablo Escobar's Story*, a 3-book series with over 1,000 pages. On his true-crime podcast on YouTube, Shaun interviews people with hard-hitting crime stories and harrowing prison experiences.